Modern Makonde Art

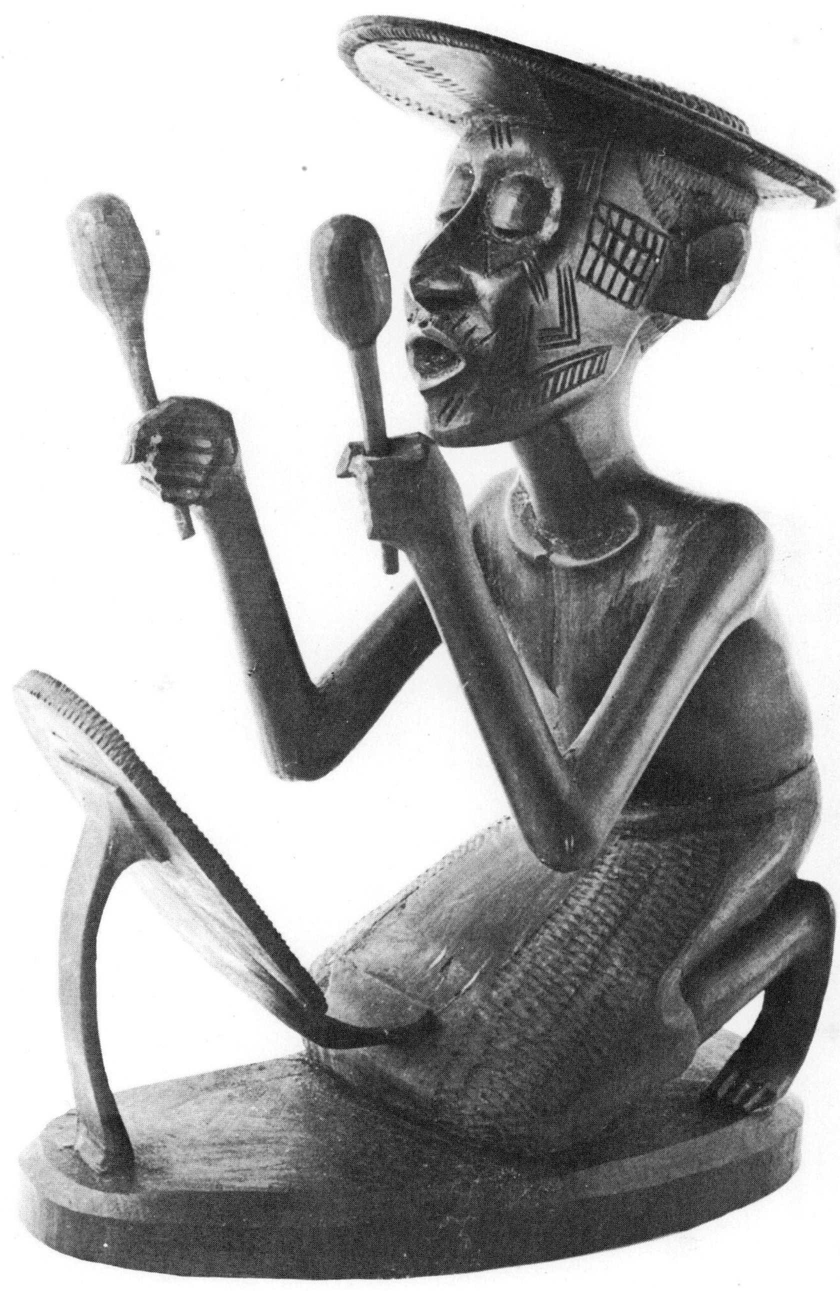

Modern Makonde Art

Jörn Korn
with photographs by
Jesper Kirknæs

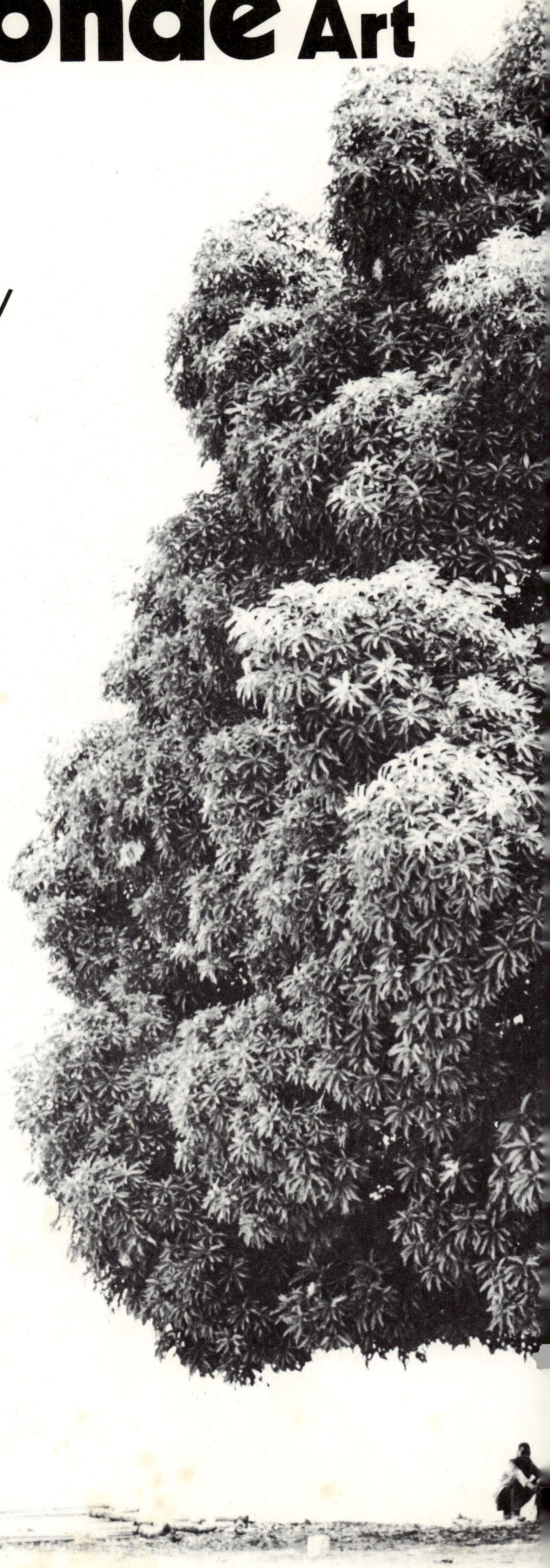

Hamlyn

London · New York · Sydney · Toronto

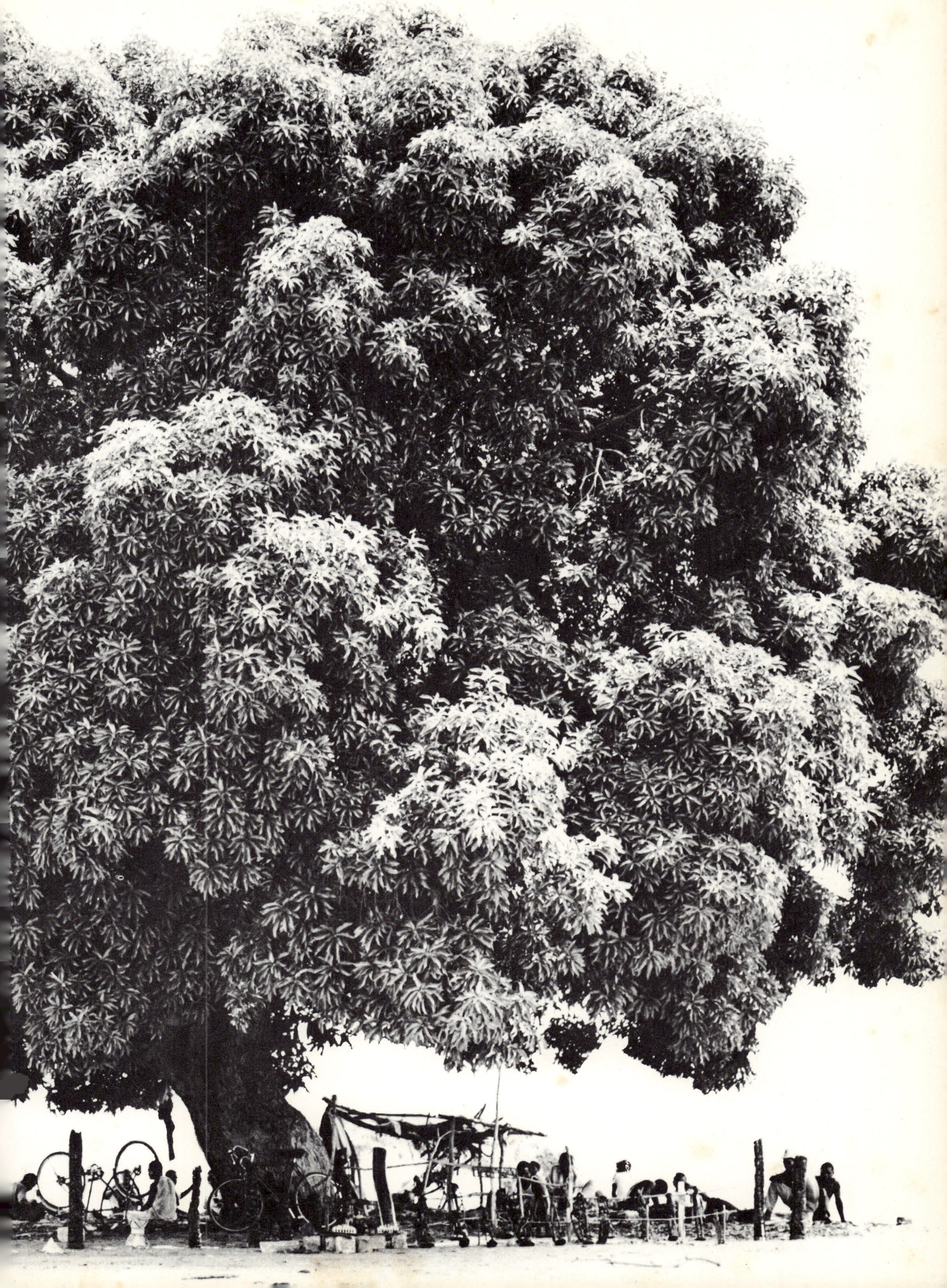

half title
The witch-doctor in ecstasy in front of the mirror through which he can see distant things and future events. (An example of Hossein Anangangola's naturalistic art.) Hossein Anangangola, 1969. 21 cm

title page
The workshop, under a mango tree

Mask. Male shetani. Yoseph Francis, 1969. 49 cm

Dedication: To the five

Published by
The Hamlyn Publishing Group Limited
London · New York · Sydney · Toronto
Astronaut House, Feltham, Middlesex, England

ISBN 0 600 36171 3

Text filmset in Great Britain by
Keyspools Ltd., Golborne.
Printed in Spain by
Printer Industria Gráfica sa, Tuset 19
Barcelona, San Vicente dels Horts 1974
Depósito Legal B. 21073/1974
Mohn Gordon Ltd., London.

Contents

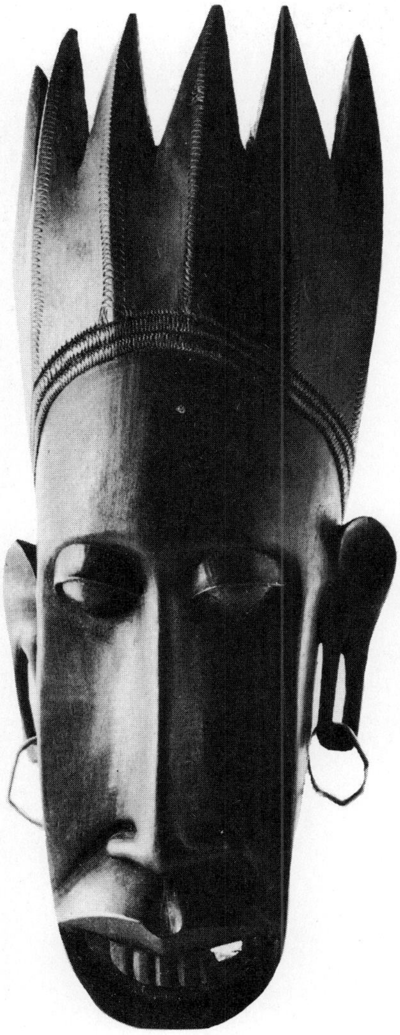

Introduction

In museums around the world you may find an occasional couple of figurines or masks which originated in the villages of the Makonde people in Mozambique, south of the Ruvuma, border river to Tanzania. And in publications on African sculpture are illustrated a few of those probably sacred figurines and dance masks carved in blond and perishable softwood, sometimes decorated with hair or with the characteristic scarification pattern or lip-plug of the Makonde. Generally the references to the purpose or age of these items are scarce indeed, and the name of their creator forgotten.

This classic Makonde sculpture has not attracted attention as has the art of West Africa. Amongst connoisseurs of African art it is still said that East Africa never contributed.

To-day something is happening. Makonde art is emerging from heaps and heaps of tourist carvings in East Africa and finding a life of its own, strong enough to bring inspiration to people far away.

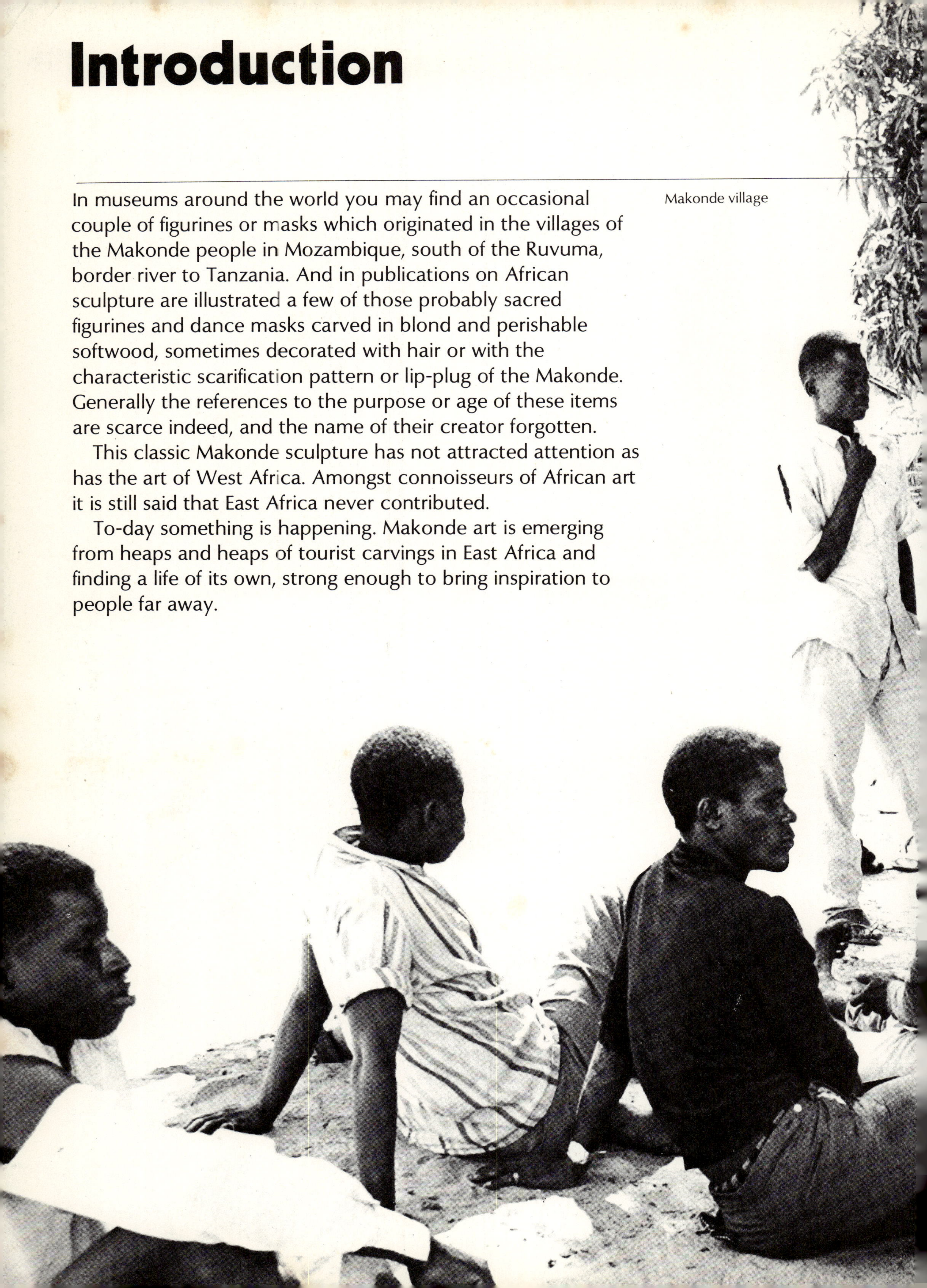

Makonde village

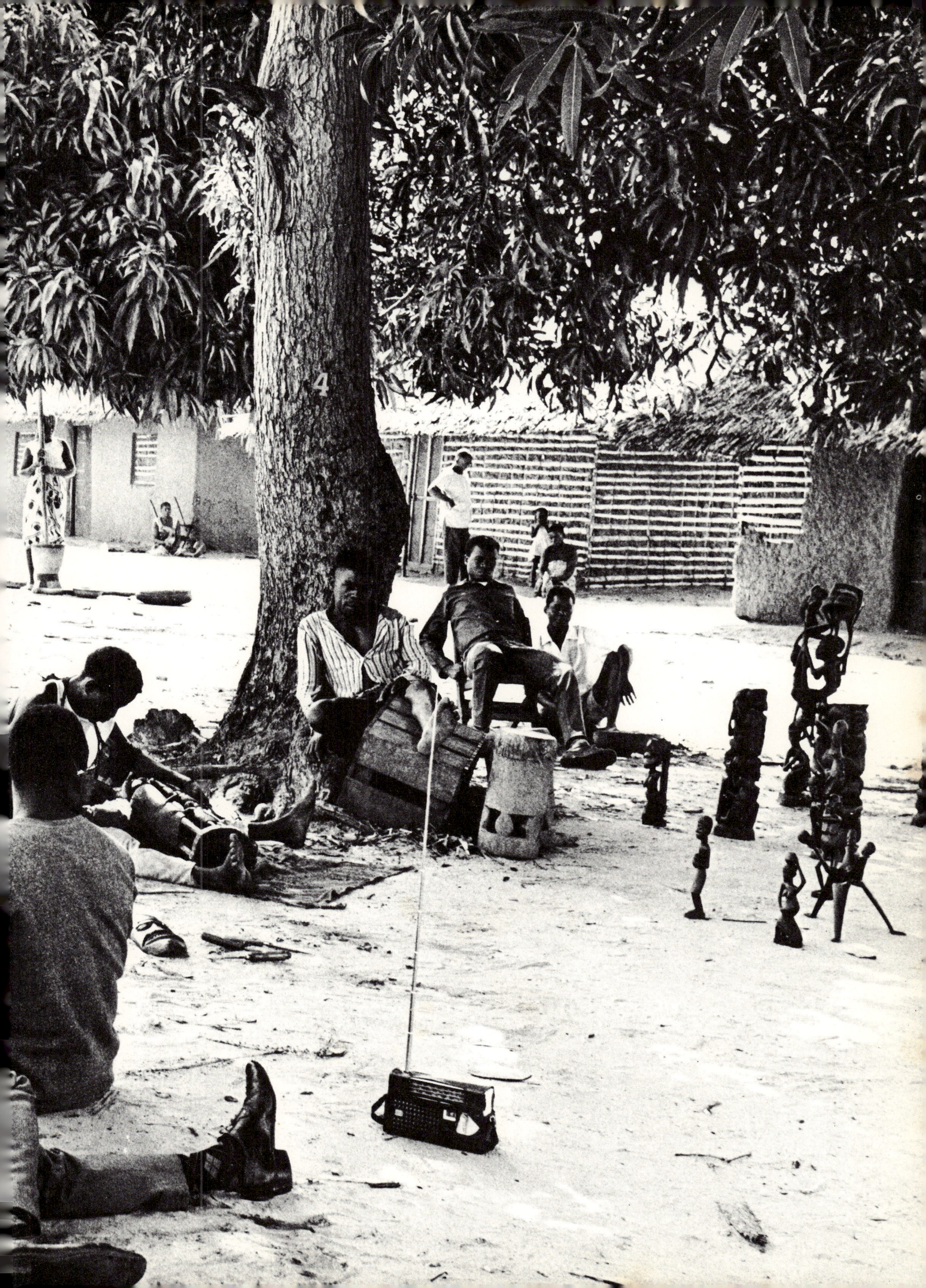

The origin of Makonde art

The Makonde people have lived in comparative isolation in their savannah highlands. Literature about them is of recent date; most has been written in the last decade. We know that ethnic groups around them called them Mahwia, the angry ones. The first Christian missionary arrived in their area in the nineteen-twenties when Islam had for some time been known to them. Before the turn of the century some Makonde people had already started to migrate north into Tanzania and Zanzibar, and, with the sisal boom in the fifties, Makonde labourers and their families were common all over the coastal region of Tanzania where they tended to form their own small communities or villages.

Old Makonde dance mask, collected about 1930

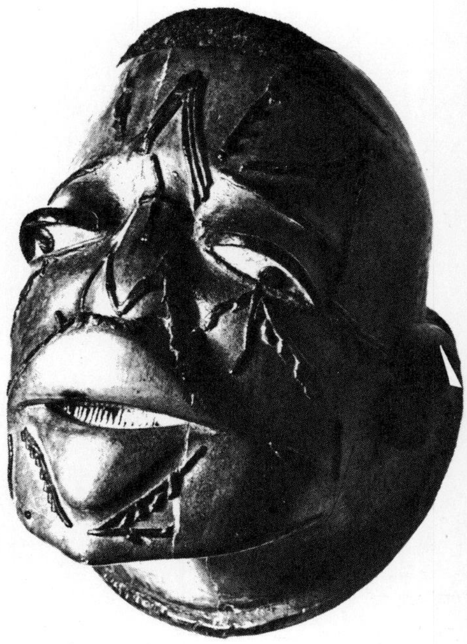

Every Makonde village in Mozambique is said to have had one or two carvers who would prepare the sculptures used at the initiation ceremonies and other rites. The skill would be passed on from father to son like that of the witch-doctor's. The first ever heard about Makonde tourist carving is probably von Stuhlmann's description of stereotyped figures of human beings in southern Tanzania by the end of the nineteenth century. According to some of the artists represented in this book, the craftsmen in the Mozambique villages had been encouraged by Portuguese missionaries occasionally to try out their trade on naturalistic pieces of sculpture in hardwood. But examples do not seem to have deserved any prominent places in the Lisbon museums.

Migrating Makonde labour took the carving tradition to Tanzania, and that is where the present wood carving industry germinated. Until 1953 an increasing number of Makonde carvers made their living from creating naturalistic pieces, mainly of human beings occupied with everyday activities such as smoking a pipe, working the pestle in the tall mortar, or carrying a baby. But most of the craftsmen were busy copying the well-known Kenya wood carvings which their agents offered to passers-by on the pavements of Dar es Salaam, main city of Tanzania, or to the curio dealers who exported large quantities of the carvings. More or less spontaneously several centres of that business (which is still flourishing) emerged. Generally the craftsmen relied upon some expatriate to buy and send their pieces abroad. Around one or two mission stations informal craftsmen's communities existed. The best-known centre was the one activated through the purchases of Mr Norman Kirk near Mtware in the southern district where few tourists ever came. Wholesale traders would often order large series of sculptures based on one model. In an attempt to control the export trade, the Tanzania Arts Council applied the same method in the sixties, ordering according to their printed catalogues.

In 1953, Mr M. Peera, a Dar es Salaam art and curio dealer, established a workshop, and supplied Makonde carvers with wooden blocks and tools as well as a steady market for their products. In this workshop the first sculpture in a new style, representing the shetani or spirits of Makonde folk culture, is said to have originated in the hands of the craftsman Samaki who one day in the mid fifties offered his patron a grotesque figure of a kind never seen before. In contrast to what might have happened in other curio workshops, the piece was not rejected. Customers in the art shop seemed to find it attractive, and more carvings of strange spirit objects were created in the shed. Today shetani carvings are produced in most of the craft communities, and many shetani carvings are to be found in Tanzania and also in curio workshops in the tourist centres of Kenya and Uganda.

What is implied in the shetani idea is hard to tell. When asked, an artist will readily name the inspiration of his work–but sometimes with a twinkle in his eye as if the creature had been invented on the spot. Quite often he might explain the background to a certain myth depicted in the wood.

Shetani (spirit or devil) is a word introduced to the coastal people of Tanzania and Mozambique by Arab tradesmen in olden days. As Herodotus described them 450 years BC, they are apparently not new in equatorial Africa. The Makonde apply the word to any creature–or spirit–not commonly identified as an animal, including several nocturnal or rarely seen creatures. Thus the noises of the black African night are interpreted, laden with fear. However, some shetani species are less mysterious–even edible. The number of their species has been recorded as some hundreds, and their size as variable from a tiny frog to a towering four to six yards. Like any other wild game the shetani would, according to several of the artists, not be particularly inclined to mix with man.

Shetani sculpture should not be seen as an attempt to describe the exact nature of those strange creatures, but rather as an imaginative interpretation of the old myths of the Makonde people.

This is the background against which modern Makonde art developed.

The artists and their work

When a thousand craftsmen carved one thousand days, would an occasional artistic talent not be expected to find its outlet? But who would notice . . .

Tourists noticed. But tourists are multifarious and are not essentially an art-conscious group. In any case, they will soon return to their home country and have little opportunity to follow up their artists in distant Africa. The temporary residents of East Africa are more likely to be in a position to cultivate a relationship with some promising Makonde carver, but even they will sooner or later leave his country. Consequently, modern Makonde art is conceived under conditions in which the craftsmen have no constant encouragement to pursue their genuine mode of expression. There are few serious channels through which Makonde artists can communicate with those who value their work in order to secure their identity.

In 1966 the author arrived in a technical aid mission to a small place called Kibaha 25 miles from Dar es Salaam. By then he had already spent some years in East Africa and his interest in local artistic products had waned in the face of the constant offerings of ordinary, slick carvings and paintings. Kibaha was surrounded by Makonde villages. Every day men from the villages would come around with their black hardwood carvings. It was obvious from the pieces that the craftsmen were striving hard to adapt their work to a form that they thought would appeal to the foreigner's taste.

For months the men kept coming and going with their work, which was monotonous, though occasionally notable for excellent craftsmanship. Some of the carvers would reveal their skill by depicting anatomical details in an extremely correct manner, and some possessed an intimate knowledge of internal organs, too. Sculptures in the shetani style were amongst the items always refused in the doorway.

But one day a sculpture was purchased at the house, a merry, flat-headed female shetani, lip plug and all, dancing on slender hands, her body twisted backwards 180 degrees to point her long legs high towards the sky. It differed so much from all that the Makonde used to bring that one would think its carver had simply given up the objective of pleasing and had let his tools play free. He was Rashidi bin Mohamed, and the piece became a two-way revelation. Once contact was established, and he felt the liberty to express himself, he began to shape sculptures like those you see on these pages. Enthusiastically, his friends tried to join the game.

Collection began. With little haggling most offers were rejected. But new craftsmen began to flock to the door, and new sculptures appeared on the shelves. A voluntary organization came to serve as a safety valve, buying (for profit to technical development projects) the works of all those carvers who did not fulfil their artistic promise in the long run.

Here, from all those craftsmen who tried their luck at Kibaha, a handful of the most self disciplined Makonde artists are introduced to you.

The tools and the wood

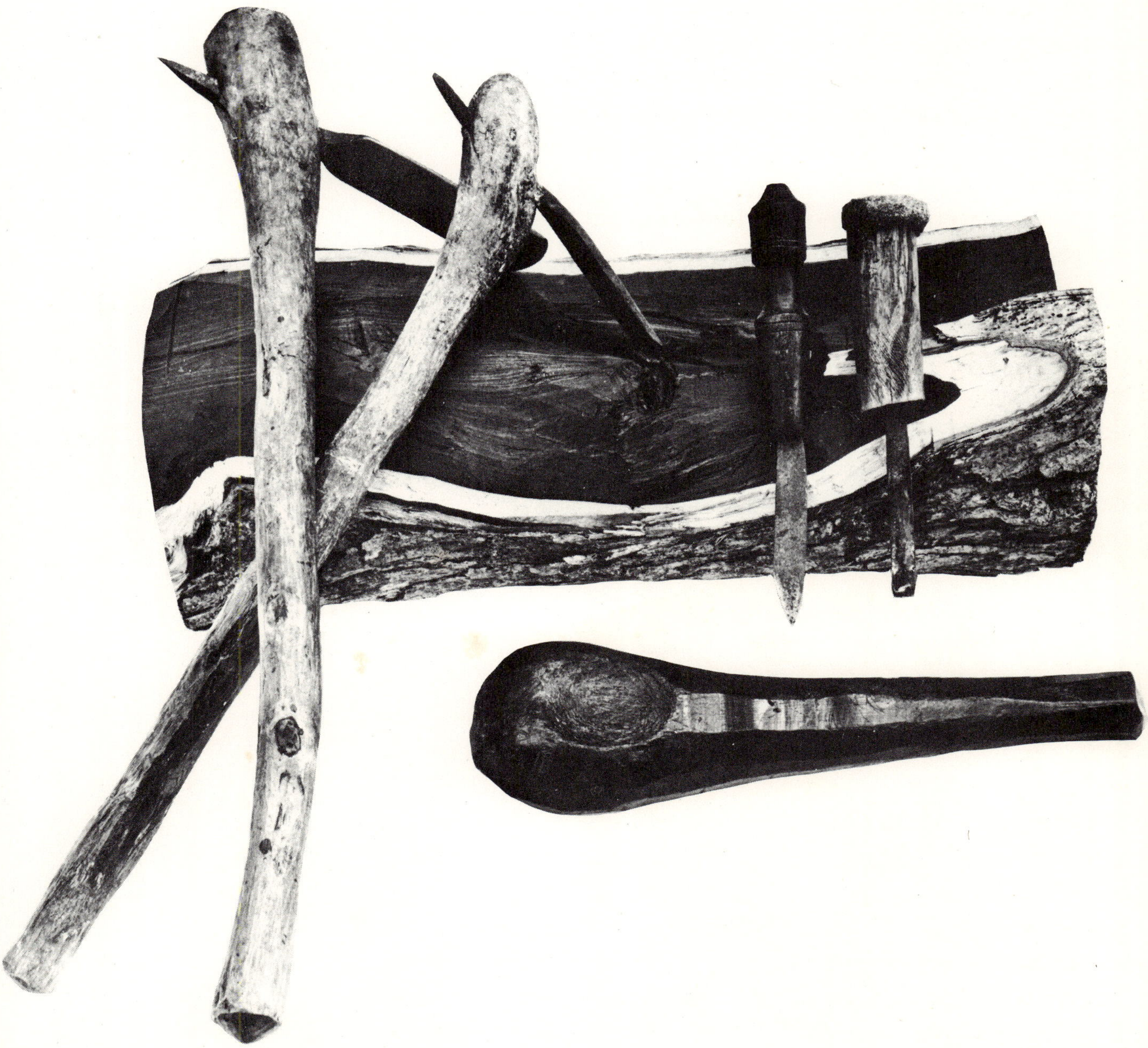

Rashidi bin Mohamed

Rashidi bin Mohamed, the son of a peasant farmer, was born about 1930 in Umande village, not far from Mueda in north-eastern Mozambique. Rashidi never went to school, but he was taught the alphabet by Roman Catholic priests. Despite the Muslim origins of his name and the influence of Christian missionaries in his early years, Rashidi is not a follower of either religion.

At the age of 12, Rashidi crossed the Ruvuma into Tanzania to find employment as a sisal cutter on a plantation close to Mtwara. He worked on the plantations for about 20 years until 1961 when Rashidi had a revelation in his dreams. On two consecutive nights, he dreamt that he made a beautiful wood carving. He interpreted these dreams as signs that he should become an artist and create wonderful objects.

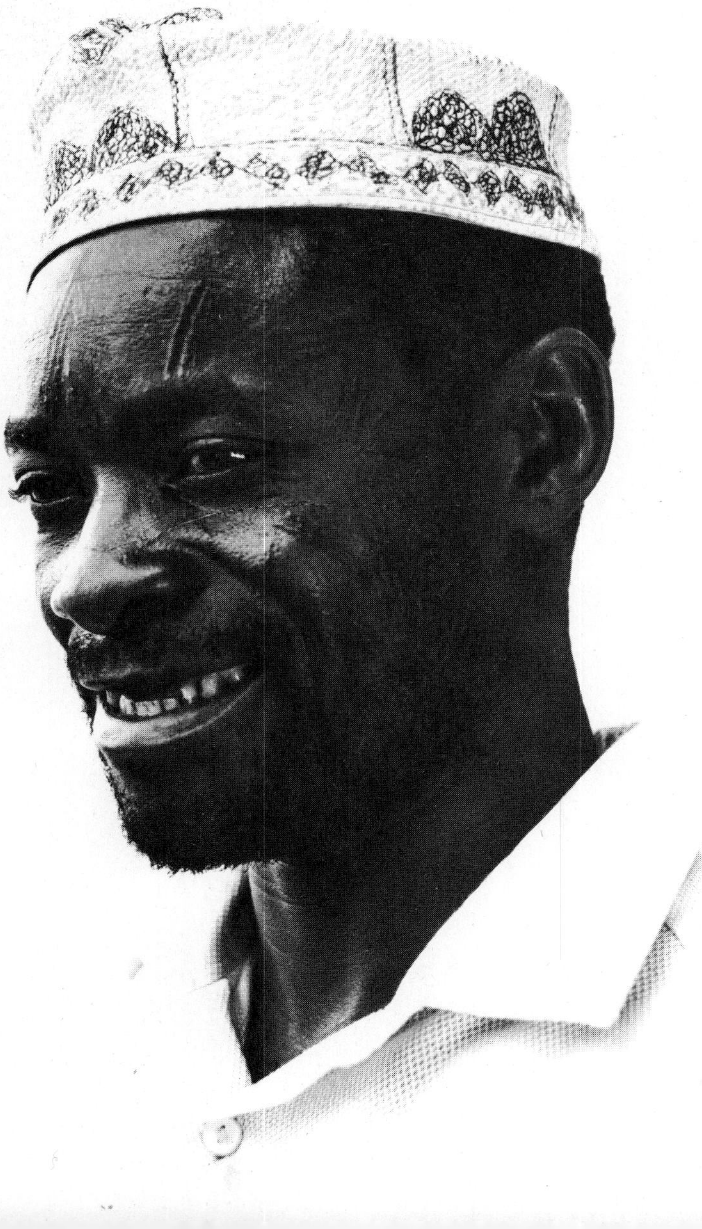

Rashidi bin Mohamed

Rashidi left the plantation and made his way northward along the coast to Dar es Salaam, the only place where a wood-carver could make a good living. He took his first sculpture to a curio dealer, who immediately accepted it to go with his quality pieces. Since collecting his first fees as an artist, Rashidi has only earned money from his creative talent and his skill with carver's tools.

In 1966, Rashidi settled temporarily in Lulanzi, a small community close to Kibaha. Makonde carvers lived in the village and would get lifts into Dar es Salaam with charcoal dealers in order to sell their carvings in the capital.

During the ensuing years, Rashidi rambled from one village to another, never settling permanently in one place. If anyone tried to find him at his home near Kibaha, he usually found an enormous padlock on the front door. The padlock was hardly necessary for the rear wall was in disrepair and one could simply look through the gaping holes to see if Rashidi was in.

Despite the disorganization of his life, Rashidi earned a good income from his carvings in the late 1960s because he worked hard most of the time. His appearance reflected his change in fortune, and he bought white shorts and a white nylon shirt. He also wore white, open mesh sports stockings and well-shined black pointed shoes. He often carried a small transistor radio which was protected by a cloth cover decorated with flowers.

Rashidi occasionally falls upon rough times, but normally he leads a quiet life with few economic or social disturbances. In 1968, Rashidi's right eye was irreparably damaged by a splinter of wood that flew off a carving. He took this incident as yet another sign that he would attain perfection as an artist. Since then he has worn spectacles made of window glass to protect his eyes while working.

Rashidi is a short, very black man, ornamented with discreet facial scarifications. Once he wore a gold alloy bridge of artificial teeth on his upper jaw, but he lost his valuable denture in a market brawl with a fish monger. In revenge, he threw his opponent's fish into the Ruvu river. The police intervened and Rashidi was arrested and kept in prison until he had raised a large bail.

His art, however, seems to be unaffected by his everchanging circumstances. As a rule his productivity is rather constant, but there are occasions when he feels creatively exhausted.

'I am completely lost,' he says, or, 'I feel absolutely empty in the brain.' Some Makonde carvers do use hashish and other euphorizing drugs to stimulate their creativity. Rashidi, however, avoids intoxicants while working, for he believes their use would spoil the clarity of his art and his skill.

An old man (mzee) who carries home an ebony block for a sculpture. (Probably intended to be a self portrait; an example of Rashidi bin Mohamed's more naturalistic art. He devoted himself exclusively to the shetani style early in 1967.) Rashidi bin Mohamed, 1967. 40 cm

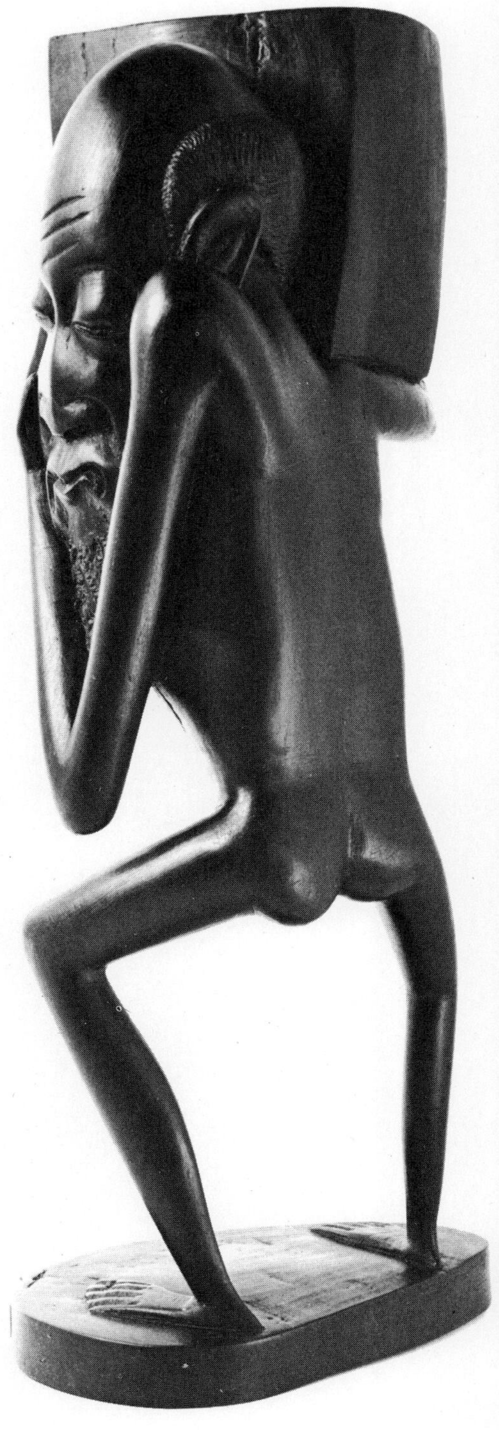

A Mozambique shetani whore holding a small male shetani. Rashidi bin Mohamed, 1969, 38 cm

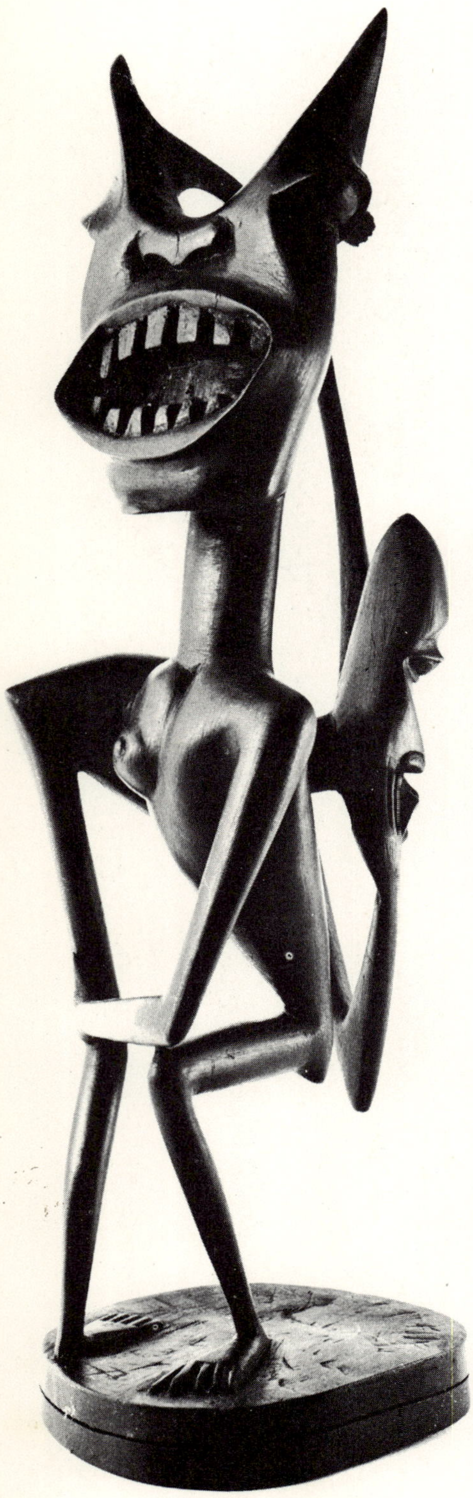

When one carving is nearing completion, Rashidi begins to think of the next one. Vague ideas germinate in his mind while he is working. He goes to sleep preoccupied with these ideas, and after a few hours, he dreams how he is going to fashion the next sculpture. In the morning, he sketches the proposed carving in pencil on a scrap of paper, including minute details. He quietly smokes a short pipe with tobacco from a cigarette as he sketches.

Rashidi says that he was never taught the principles of wood-carving. His father possessed no carver's tools. He claims that he learned his craft by scrutinizing the objects of nature and imitating them again and again in his sculpture. 'God taught me,' is his uncomplicated explanation of the origin of his skill.

For the roughest part of his work, Rashidi sometimes employs a few casual labourers. He takes a sketch of the proposed sculpture with him and together they go into the shrub forest to select an appropriate log. Rashidi critically examines the asymmetrically twisted trees. He orders the labourers to fell the suitable tree, cut the log clean and bring it to his workshop. When working in town, Rashidi usually buys a wooden block from one of the curio dealers.

He sets to work in the shade of a grass-thatched roof or of a large tree. At first he uses a big saw, then a small saw. Thereafter he shifts to a big *teso*, the locally made light adze which is the main tool of all Makonde carvers, and to a small *teso*. Next a coarse rasp, then a fine rasp are used, followed finally by coarse-grain and fine-grain sandpaper. If in the course of his carving he realizes that an unsuitable block was selected for the intended sculpture, Rashidi abandons that block without hesitation and starts afresh. He works intensely and seriously and without break. Considerable time and concentration are devoted to a large sculpture. Sometimes he works for a month on a single piece.

As soon as a sculpture is finished, he puts on his best clothes and takes it to his patrons. His facial expression and body posture show satisfaction and great expectation. He also likes to compare his older pieces with his new ones. A wife or occasionally an apprentice or friend is taken to see the collection of his works. His attitude toward his own sculpture does not change—a success remains a success.

Rashidi never attempts to carve something abstract or artificial. He criticizes some of his fellow carvers for their deviations from the world as he visualizes it. His carvings are studies from life. He never imitates from a book or catalogue. While his first creations were excellently carved human situations, he soon changed to shetani sculpture.

There are numerous spirits in Rashidi's world, perhaps over 300 species. He claims a thorough knowledge of only one section of shetani fauna. It would be impossible for one person to know all the shetani for they are notoriously changeable in occurrence and habit, he says. The spirits of Rashidi's homeland resemble those found where he now lives. They are nocturnal and are comparatively harmless and are reluctant to interfere with humans.

In Rashidi's home village people worshipped carvings placed under a big tree. He remembers them clearly, and occasionally tries to imitate them. While the carvings in the village had supernatural powers, Rashidi says that his own carvings do not.

Rashidi specializes in chameleon shetani sculpture. The chameleon is a familiar figure in African mythology. There are many stories about the chameleon: that they were God's messengers; that they helped in the creation of mankind; that they are really disguised witches who bite women's nipples and never let go.

There are several types of chameleons known to Rashidi. First, the small ones, the size of a finger, are true reptiles and are quite common. The second type is arm-size, is less common and in fact is a shetani. The third type, unknown to science, is the chameleon shetani, which is the size of a cow and is dangerous to humans if encountered in the bush.

In Rashidi's childhood shetani were familiar to everyone. In the villages everybody knows them, but few people see them, for they take precautions not to. The chances of survival after encountering one of the powerful species are slight. Several unfortunate people who saw shetani gave detailed descriptions of their appearances, which have been passed on to succeeding generations. Most of the background information for Rashidi's art is supplied by these tales, but he has also carved shetani which he has seen himself. His beliefs about shetani probably do not differ from commonly held beliefs in contemporary Makonde villages. Villagers build small temples for the spirits in their gardens. Offerings of boiled rice, maize-cobs, honey-combs and other foodstuff are put in the temples to appease the shetani who usually collect these supplies at night.

Rashidi thinks that most shetani are indifferent to human beings. Spirits watch the village day and night, but rarely intervene in the villager's lives. They do not seem to exert any influence over what happens after death, nor are they concerned with people's behaviour towards one another. Benevolent shetani are extremely rare; they are worshipped but their powers seem negligible.

Old mother-shetani from Mozambique. (Anterior surface of the lip-plug is covered with aluminium foil.) Rashidi bin Mohamed, 1967. 50 cm.

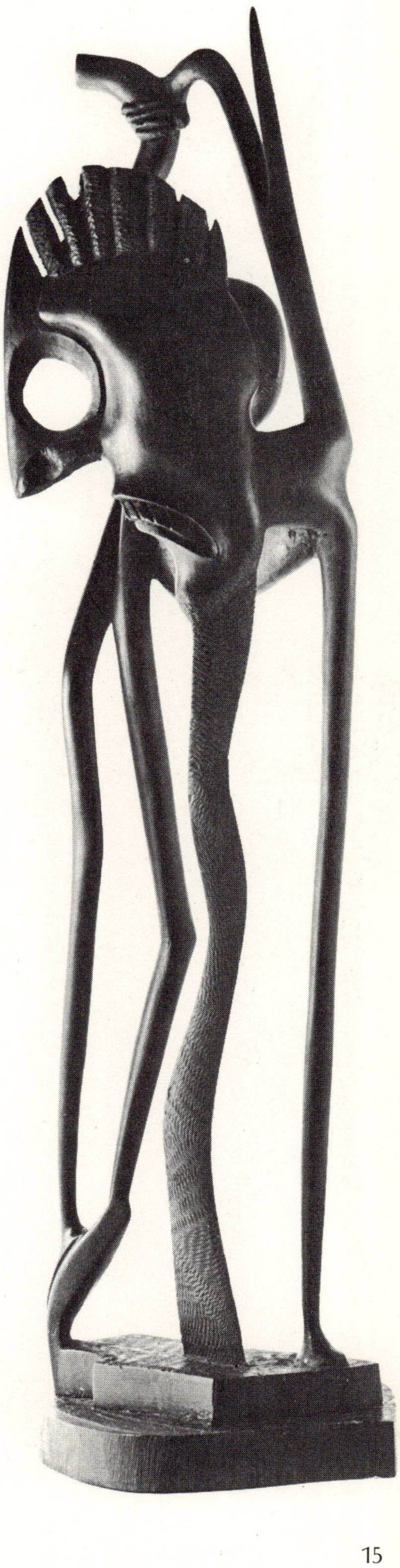

Shetani love scene. Mozambique shetani, secretly together in the bush. The tongue plays an important part in shetani erotics. Rashidi bin Mohamed, 1969. 45 cm

Mozambique shetani. The chamelon shetani provides transport for his master on a kind of table that rests on his back. Rashidi bin Mohamed, 1969. 38 cm

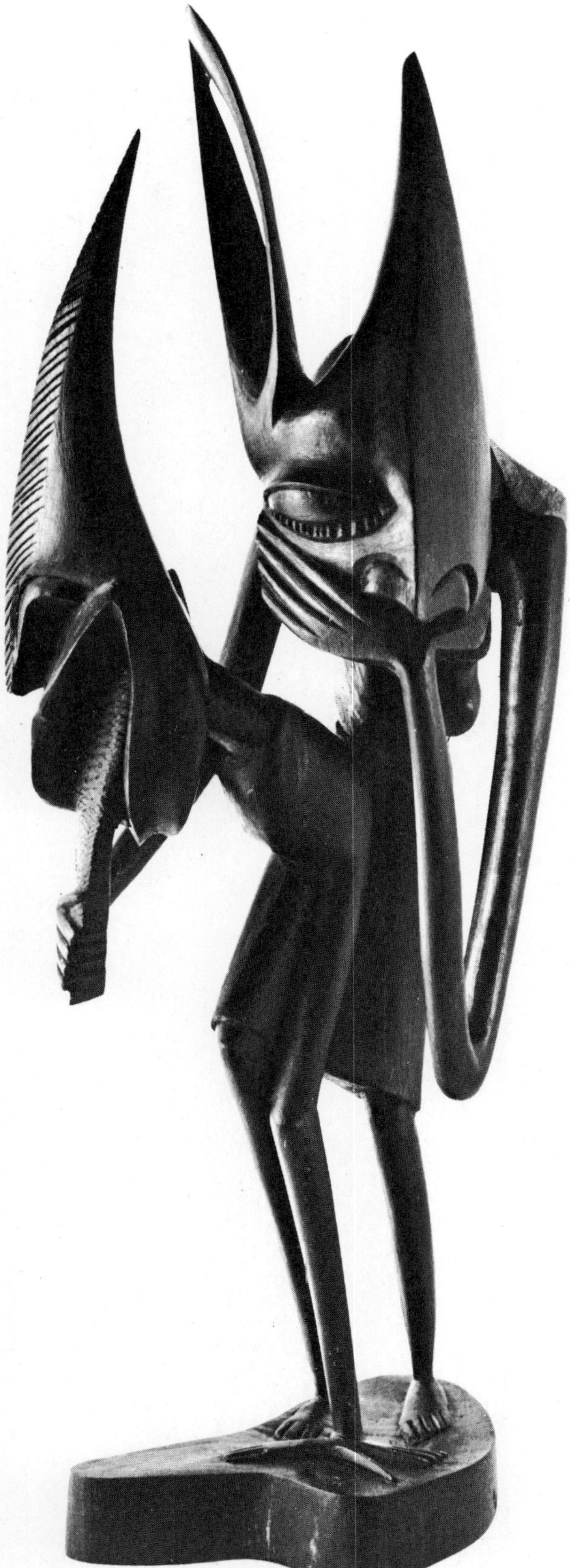

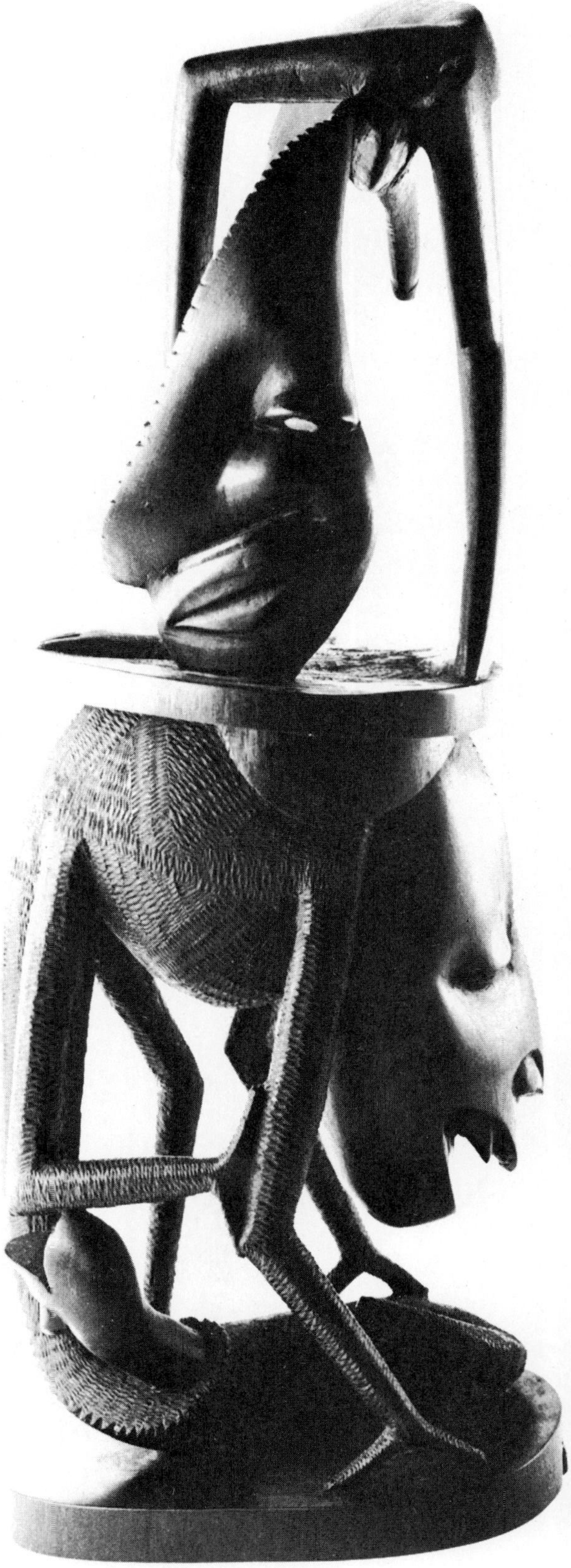

Kifuli. A famous jogoo (cock) shetani. The Kifuli live in the forests of the Mtwara region but roam all over the coastal parts of the country, moving with a very light, swift gait. They are more feared than most other species of shetani because of their capricious habits, their bad temper, and their tremendous appetite. People tremble in horror when the visit of a Kifuli is anticipated for great losses will invariably incur when they are in the vicinity of the village. Rashidi bin Mohamed, 1969. 63 cm

A city shetani. One of the few modern species of shetani. Dressed in a policeman's uniform he will roam the streets of the town when people have retired to their houses. Sometimes he will make use of a loudspeaker when announcing the kill of a victim to his fellow shetani, and the sound of his voice will be horribly amplified. Even by day he may appear, by then not distinguishable from an ordinary policeman. Rashidi bin Mohamed, 1969. 48 cm

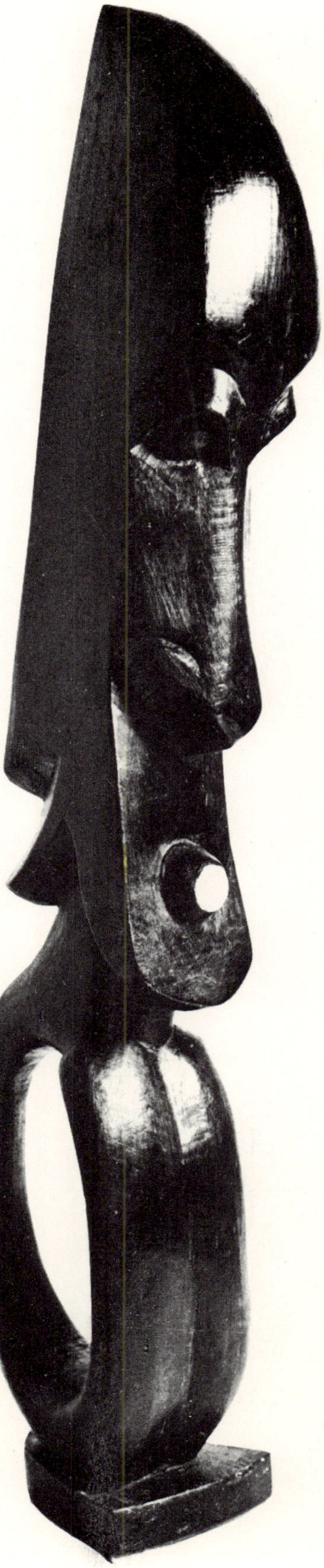

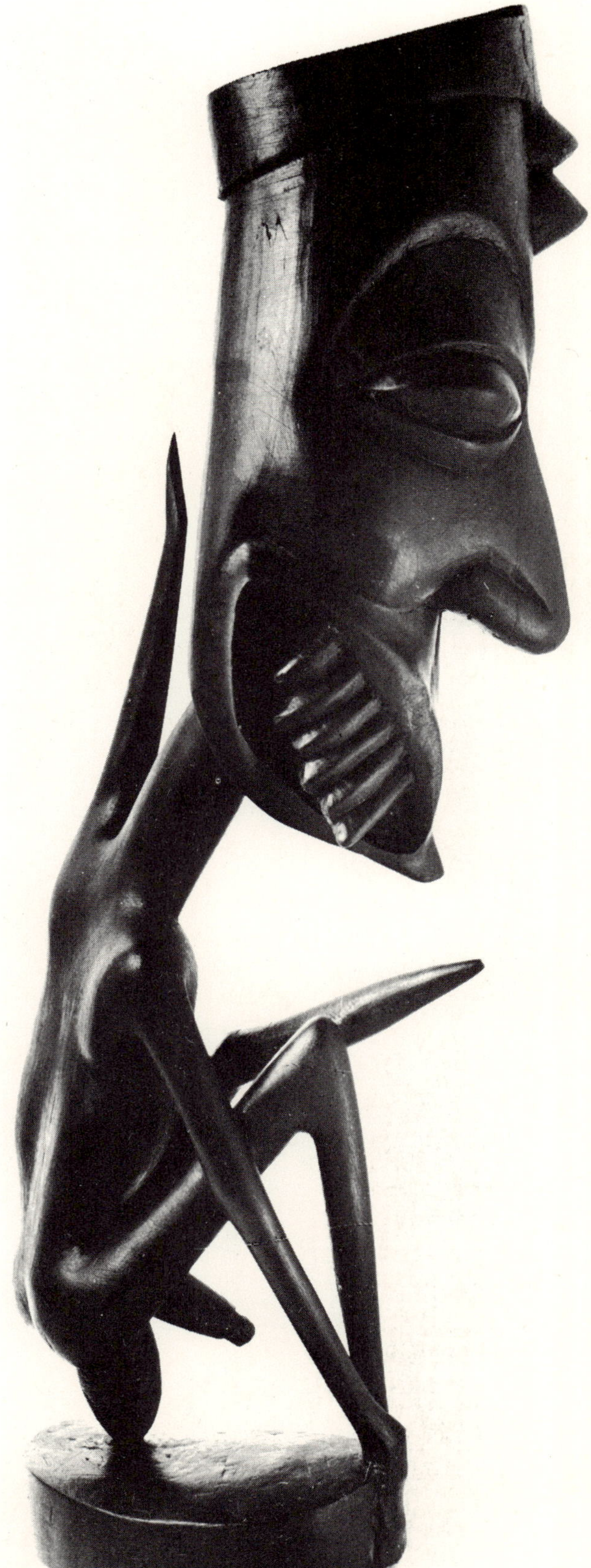

Mozambique shetani love scene. The large female (with lip-plug) has got her will with the smaller male shetani (the enormous left ear of the male distinguishes him from a human being). Rashidi bin Mohamed, 1969. 44 cm

Anonymous shetani couple. Rashidi bin Mohamed, 1969, 38 cm

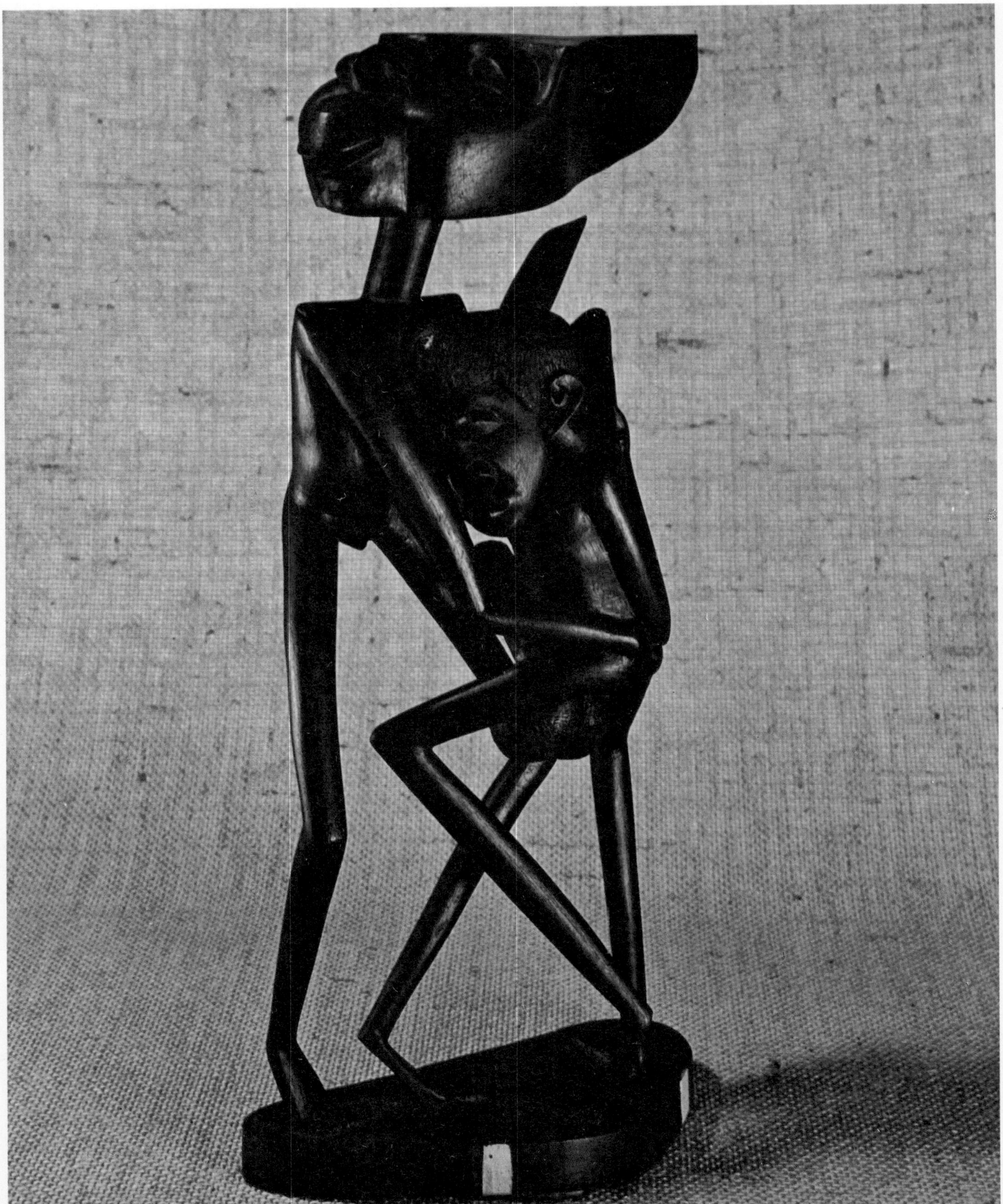

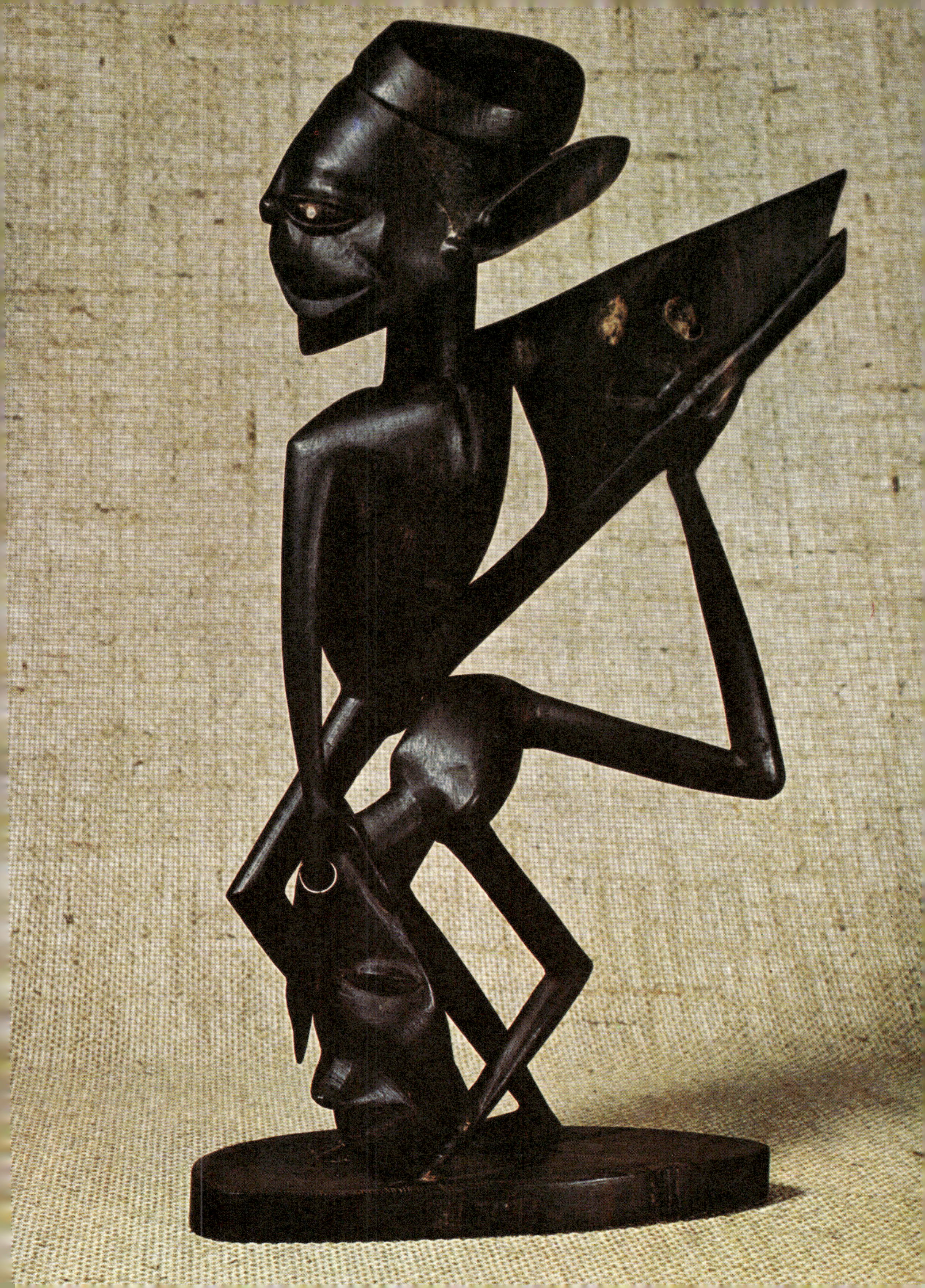

Mozambique shetani couple about to make love but—as will often happen—disturbed by a chameleon shetani pictured below. Rashidi bin Mohamed, 1968. 64 cm

A group of Ruvu fishing shetani occupied in an erotic play. Rashidi bin Mohamed, 1969. 49 cm

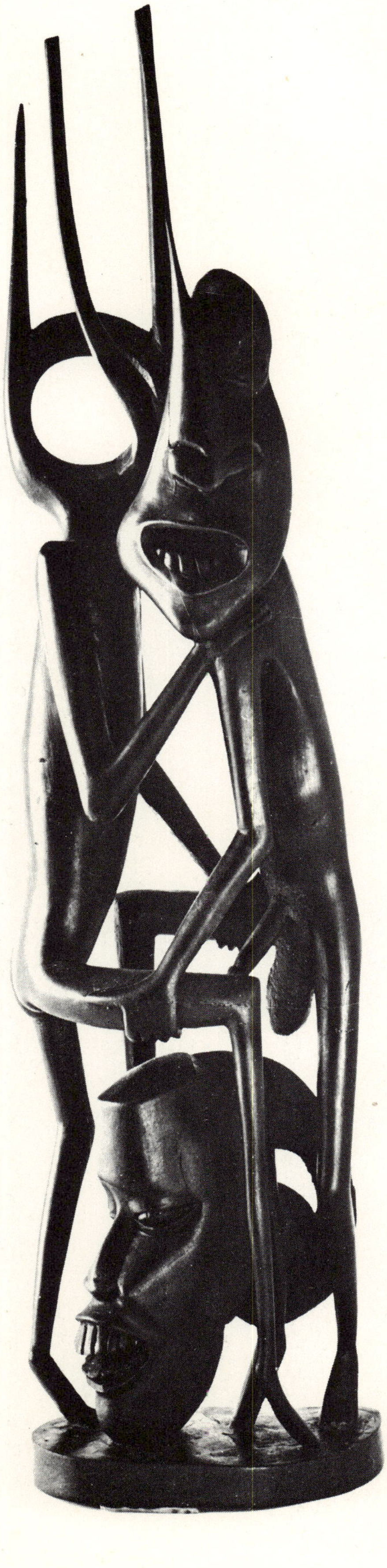

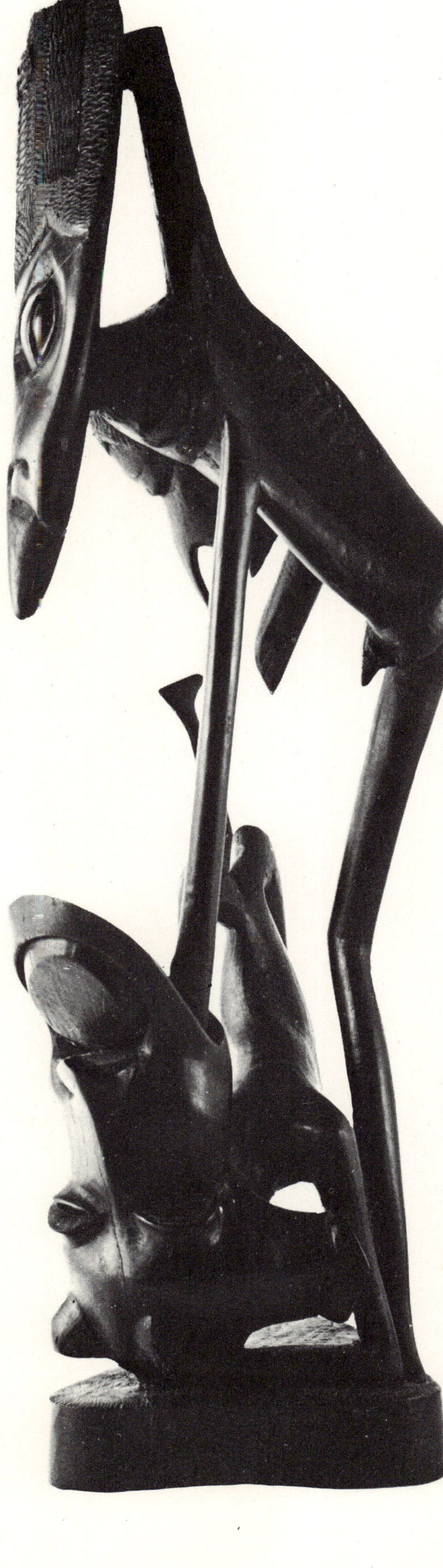

Shetani love scene. The male is not quite willing to cooperate. Rashidi bin Mohamed, 1969. 47 cm

Shetani love scene. Rashidi bin Mohamed, 1969. 62 cm

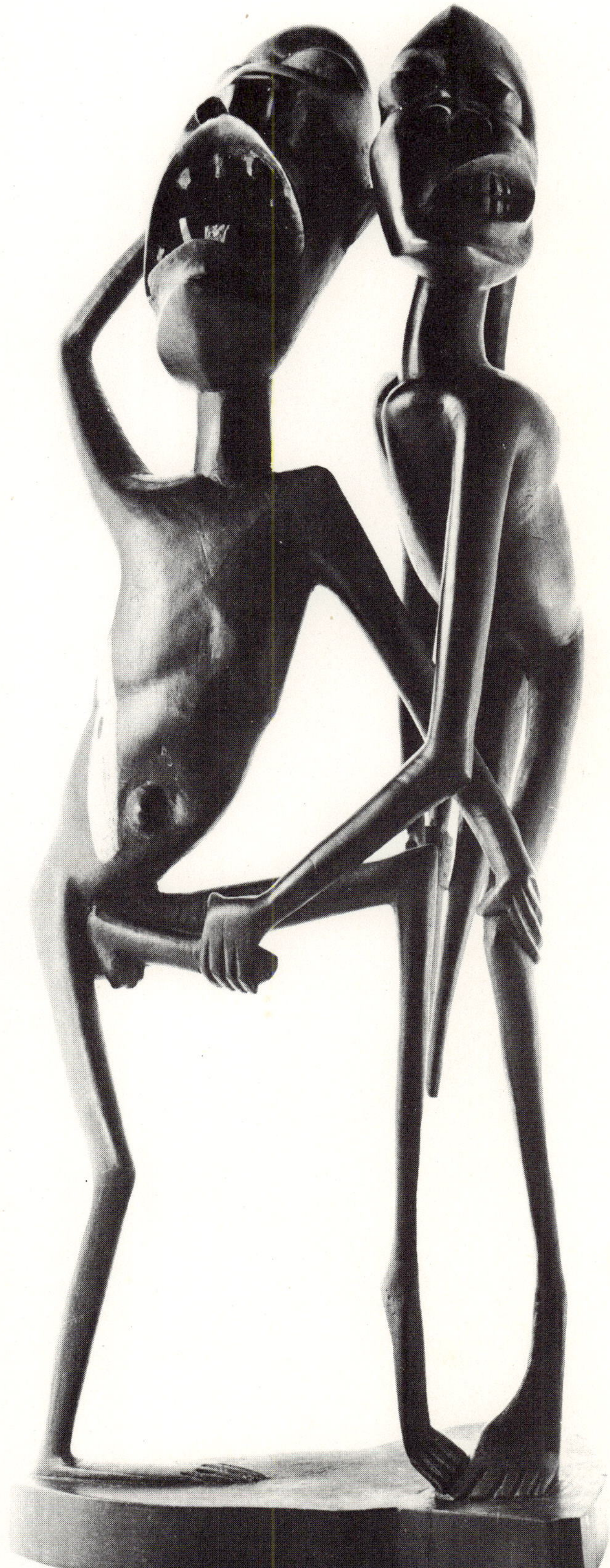

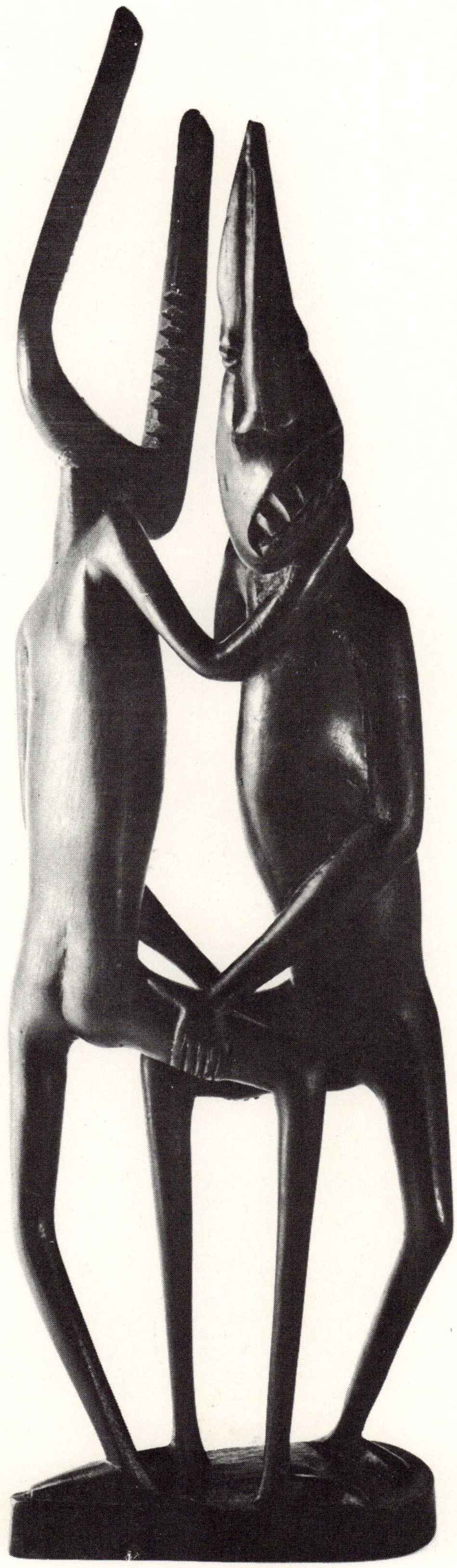

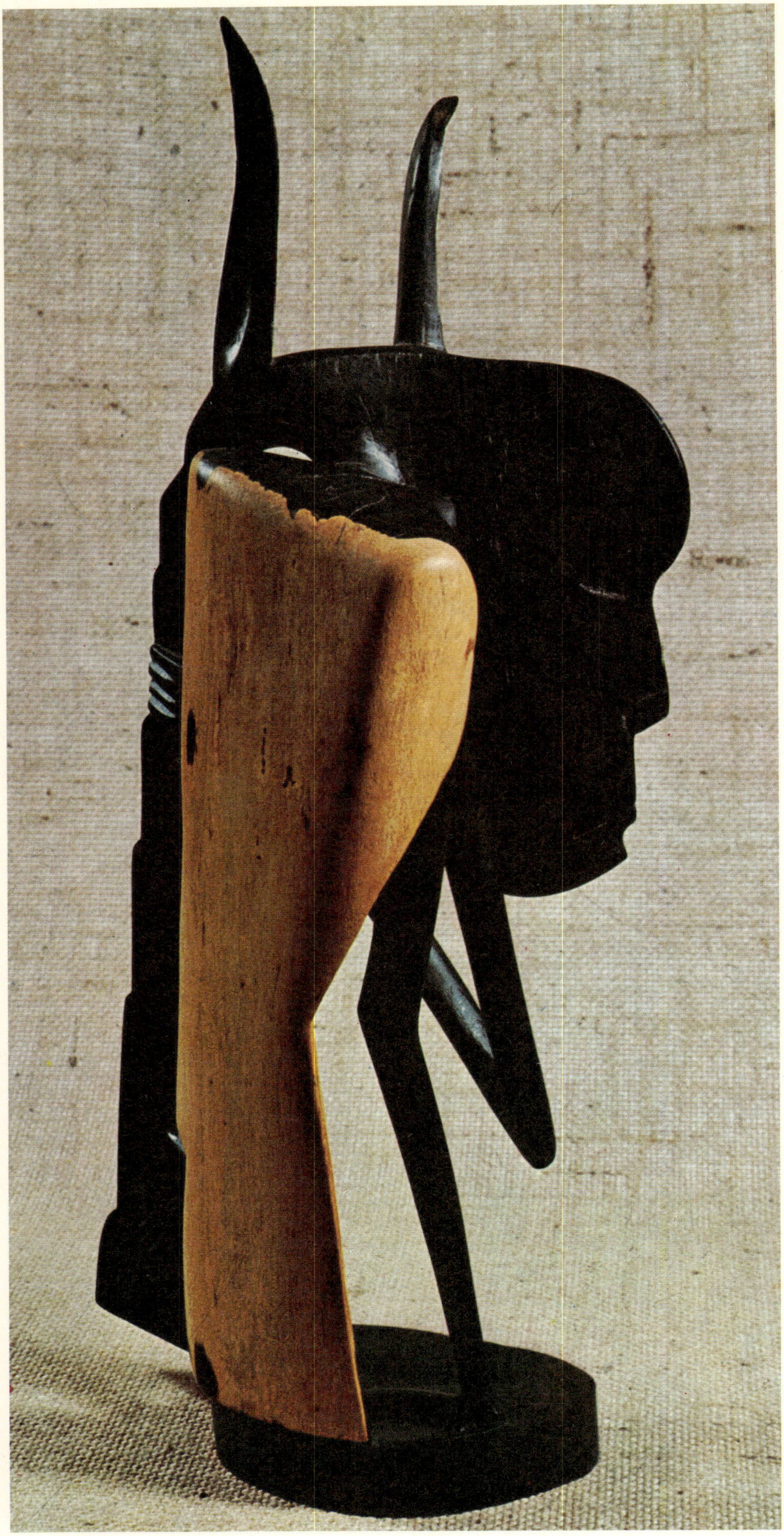

Anonymous Mozambique shetani. Rashidi bin Mohamed, 1969. 47 cm

Shetani whore. The cranium of this shetani is completely flat, and Rashidi bin Mohamed has glued dirt inside the mouth of the figure. Her name is Kunama. She is the daughter of a king-shetani. She is quite a harmless creature who lives from the dry flour of the cassava tuber. Rashidi bin Mohamed, 1969. 32 cm

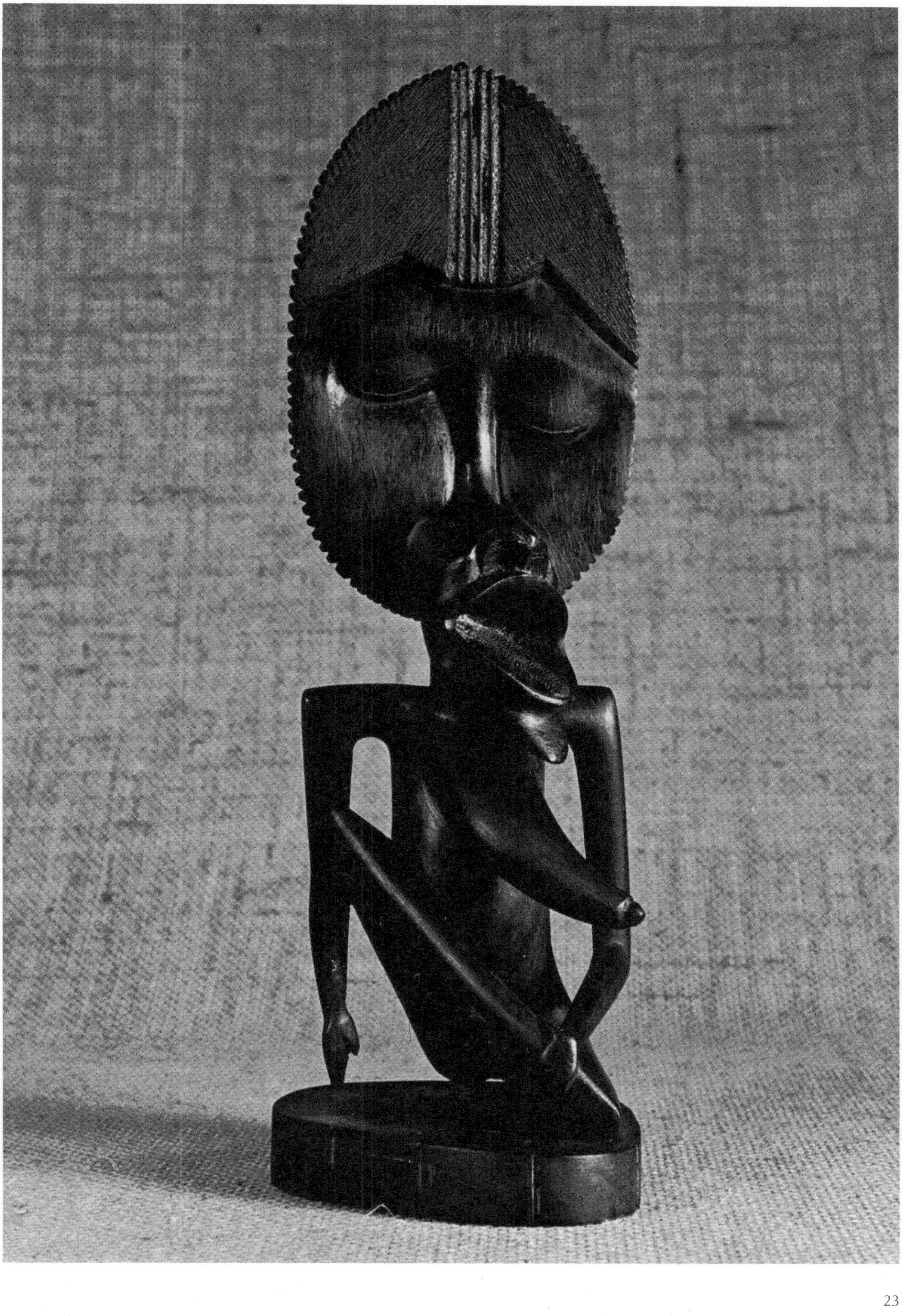

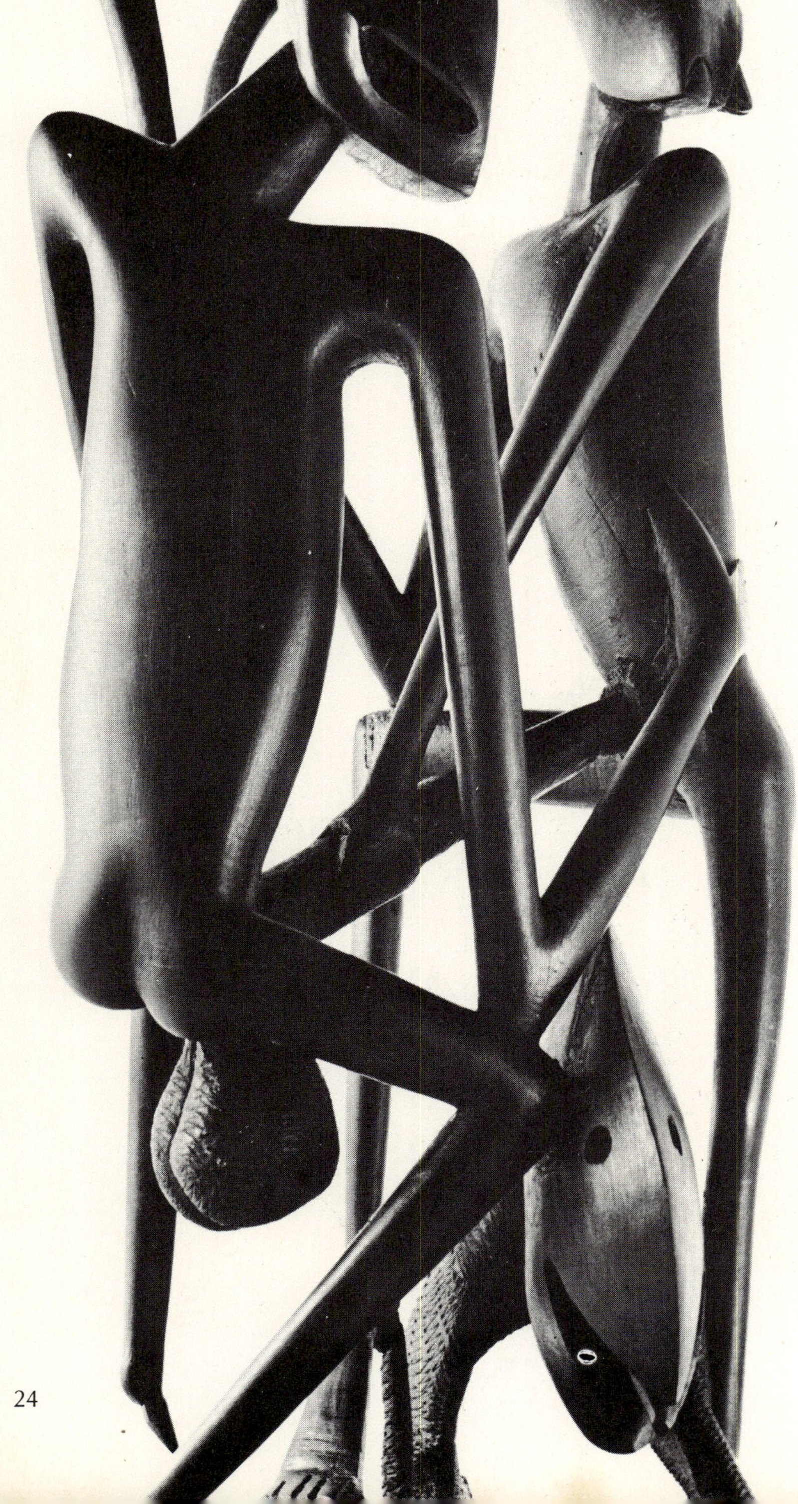

Shetani love scene. The chameleon spirit below did not quite succeed in interrupting the affair. Both species are from Mozambique. Rashidi bin Mohamed, 1969. 41 cm

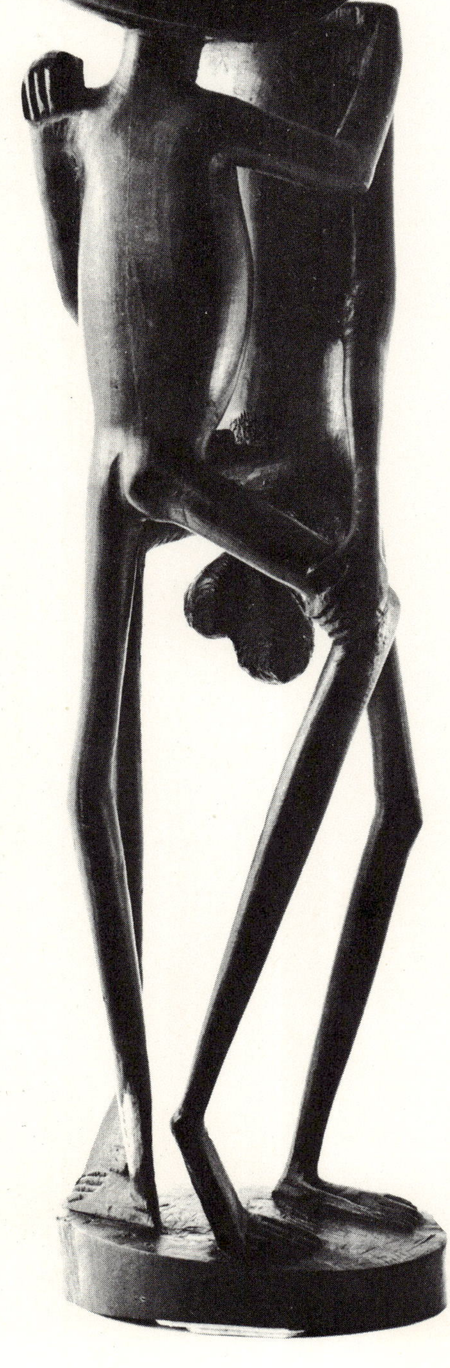

Shetani love scene. A Mozambique shetani couple Rashidi saw on his way from his home region to Tanzania. Rashidi bin Mohamed, 1968. 60 cm

Shetani love scene. Rashidi bin Mohamed carved this picture of the strange love of Lulanzi shetani and included the penis in the picture. Rashidi's wife objected when he wanted to take the sculpture away for sale: What would the wife of his patron say! So, before leaving the workshop, Rashidi had to cut off the penis. He kept the two missing segments for a long time. Although urged to bring them later, he never did so.
Rashidi bin Mohamed, 1968. 45 cm

A good shetani found everywhere. He is called 'The Father of God'. His body is complicated with something that looks like an additional head and a wing. His face is like the sun itself.
Rashidi bin Mohamed, 1967. 47 cm

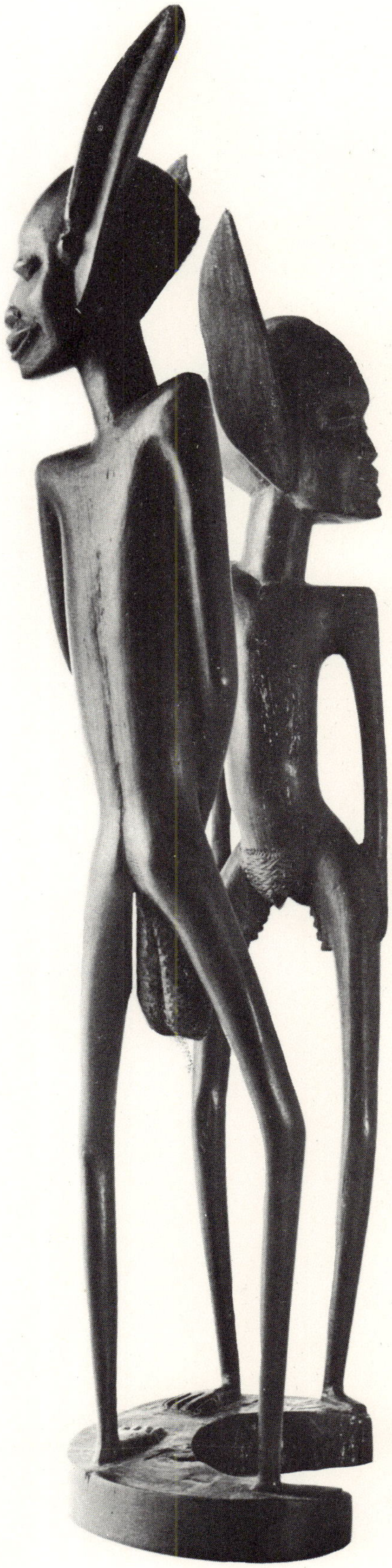

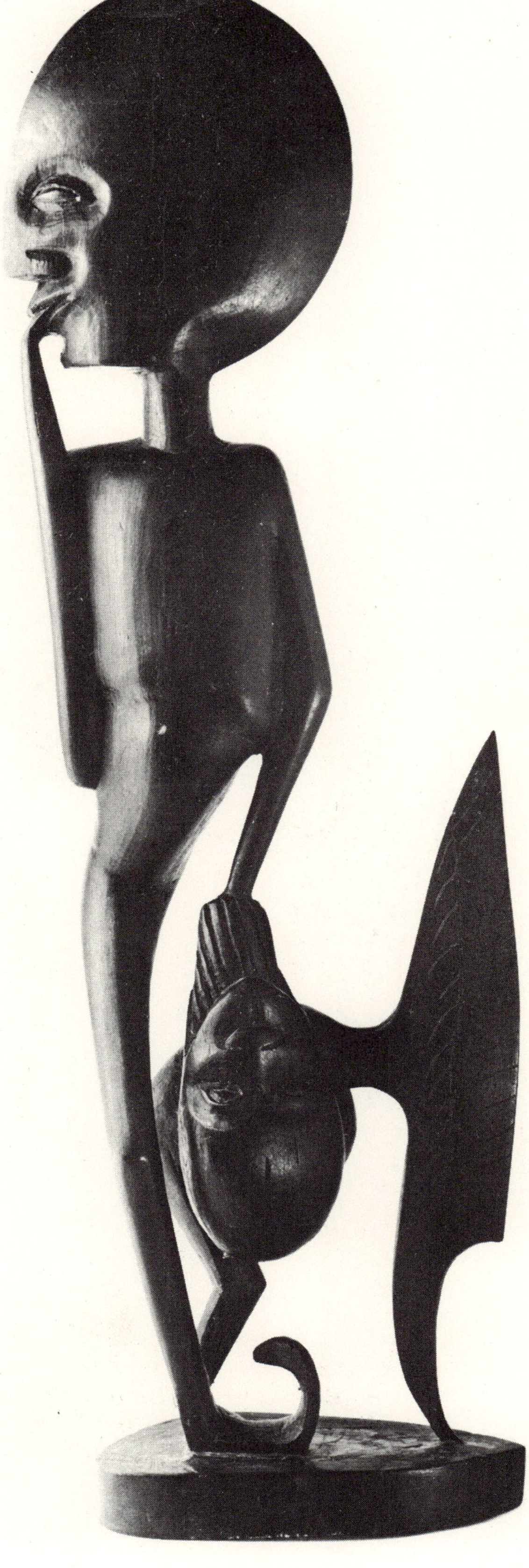

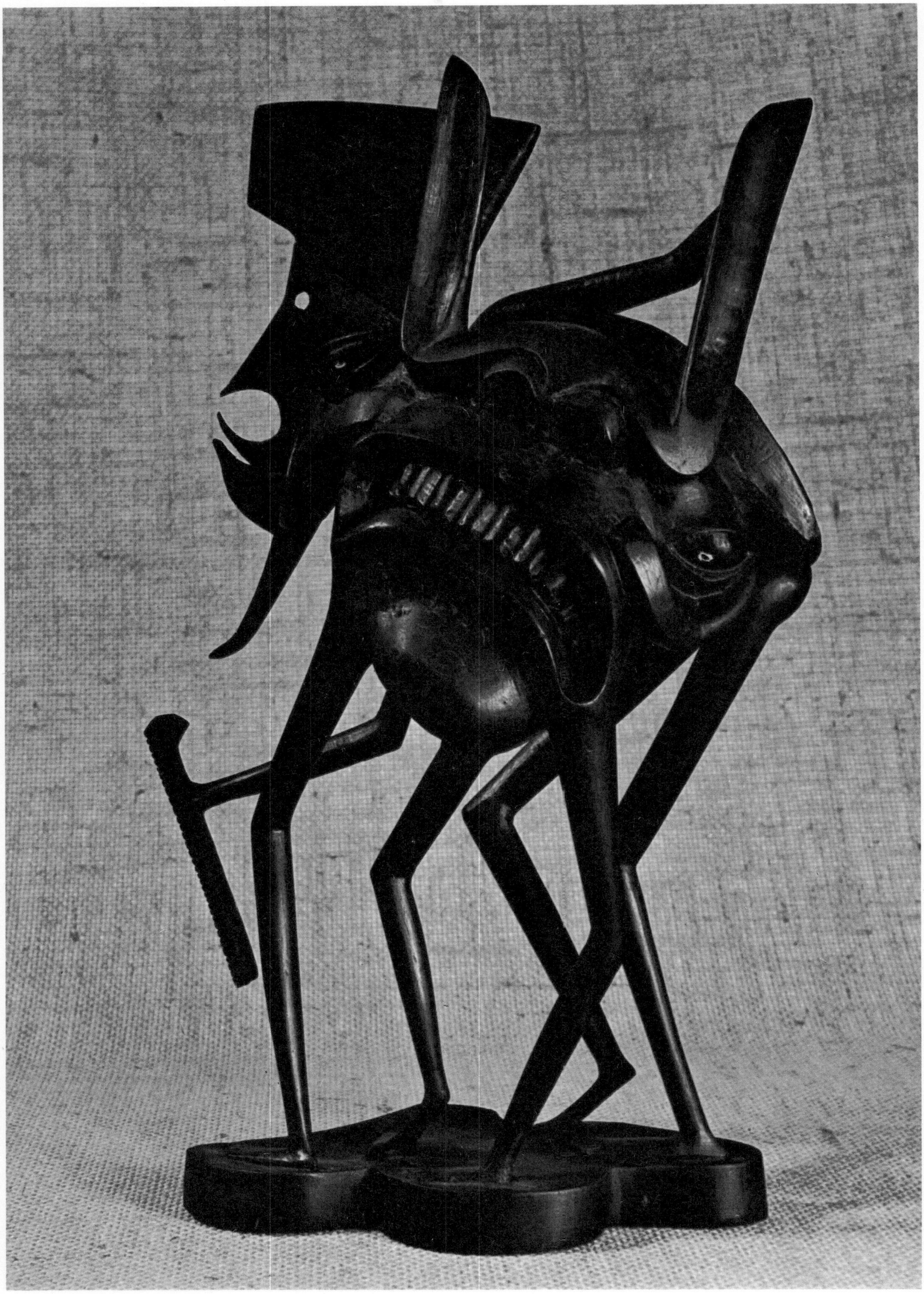

A complicated shetani unit. Rashidi bin Mohamed, 1969. 40 cm

Mask. A witch-doctor. Rashidi bin Mohamed, 1968. 28 cm

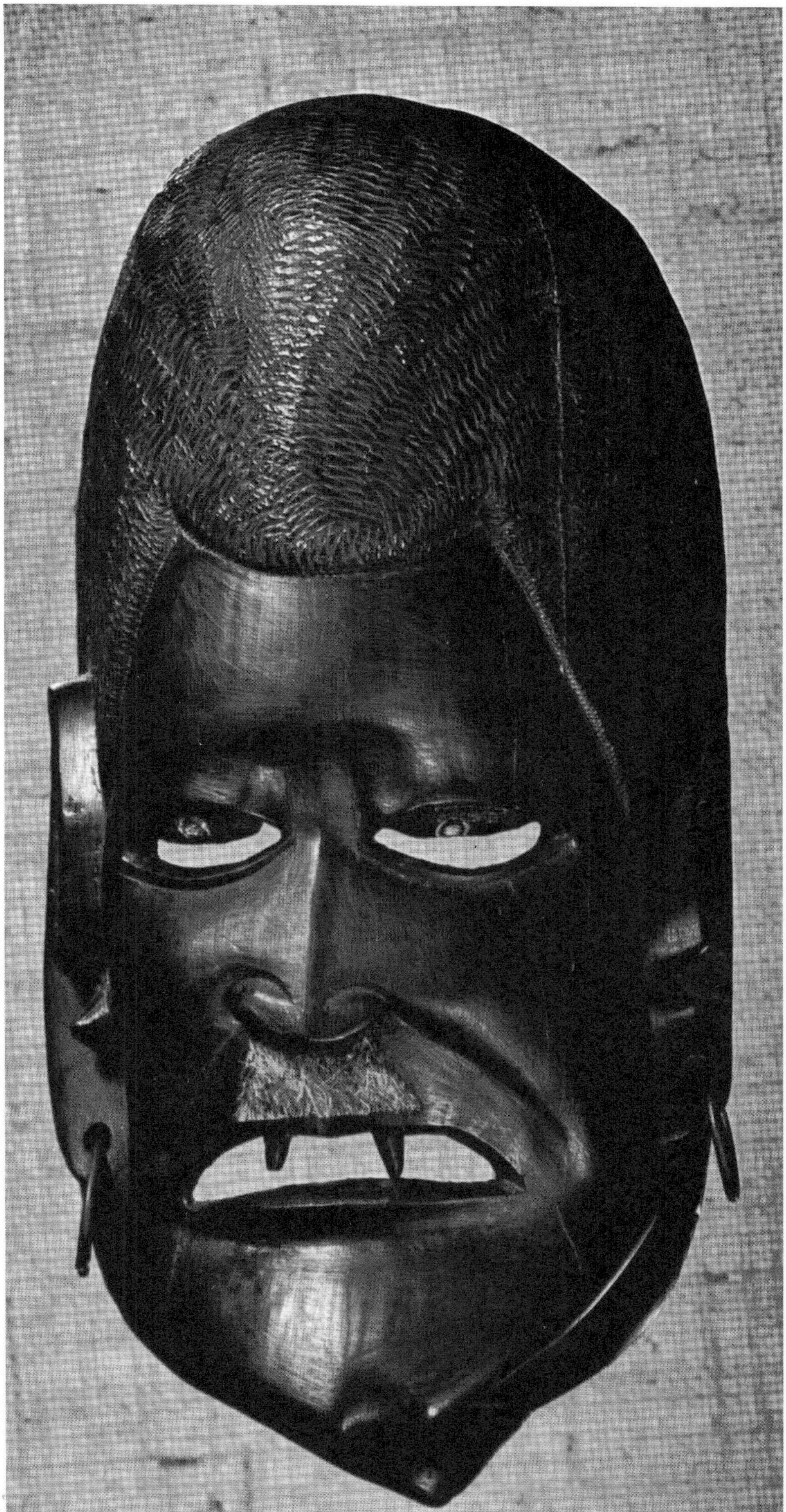

Mozambique shetani. An old shetani stood like a tree in the forest. A chameleon shetani came along and did not notice him. The chameleon began to walk up his legs and belly, and the old shetani curved backwards in surprise crying 'No, no, Sir' ('Eh-eh, Bwana!'). Rashidi bin Mohamed, 1968. 48 cm

Kisarawe shetani from near Pugu railway station. This man-like shetani was walking along with a heavy board and became tired. He is now resting, preparing himself to such blood from the chameleon which accompanied him on the journey. Rashidi bin Mohamed, 1967. 38 cm

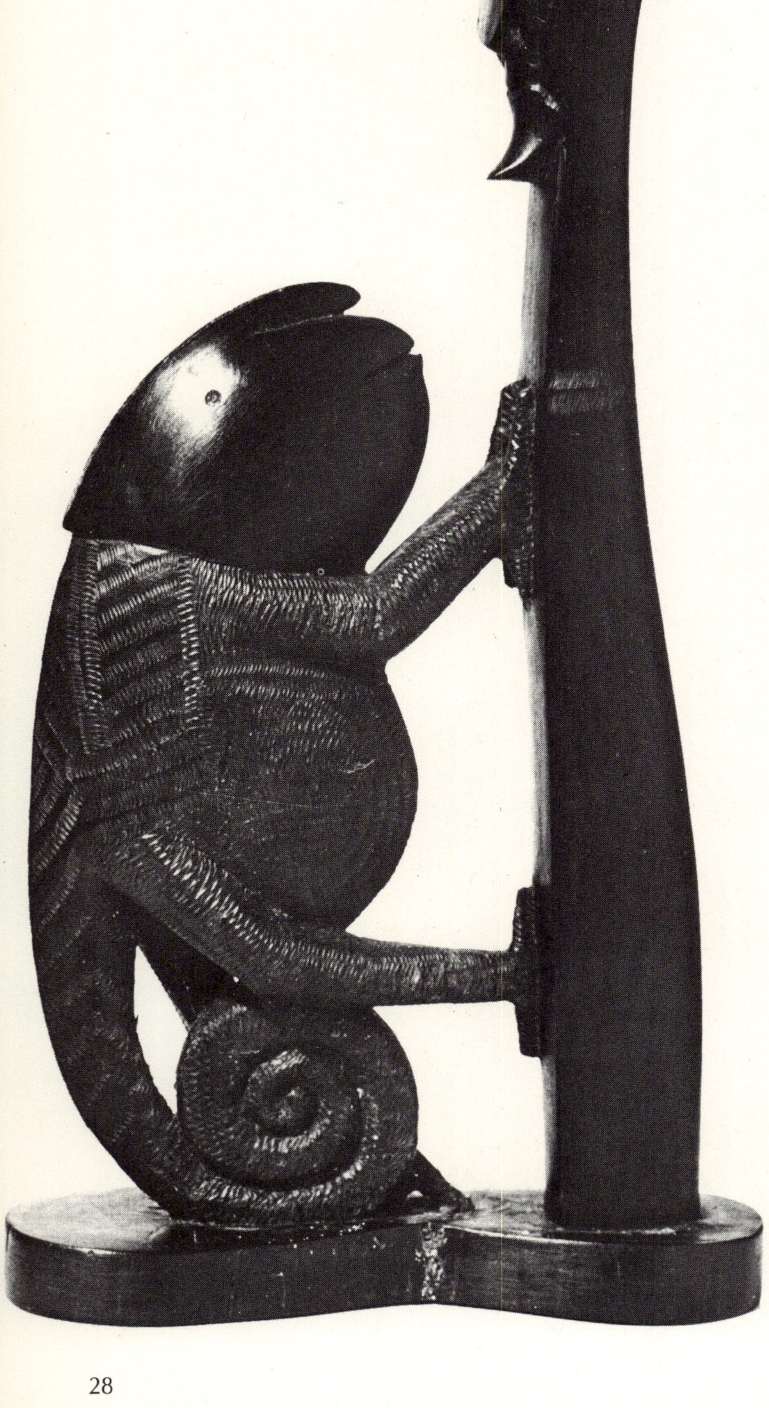

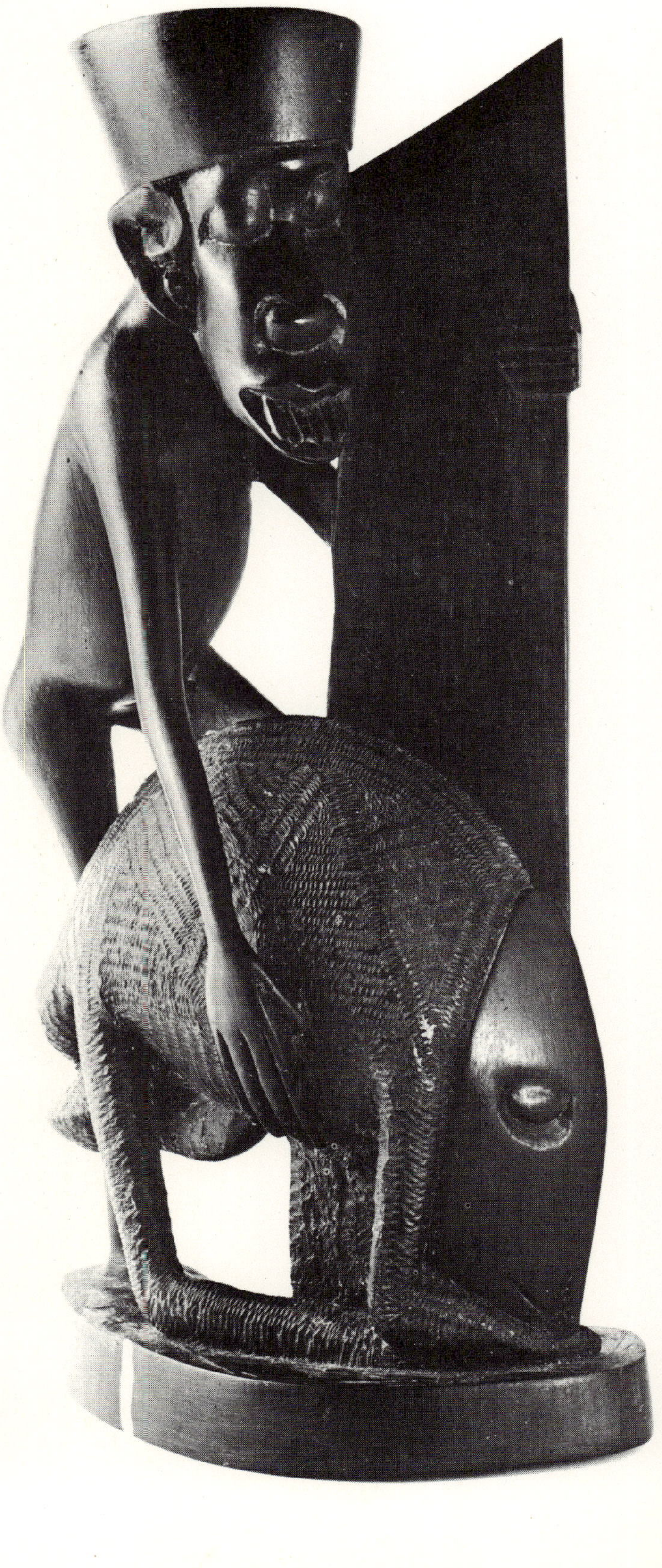

A Mozambique shetani unit. The upper part is male, the lower is female. The female is shaped like a chameleon and transports the unit. The upper shetani-part sucks blood from the lower one through his pointed chin. In this way, the unit is partly self-contained. Rashidi bin Mohamed, 1968. 34 cm

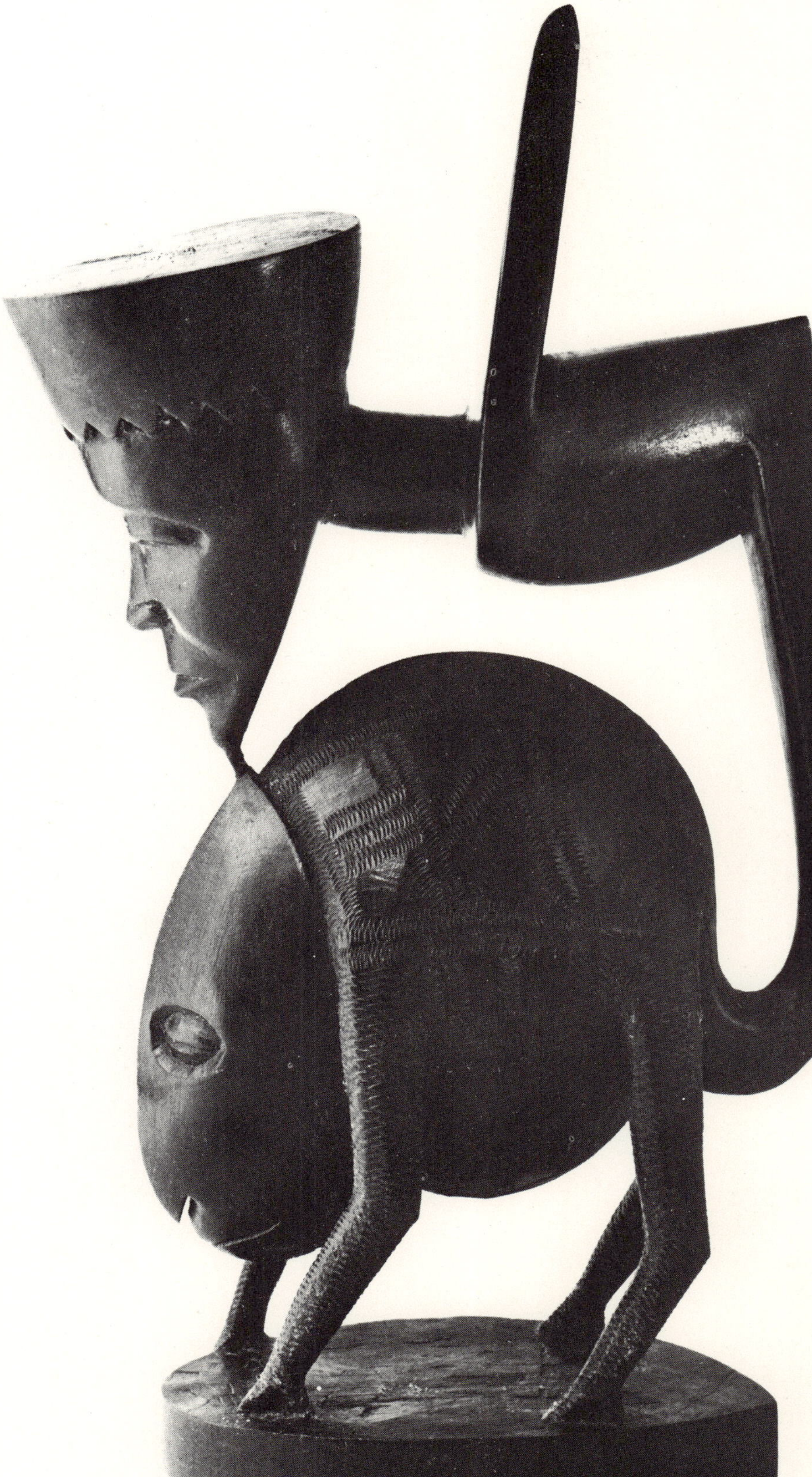

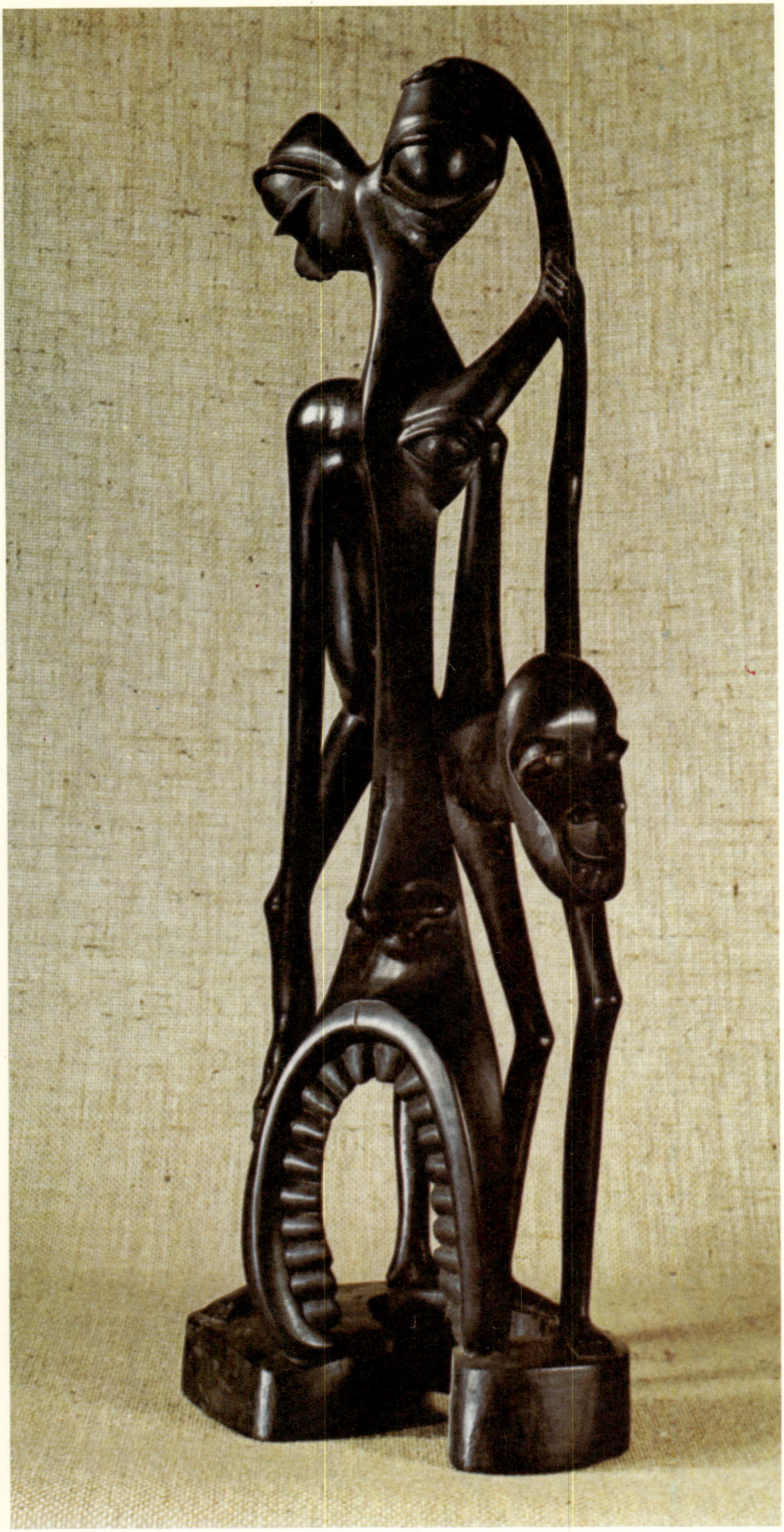

Pair of Kubwengu shetani. Enormous forest species. Prefers bush-pigs as prey. Yoseph Francis' father saw one once when walking together with a man and a woman. Yoseph Francis, 1969. 77 cm

Mask. Female shetani. Yoseph Francis, 1969. 49 cm

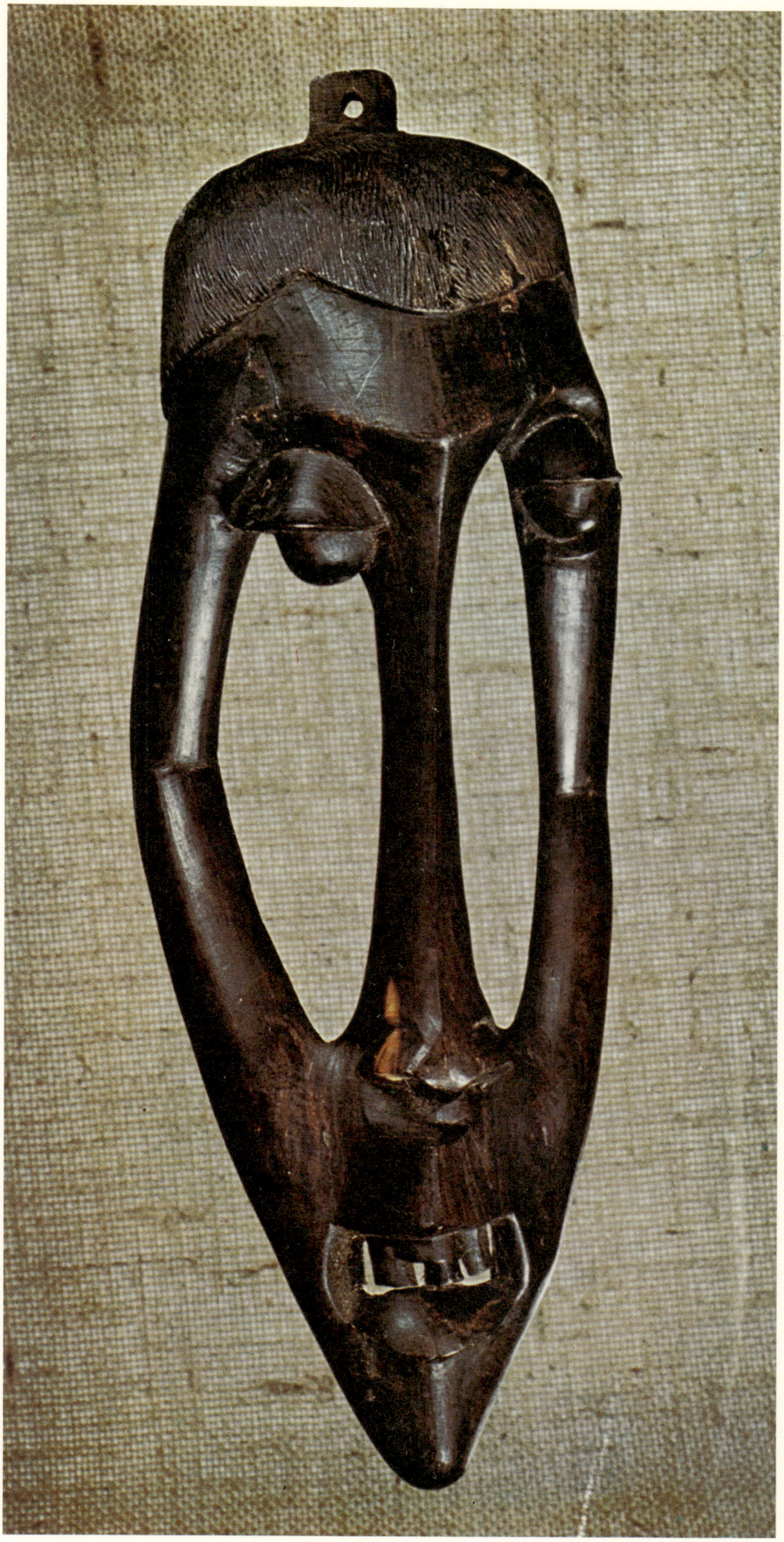

A female shetani from Lindi. One of the largest and most cruel species. Will kill people in their houses by night. Rashidi bin Mohamed, 1969. 58 cm

Chameleon shetani. Lion-sized, and common in the bush forest around Kibaha, Dar es Salaam. Rashidi bin Mohamed, 1967. 25 cm

Ukunduka couple. Ukundukas are a large and dangerous species of shetani which will occasionally interrupt the pregnancies of village women. Ukundukas feed only through sexual intercourse. Kashimiri Matayo, 1969. 81 and 76 cm

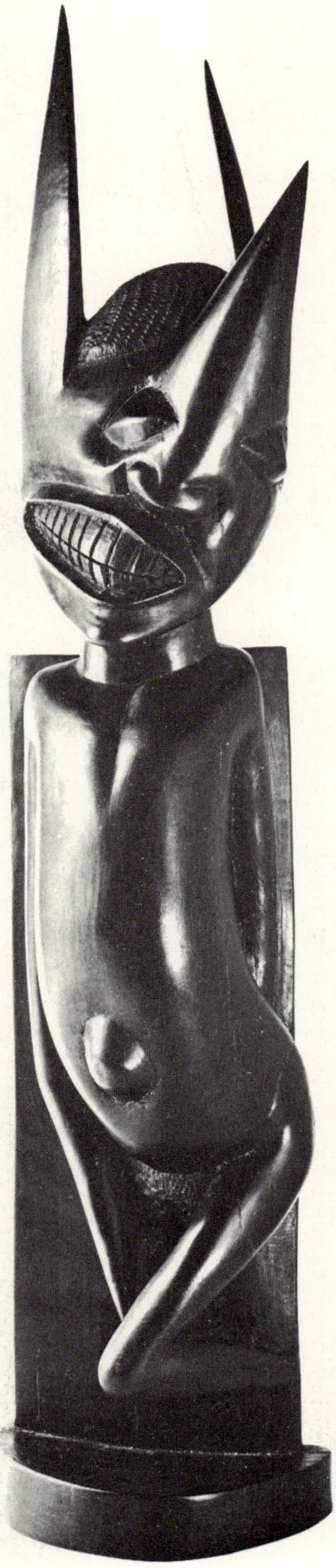

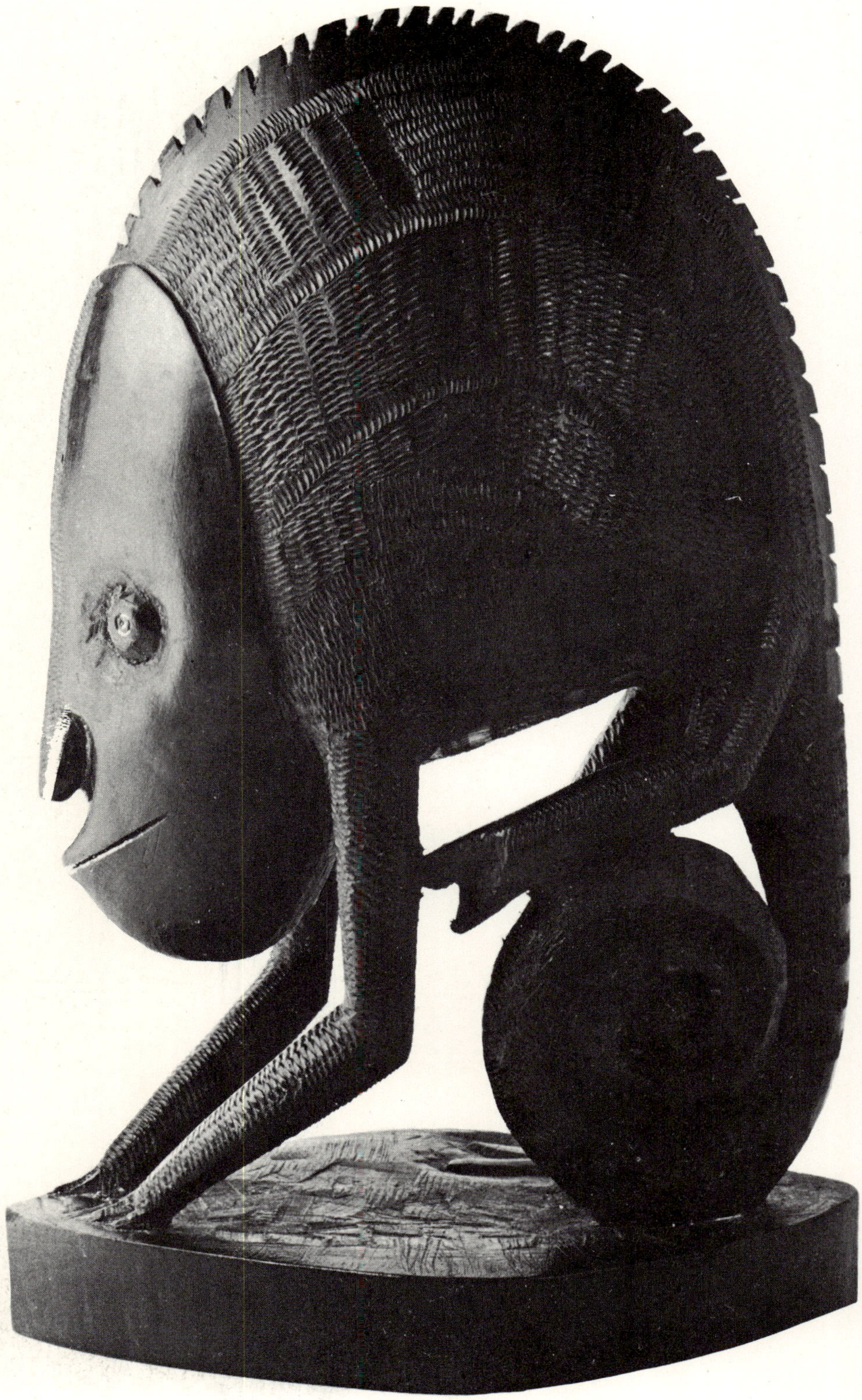

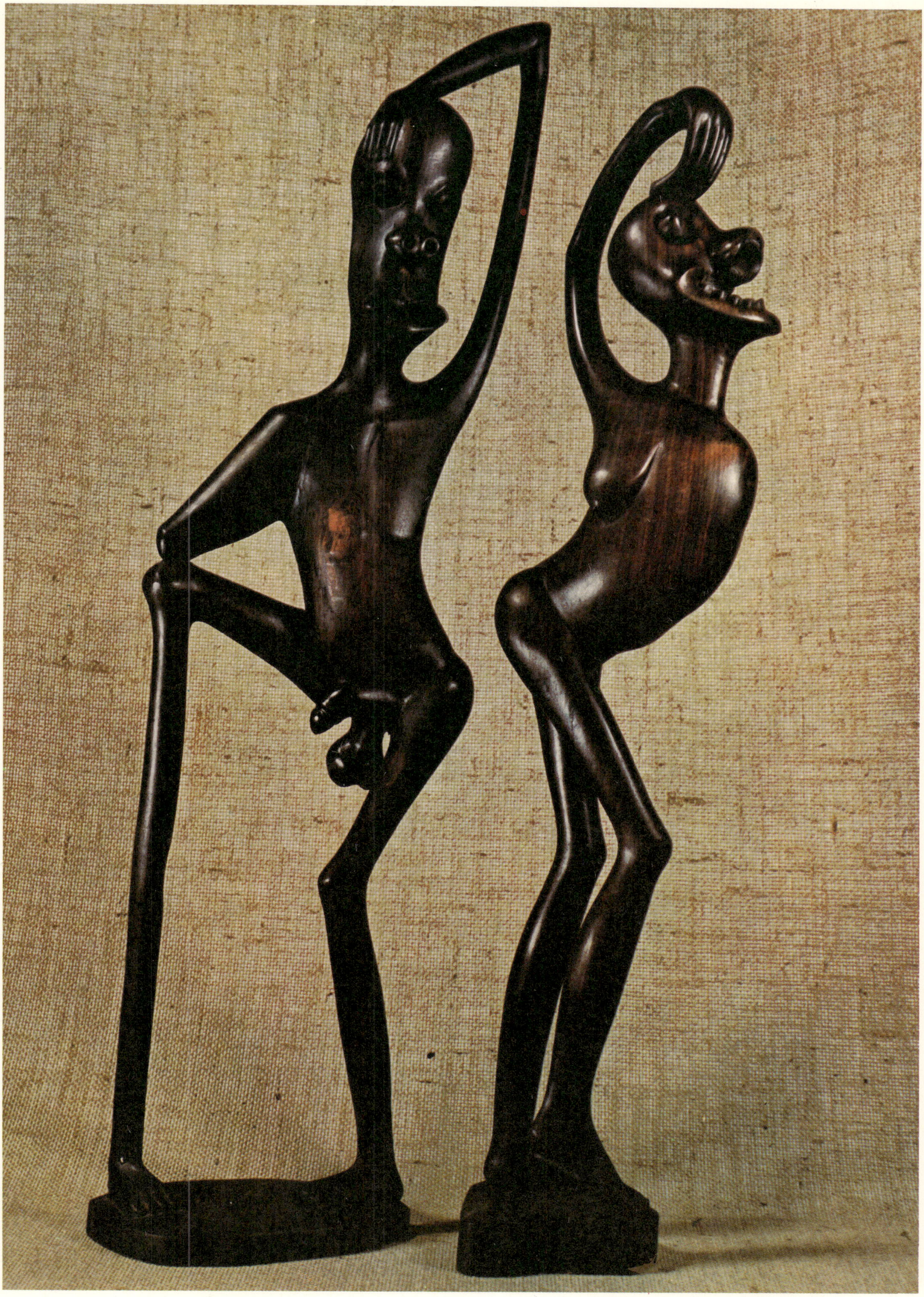

Kashimiri Matayo

Kashimiri (or Cosmel) Matayo learned to carve in his father's workshop in Mueda, Mozambique, along with his older brother Yoseph Francis. As soon as they were old enough, the brothers joined their father in the family workshop where they carved softwood, then hardwood sculptures for Portuguese patrons. Kashimiri and Yoseph have only earned their livelihood through wood-carving. They have always lived and worked together and few people can distinguish between their work until 1969.

In 1955 the brothers migrated together from north-eastern Mozambique to Dar es Salaam, the major market for Makonde carving. By the late 1960s they had moved to the village of Kaubwa near Kibaha where the author met them. Kashimiri now lives in a house by the main road with his wife and children. A thatched shed behind the house is his workshop, which is also shared by his uncle, Shuruma Masheka, a specialist in carving masks.

At 33 years old, Kashimiri is a handsome man with an easy, full smile. He is polite, modest and self-conscious. He is very hard-working and conscientious about his work. He does not have much contact with other Makonde craftsmen who seem less disciplined and organized than he is.

Unlike Rashidi bin Mohamed, Kashimiri rarely selects his block of hardwood from the shrub himself. To fell a *mpingo* tree requires a government licence which is bought for 30 shillings. Instead, Kashimiri will usually pay about 8 shillings for a block selected from the stock of a curio dealer. He chooses his blocks carefully and rejects anything faulty. He works by himself until his sculptures are ready for the finishing touches. He uses the ordinary tools of all Makonde carvers and sometimes employs sharp instruments made by himself or villagers from car wrecks which abound along the Dar es Salaam–Morogoro road. The finishing touches are often accomplished by his wife Rusia. She works with glass-paper and brush. The finish on the dense ebony-like structure is so fine that the piece looks as if it were polished, which is not the case, for Kashimiri never applies wax or oil to his carvings.

Kashimiri usually works from 6 a.m. to 6 p.m., hardly allowing himself time off to eat or rest during the daylight hours. He works continuously on a sculpture until it is completed. On the average, one sculpture requires slightly more than a week of his

Kashimiri Matayo

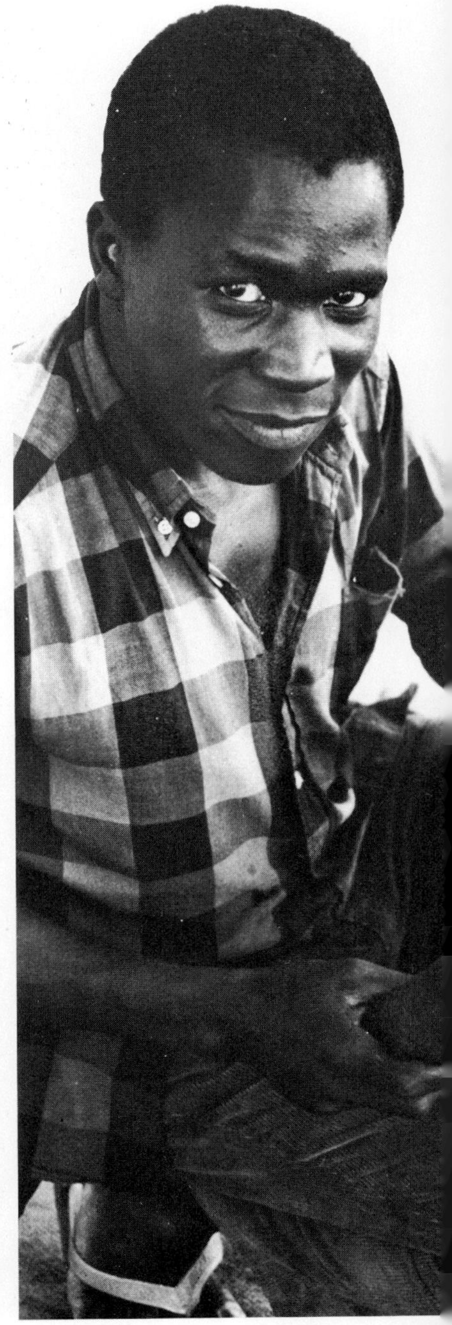

labour. As soon as one is finished, he takes it to a patron for review, then returns home immediately to see what is 'inside' the next block of hardwood. Thick horny pads of skin on his hands where his tools rest are testimony to his hard work.

Each of his sculptures cost several hundred shillings. Considering the skill and time involved, his comparatively high prices seem inadequate compensation for Kashimiri's skill and imagination. His wife may request a token of 50 cents from a buyer for her part in the achievement. Kashimiri uses his earnings mainly for his family and his parents in Mozambique. He cannot afford luxuries such as a bicycle or cigarettes.

According to Kashimiri, Makonde art originated many years ago when the Portuguese encouraged his ancestors to make replicas of sacred figurines that were used in Makonde ceremonies. His father used to produce such carvings, but Kashimiri only vaguely remembers what they looked like. He recalls that they depicted scenes from village life, the original topic of his own art.

Kashimiri only began to carve shetani after his migration to Tanzania. He has never seen a shetani himself, but an incident that his father describes remains vivid to him. His father was walking home through the bush one evening when suddenly a huge creature blocked his way and struck him to the ground. He lay unconscious for some time before he managed to struggle to his feet and walk home. He was still shivering when he reached his house. This event made a strong impression on both Kashimiri and his brother Yoseph Francis.

Shetani were a fascinating subject for conversation and story-telling. Kashimiri believes they existed at one time, but rarely do to-day. There were about ten types of spirits in the traditional tales told by his father and grandfather. They were described in such detail that he has no difficulty in producing images of them. He does not work in a pre-set pattern, but lets his imagination play freely with the mythical creatures. None of his sculptures has magical powers, Kashimiri says.

At first his sculptures were of medium size. They bore no significant sexual characteristics other than female breasts and the lip-plug which is still common among Makonde women.

Since 1969, he has developed a special style of his own. The sculpture increased in size and he began to elaborate the male sexual organs of the shetani. The first one of this type he wrapped up in a cloth in order to take it to a patron. He hid the sculpture, not for religious reasons, but to save himself shame and embarrassment if his wife should see such a thing. Kashimiri is a Roman Catholic, and he thanks God for his power to depict shetani.

The shetani Ngong'aijia nursing her child. Kashimiri Matayo, 1969. 73 cm

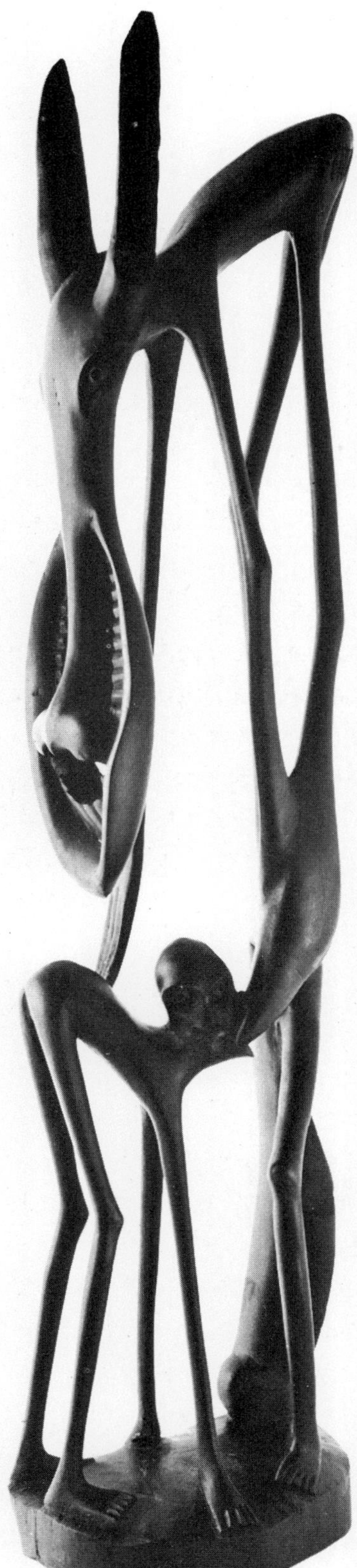

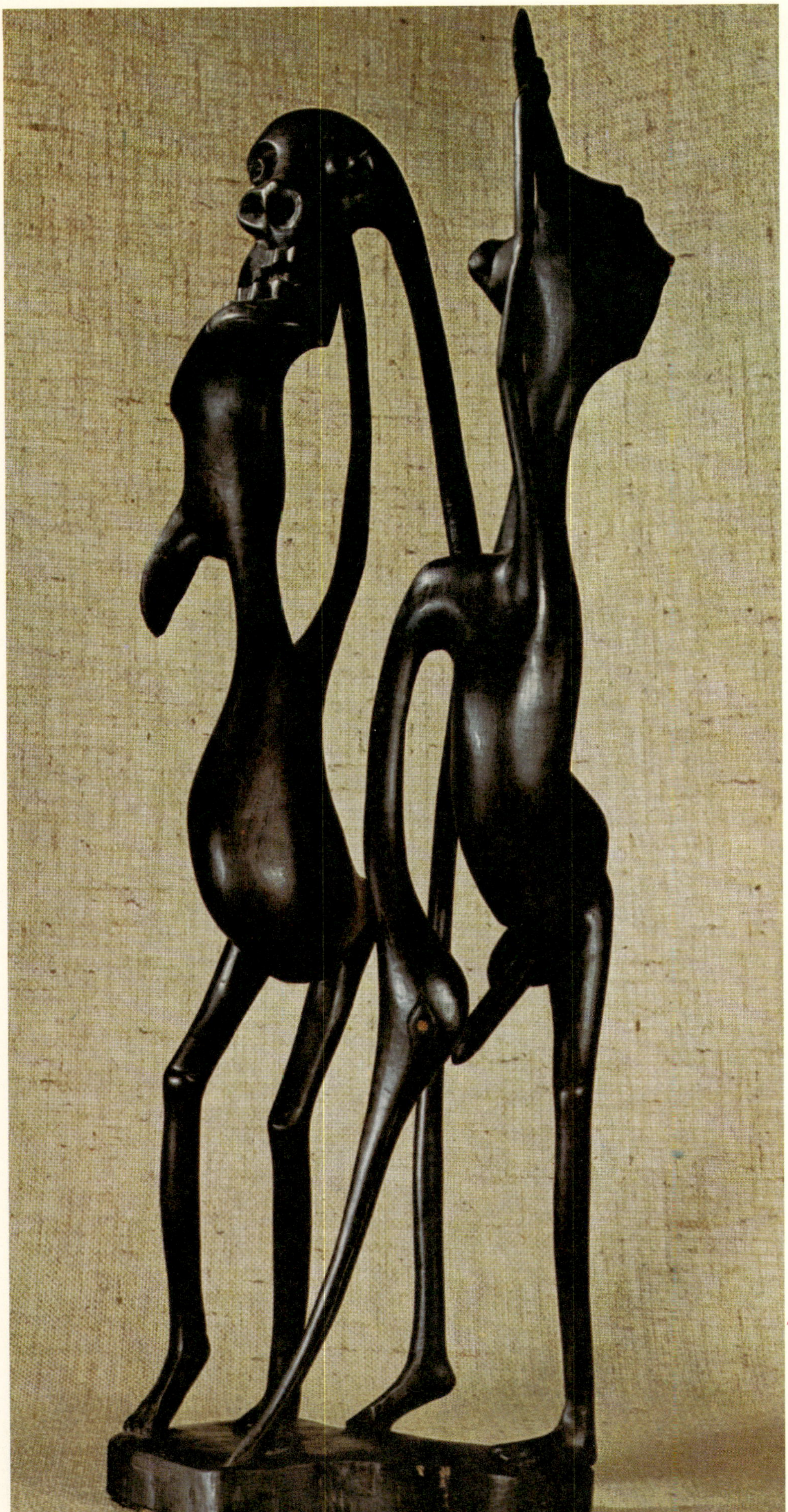

'Baba na Mama' shetani.
Kashimiri Matayo, 1969. 92 cm

'Baba na Mama' shetani.
Kashimiri Matayo, 1969. 92 cm

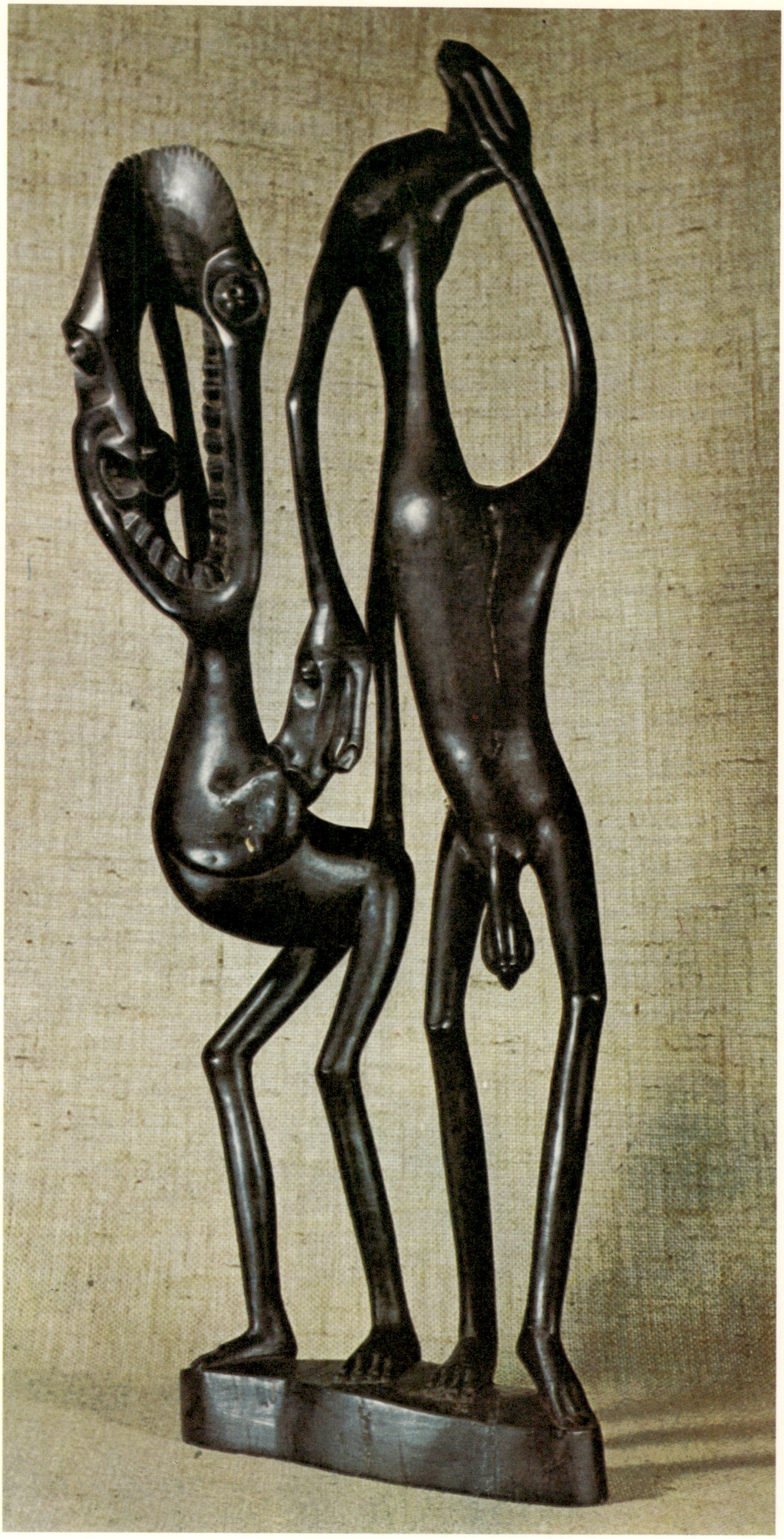

Shulwele shetani unit. Shulweles are 'doctor-shetani' who collect and feed on medicine-herbs. The smaller Shulwele below is named Muntela. Muntela is here being fed by the upper shetani after having helped to fill the jar with herbs. Shulweles usually dwell in and around large trees. Kashimiri Matayo, 1969. 56 cm

Chipinga shetani unit. Shetani of this type are common around Dar es Salaam. Clay is their main food, but they are dangerous to human beings. Their habitat is deserted warthog holes. Kashimiri Matayo, 1969. 84 cm

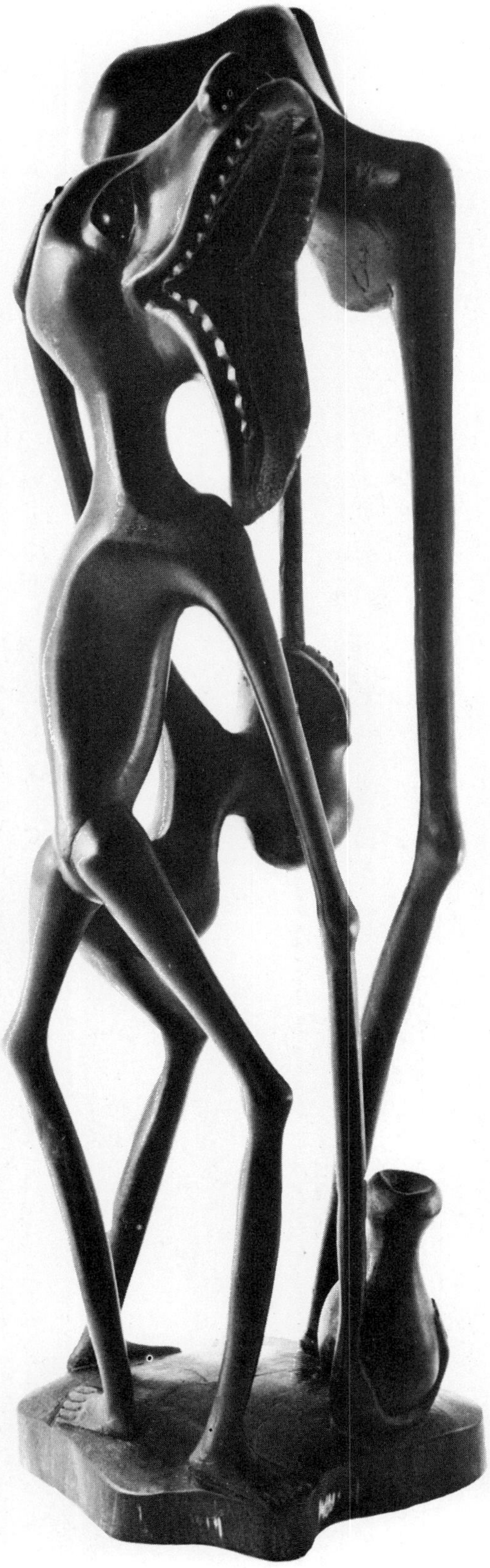

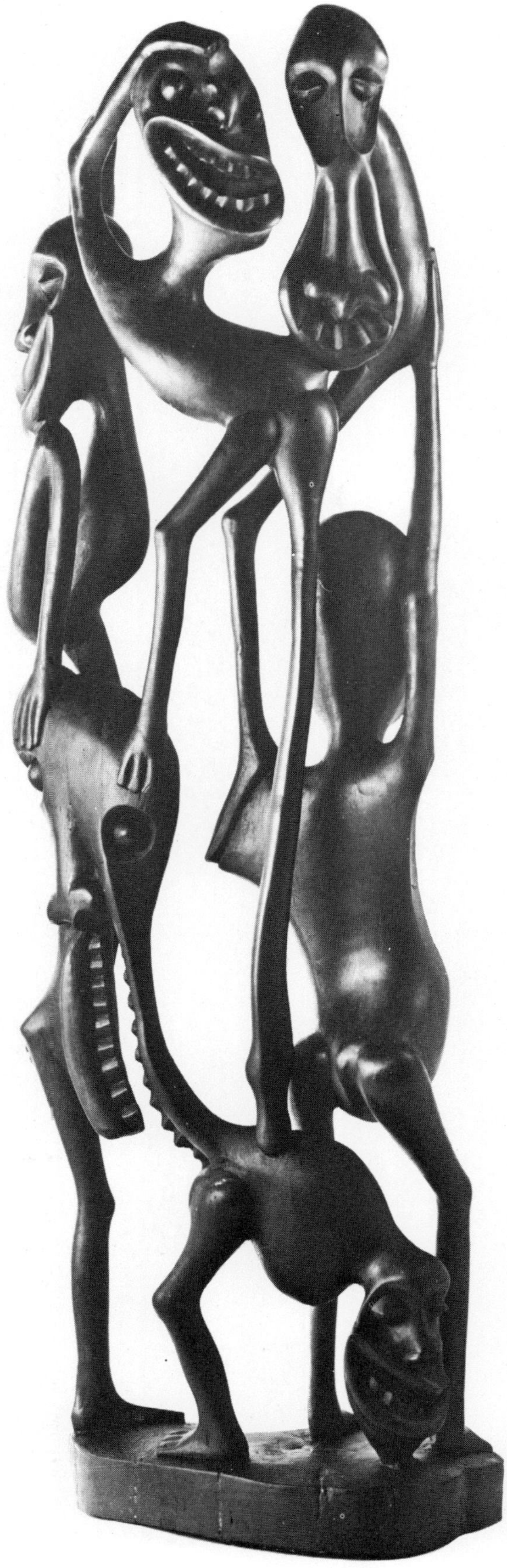

Manganyu shetani unit. Carnivore shetani species from the burnt-off savannah areas. Kashimiri Matayo, 1969. 84 cm

Adinkula, a forest shetani from Mozambique. Very large but not very dangerous. Also called Aidimhulla. Kashimiri Matayo, 1968. 56 cm

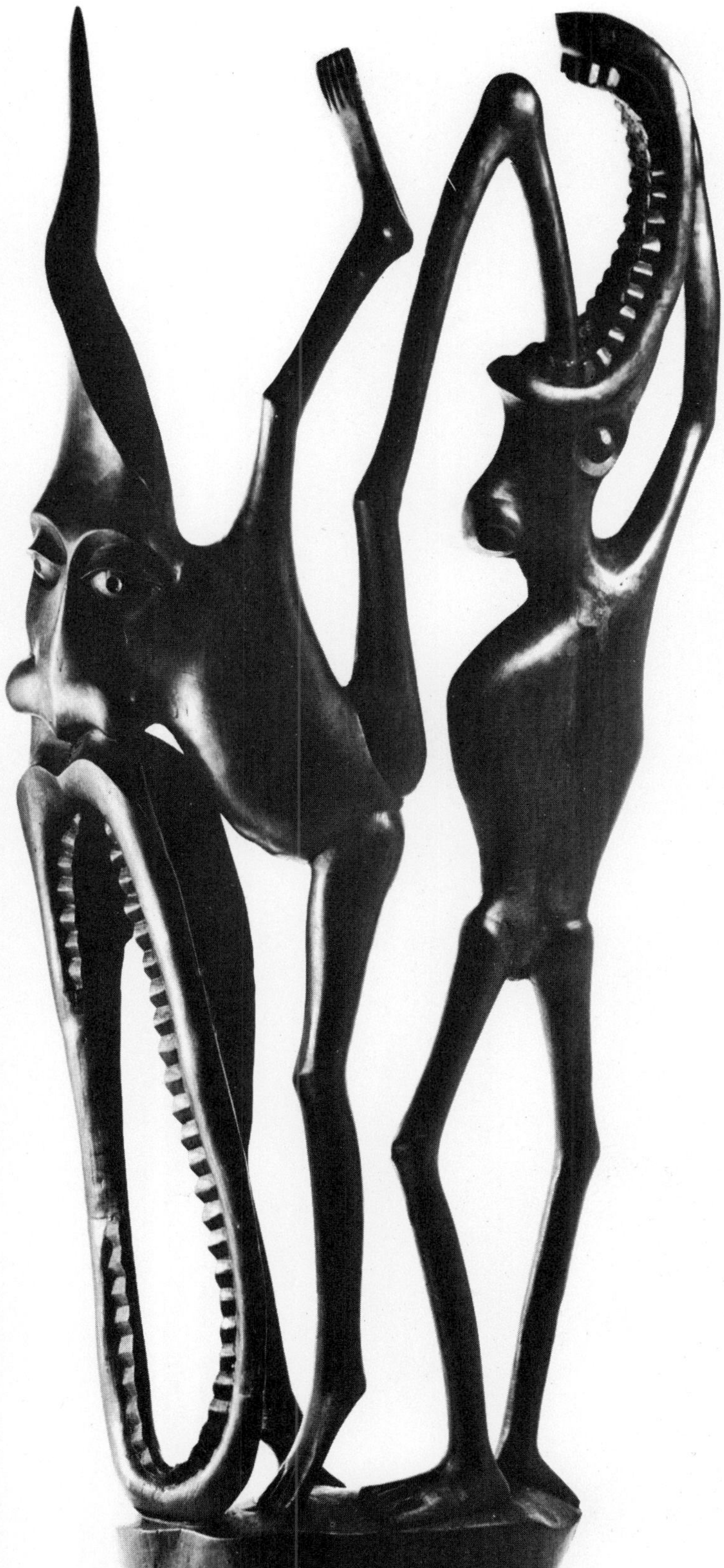

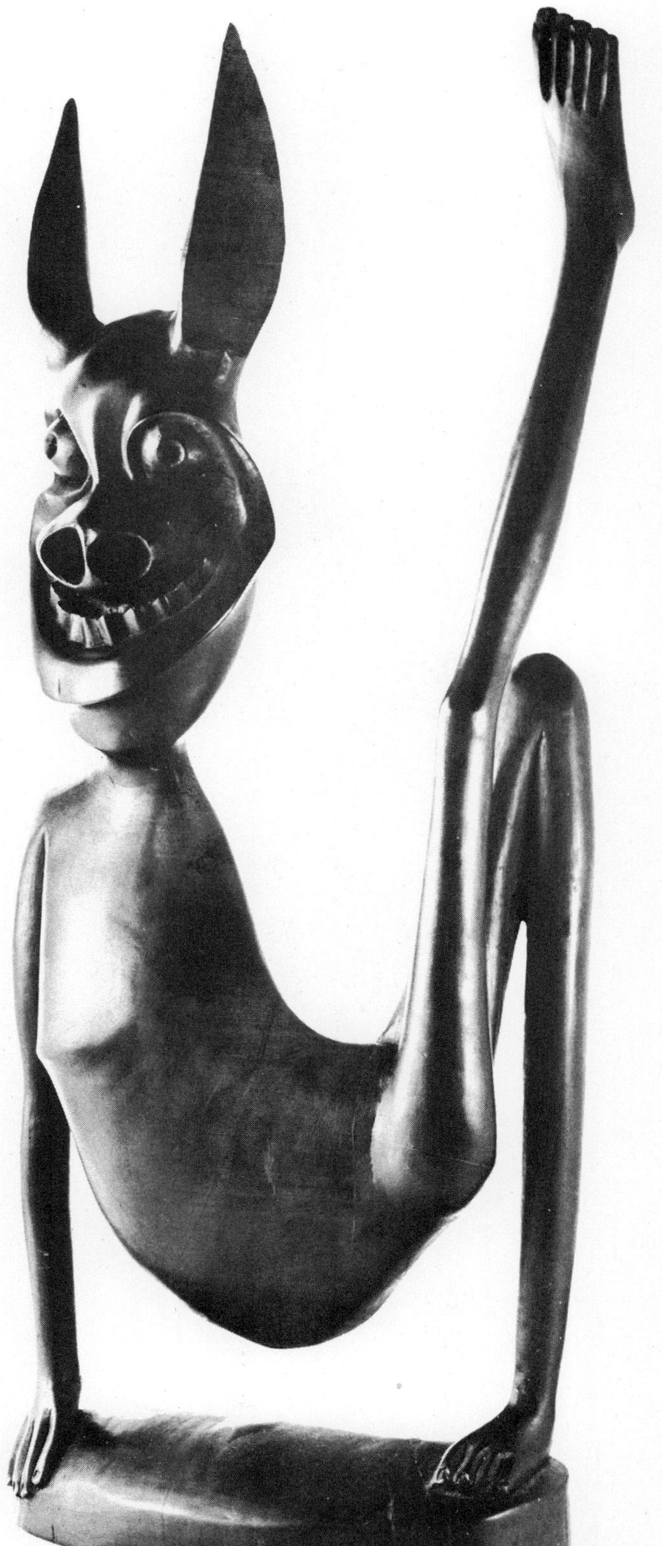

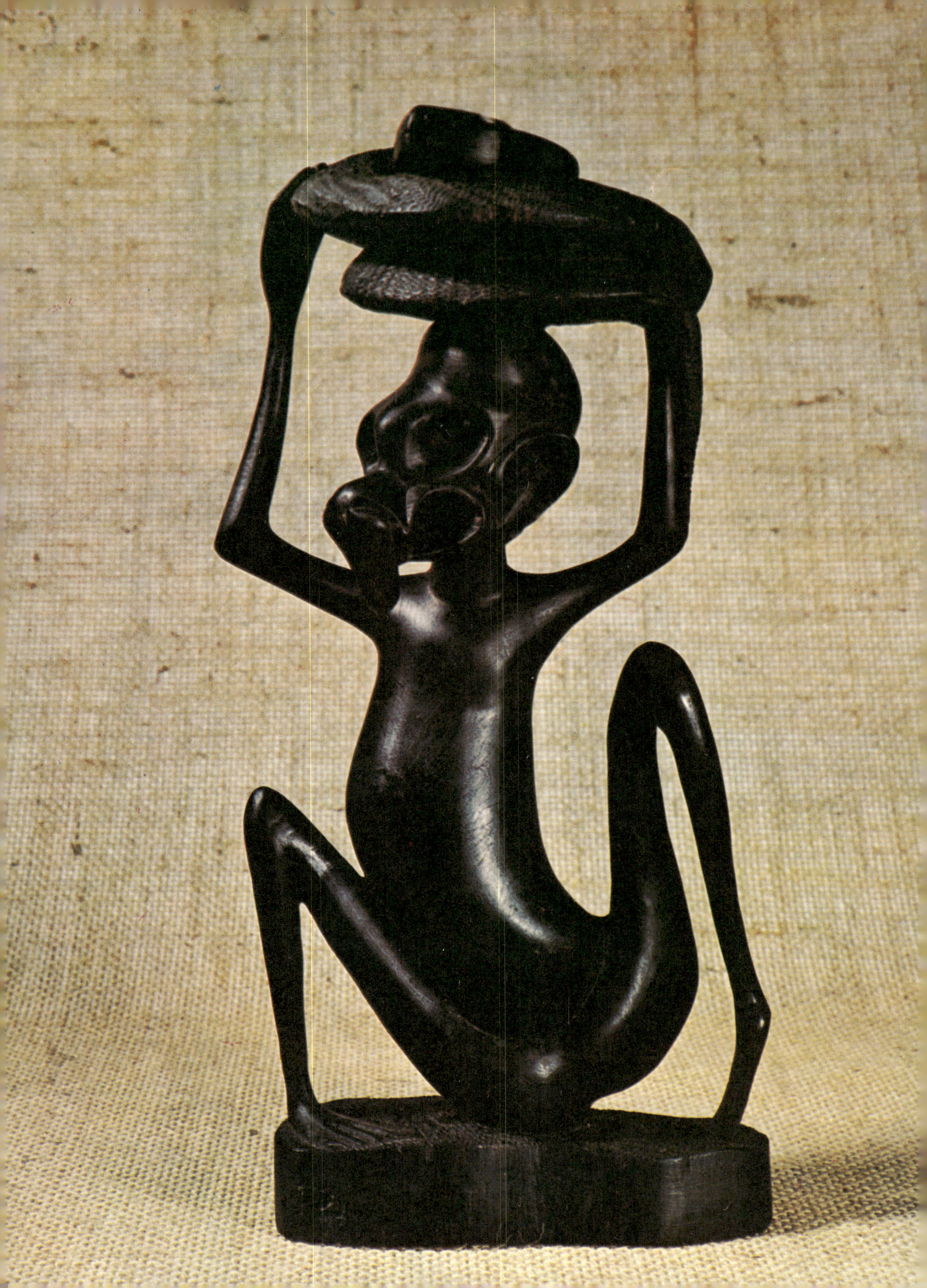

Mbilika shetani. The Mbilika carries home a large puff-adder from his hunt in the barren bush-lands. Mbilikas live almost exclusively from snakes. They eat them raw; shetani never use fire for cooking. Nafasi Mpagua, 1968. 31 cm

Aija and Mwituao. The larger Mwituao shetani is performing an erotic play with the tongue of the Aija, who supports his hydrocele (water-hernia of the scrotum, caused by filariasis). Nafasi Mpagua, 1969. 52 cm

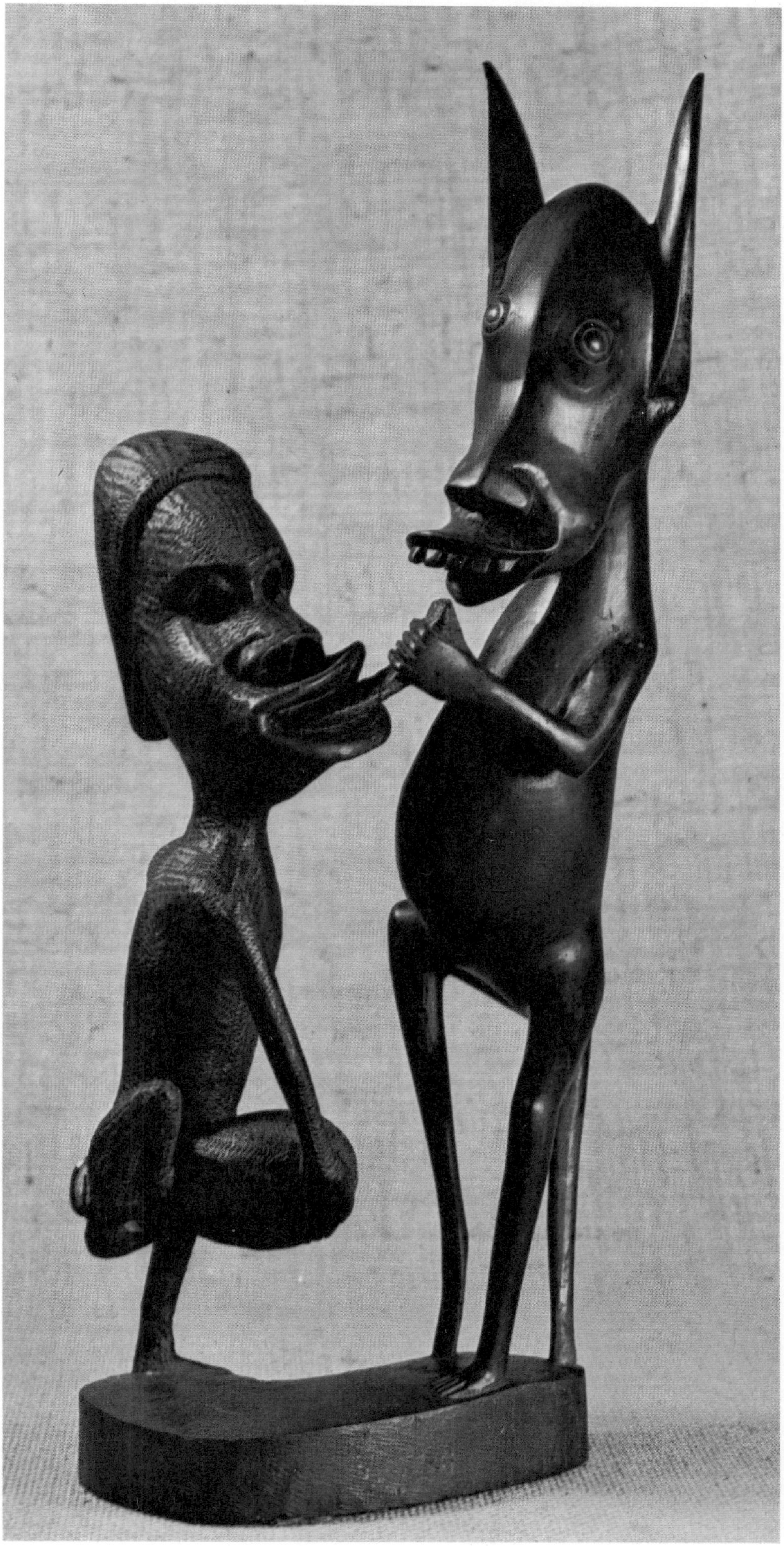

Korongo and Nkombele. The female shetani Korongo (head up) was left at home when her husband Nkombele went out. As he returned from the day's business, he found that Korongo had eaten up every bit of their food all by herself. So he thrust his fist (seen raised) into her face. And now Korongo weeps and screams eternally from the pain. Kashimiri Matayo, 1969. 53 cm

Ndonja shetani unit. The Ndonja mother orders one of her sons (below) to take water to his sick brother (above). Ndonja shetani will often scare people who travel alone through the bush-land. Kashimiri Matayo, 1969. 56 cm

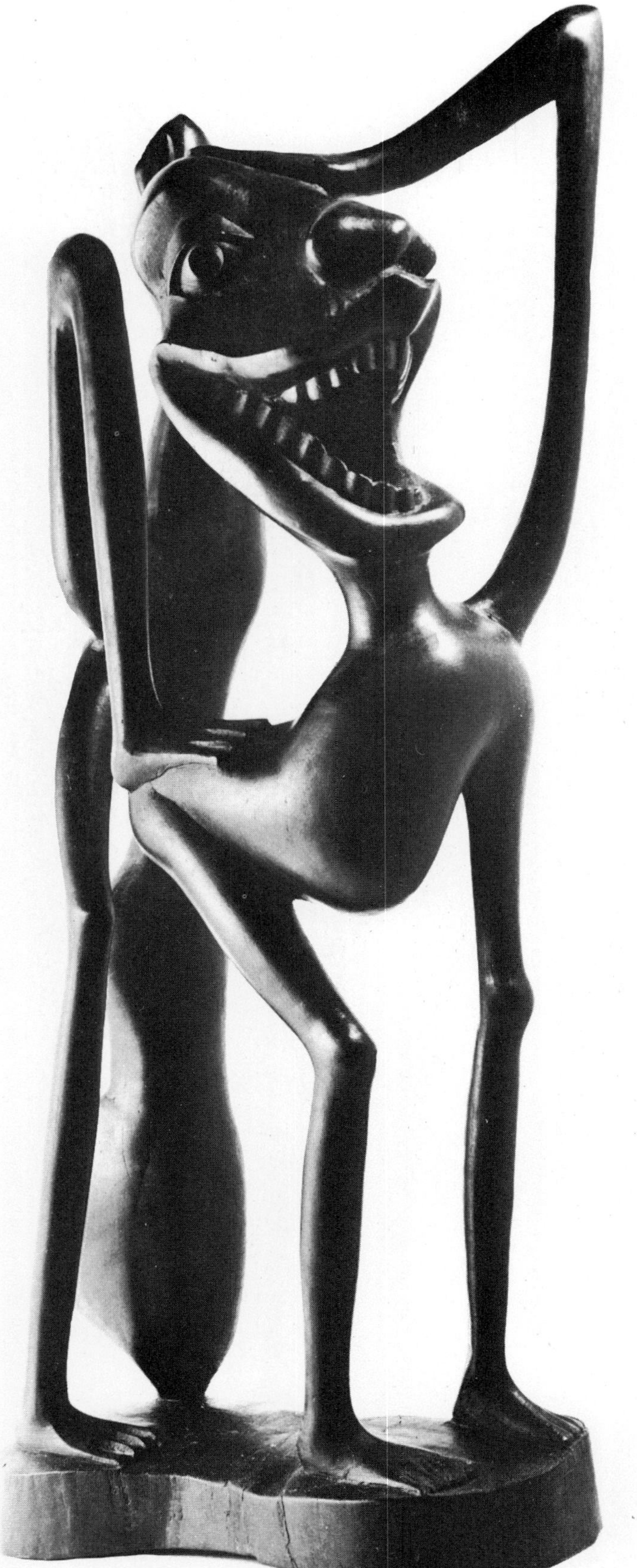

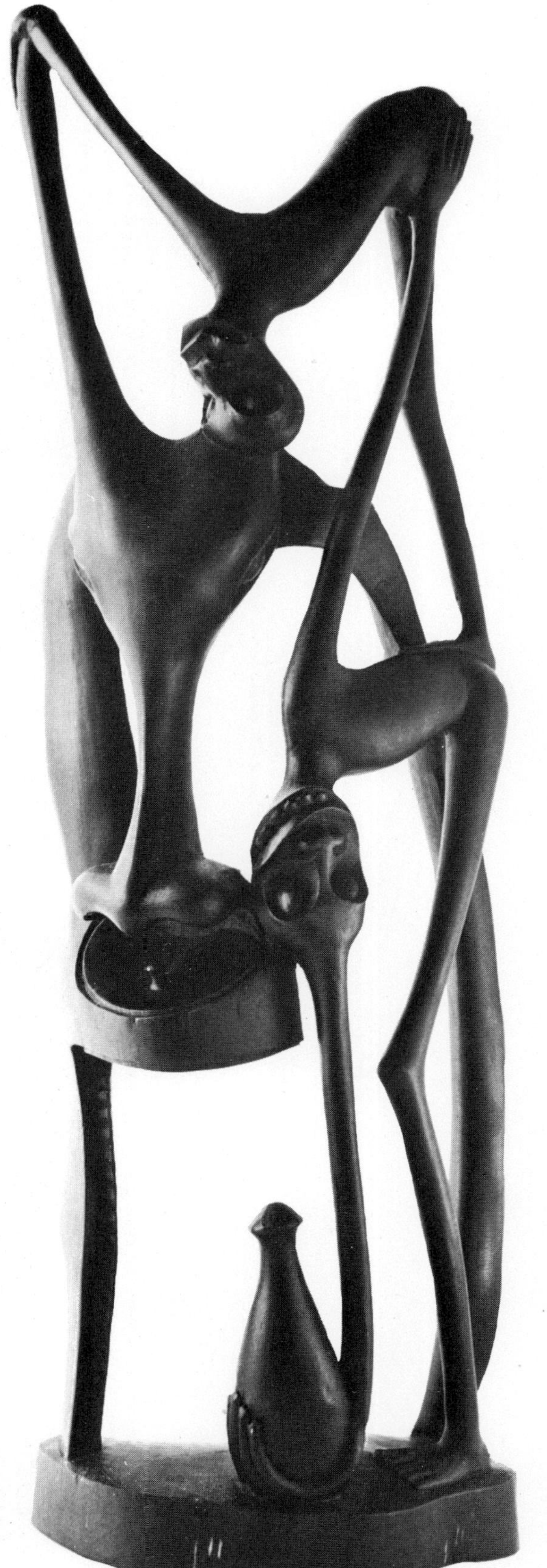

Makanuya. Makanuya shetani are as large as a tall man. Although they live on pure water only, they are terrifying to meet. Kashimiri Matayo, 1969. 71 cm

Kibwenge shetani couple, standing on the beach. The Kibwenges live on fish and dwell in the coastal forest. Kashimiri Matayo, 1969. 56 cm

Mchawe shetani couple and their child. Mchawe means witchcraft, and these shetani do exert witchcraft on the people who meet them in the bush. The Mchawe shetani eat large amounts of clay, herbs and water. Kashimiri Matayo, 1969. 61 cm

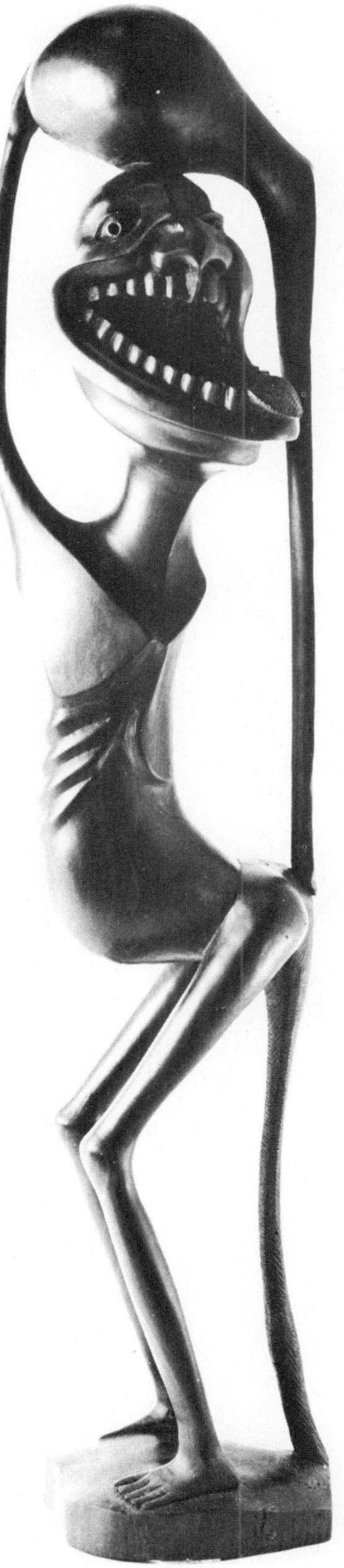

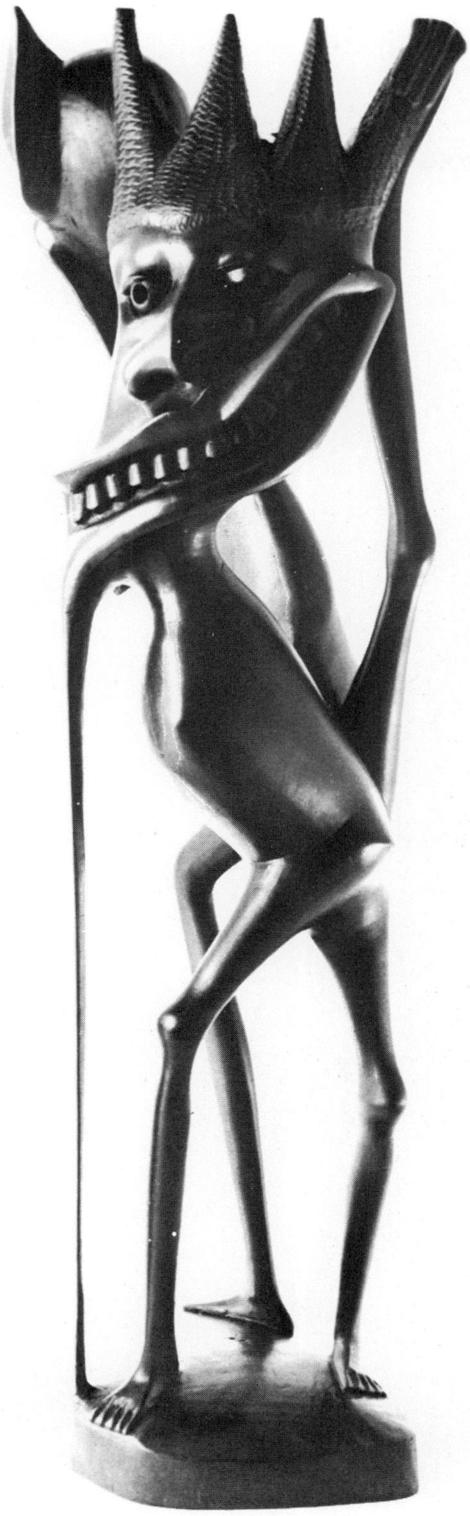

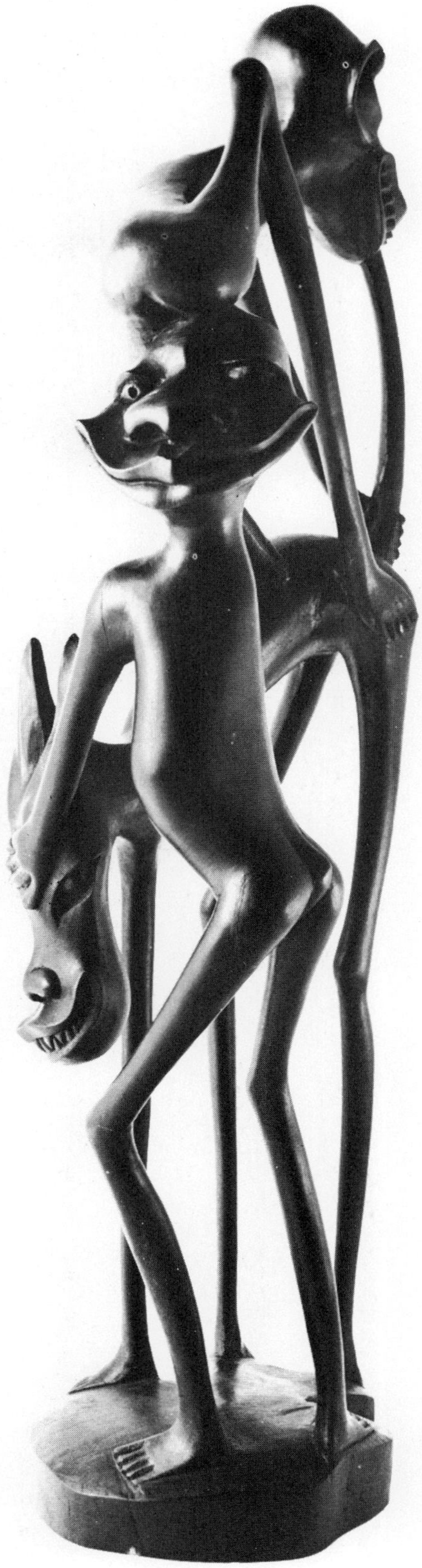

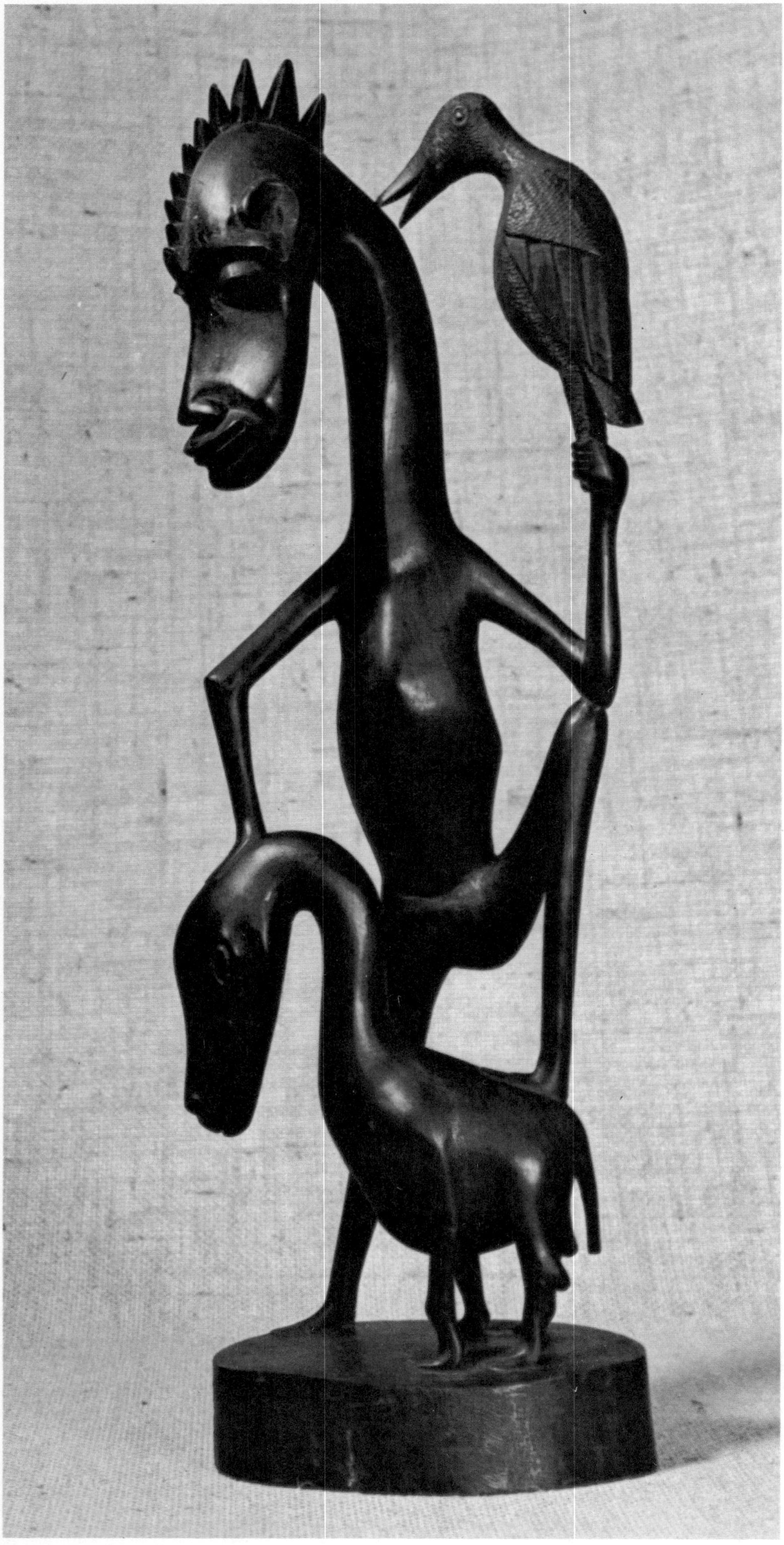

Liyama shetani mounted on his shetani-beast. Liyamas never walk. They are always seen with a kind of shetani bird as a stick or symbol same way as chiefs usually parade a stick or a fly-whisk. The bird is called Shuuni. Nafasi Mpagua, 1969. 57 cm

Siwawi shetani. The Siwawi are fish-eating ocean-dwelling species. By night they ascend the dry land and roam about in couples. Whenever they become exhausted, they will suck energy out of each other's tongues. Nafasi Mpagua, 1968. 48 cm

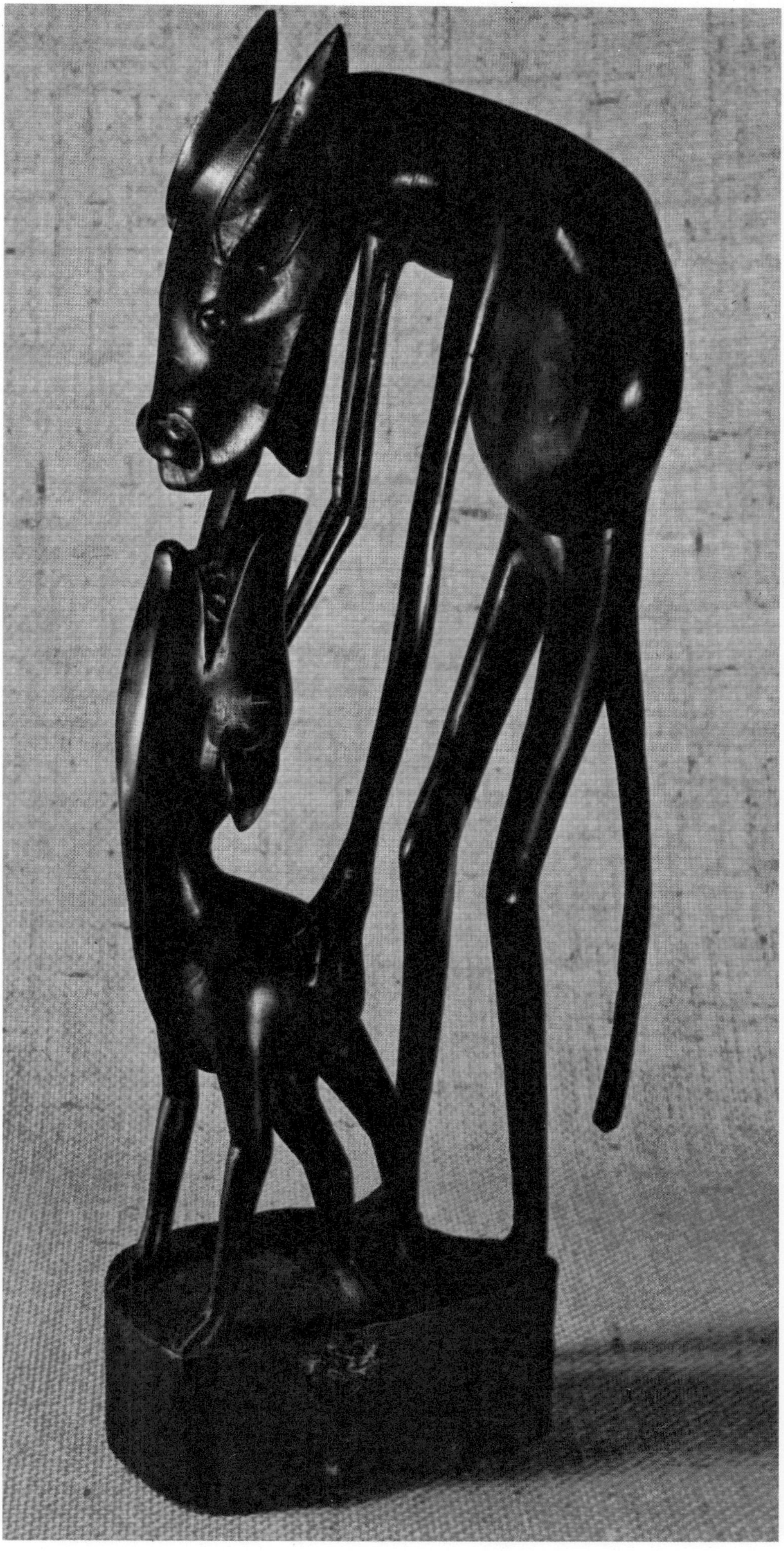

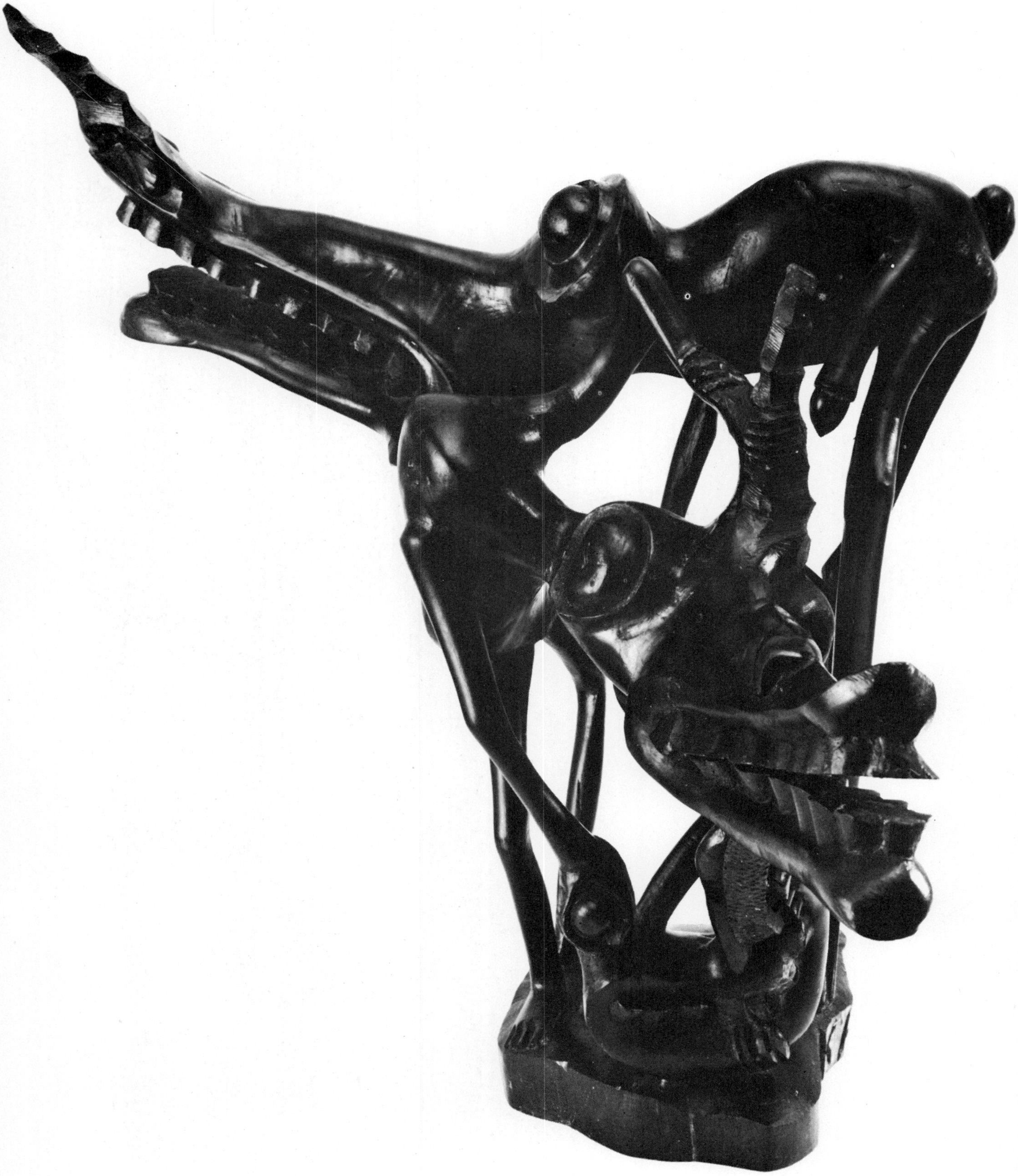

Shetani unit from earth. (This sculpture is carved from the upside-down root section of a blackwood tree-trunk, taking advantage of its irregular shapes.) Kashimiri Matayo, 1970. 51 cm

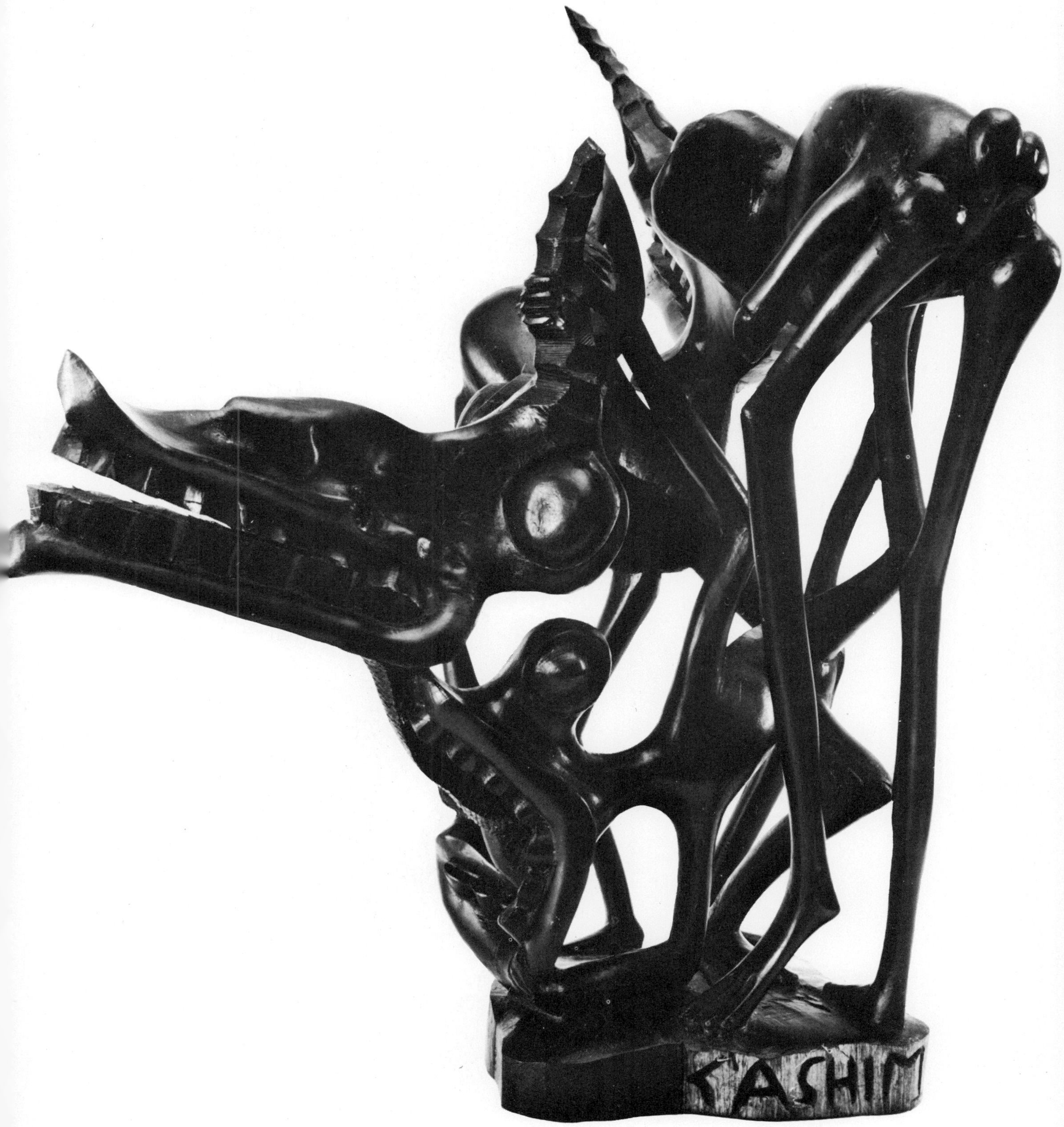

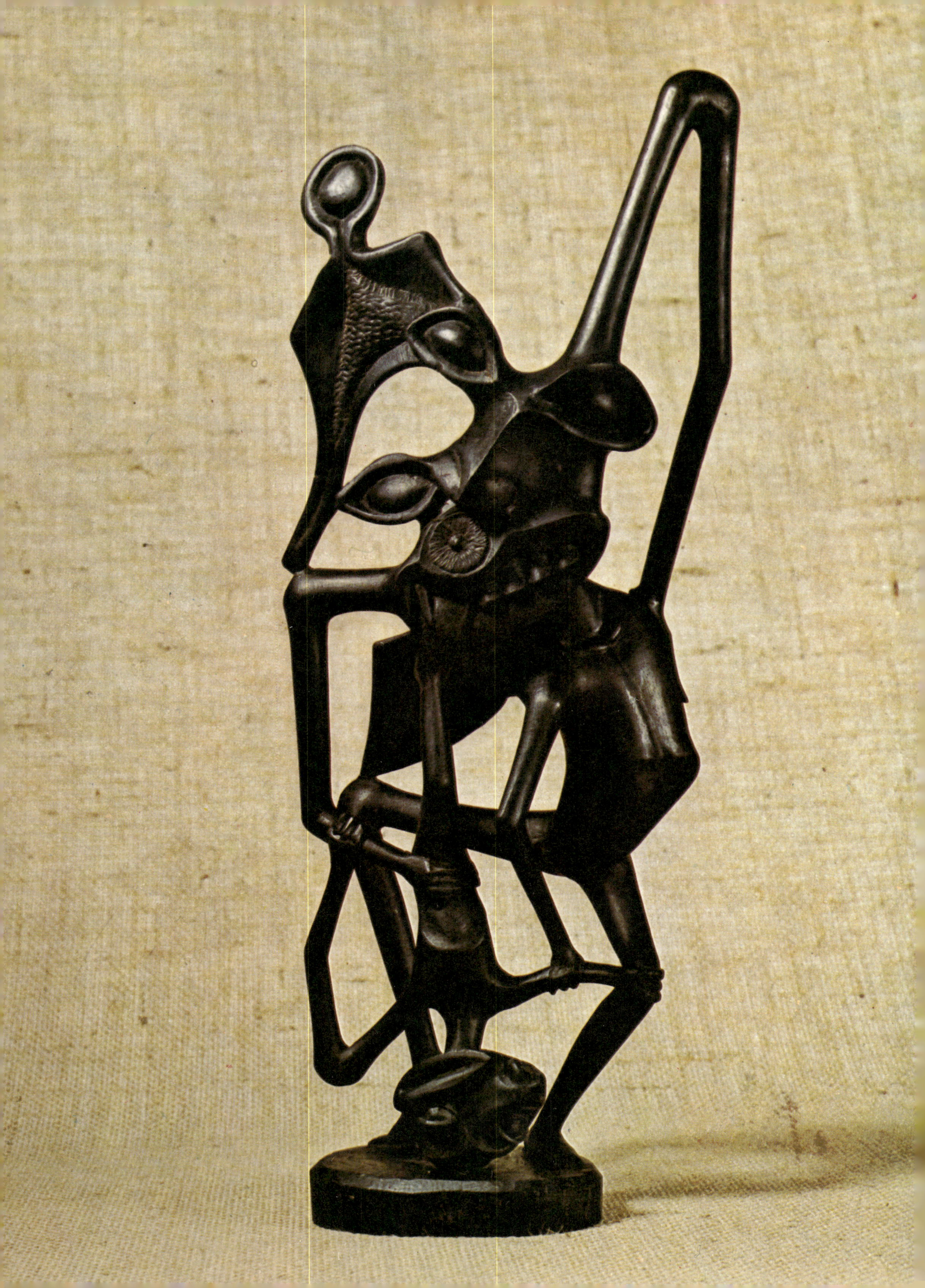

Anonymous shetani (female, with lip-plug) devouring her prey, a young one of another shetani species. Hossein Anangangola, 1969. 40 cm

'Mama na Baba'. Shetani couple. Kashimiri Matayo, 1969. 70 cm

Namangonye shetani unit. The species live in the vicinity of villages and steal food from the gardens. Common around Kibaha. Kashimiri Matayo, 1969. 80 cm

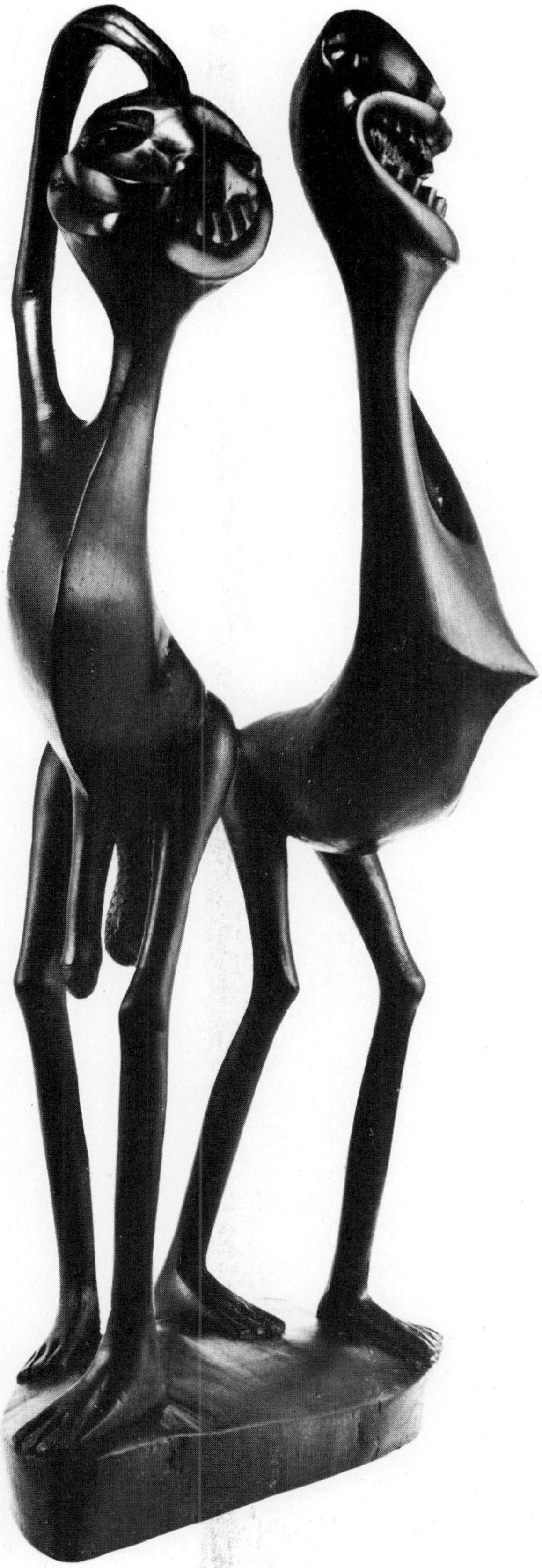

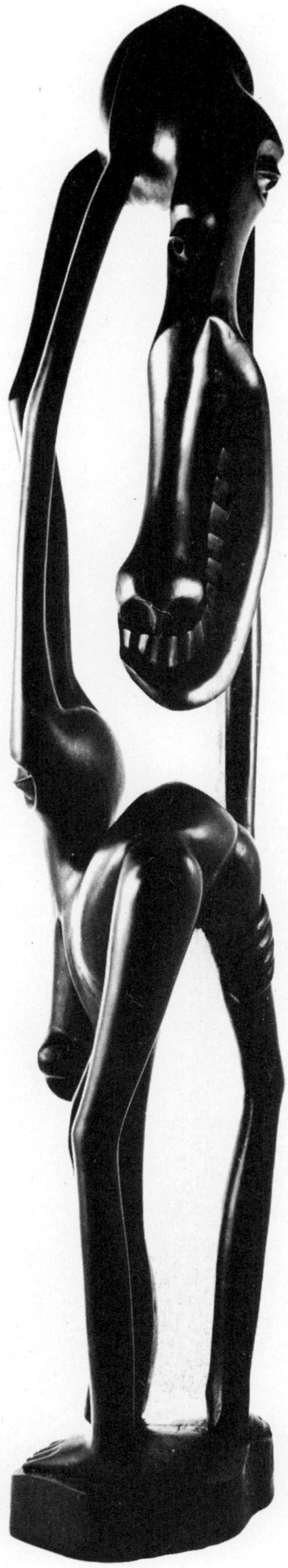

Yoseph Francis

Yoseph Francis

Yoseph Francis, or Alimazi, is the elder brother of Kashimiri Matayo. The lives and art of the two men have been intertwined since they began carving in their father's workshop in Mozambique when they were about ten years old. Yoseph Francis is about 40 years old, but is unsure of his exact age. In many ways, Yoseph has been his brother's teacher and mentor. They migrated together to Dar es Salaam in the mid-1950s and Kashimiri followed his elder brother to the outskirts of Dar where Yoseph had acquired patrons to support his art.

Yoseph's first carvings depicted naturalistic scenes of life and animals, such as frogs and chameleons. Upon his move to Dar es Salaam, he turned to shetani carving, which was more sought after by buyers and curio dealers. Yoseph became a

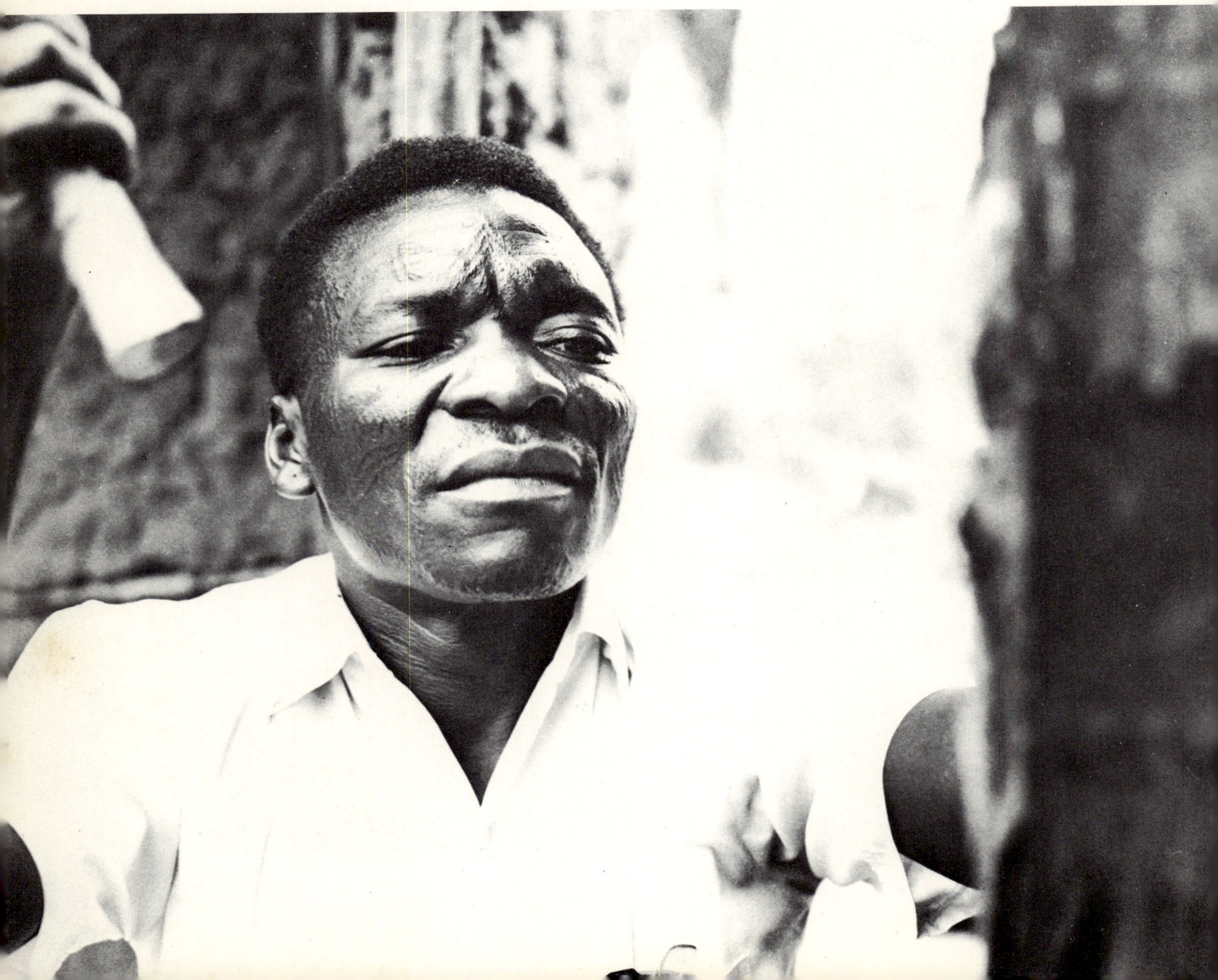

Roman Catholic in 1952, but he does not think that religion has altered his artistic creativity. He admits, however, that if he decided to carve an obscene figure, he would work on it hidden away in the bush. As a young boy in Mozambique, Yoseph saw wooden figurines which were said to have supernatural powers. His own carvings lack any magic or powers over others, he says.

His views about the existence of shetani differ from those of his brother Kashimiri. Yoseph believes that shetani fauna was introduced to East Africa by Arab traders who landed on the coast of Mozambique hundreds of years ago. Nowadays, he believes, they are extremely common throughout the coastal region. The shetani around Dar es Salaam strike him as being a particularly tough species. It is more common for him to hear shetani around the houses at Kaubwa at night, than to hear the roar of lions, which is occasional. Shetani are increasing in number and only those men who inherit their ancestor's knowledge of magic have any power over them, according to Yoseph Francis.

left Mask. Portrait of a girl. Kashimiri Matayo, 1969, 30 cm

below Kwimijenge and his large wife Nankwena (with the lip-plug). Mozambique shetani; large and dangerous banana-eating species. Yoseph Francis, 1969. 53 cm

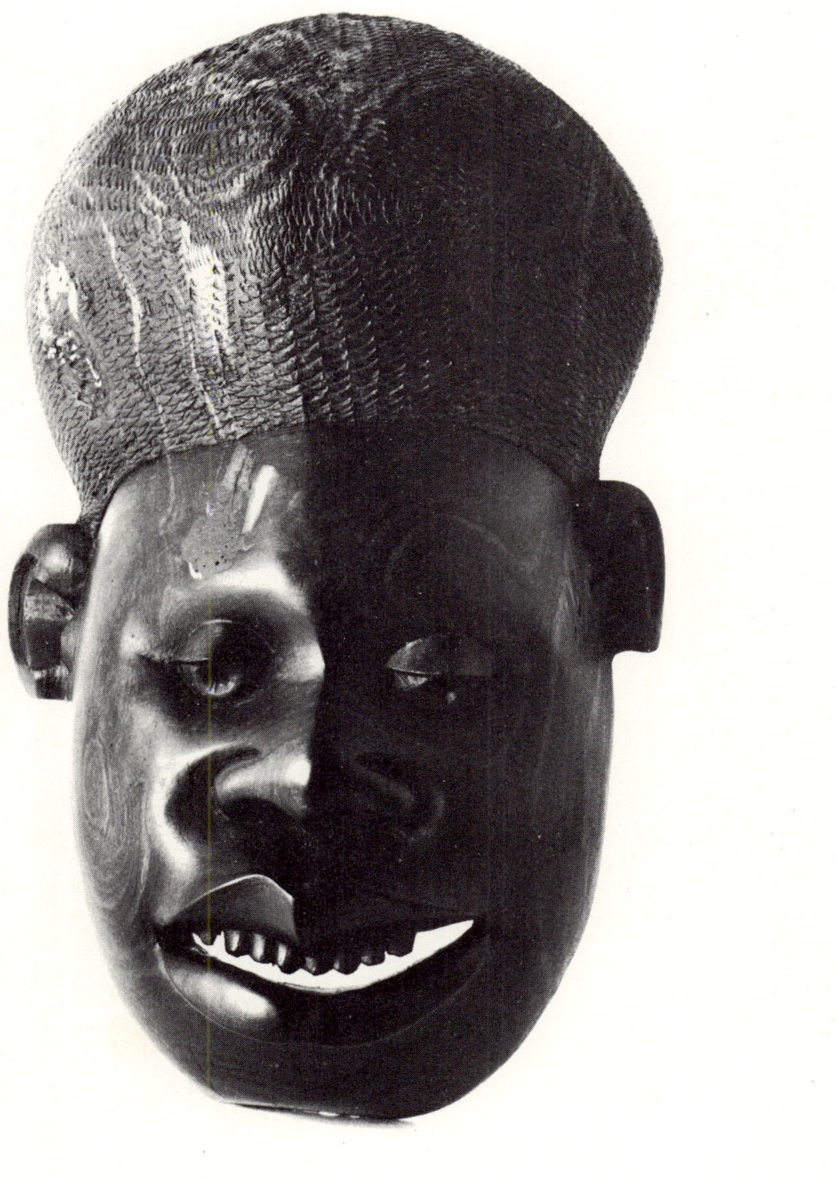

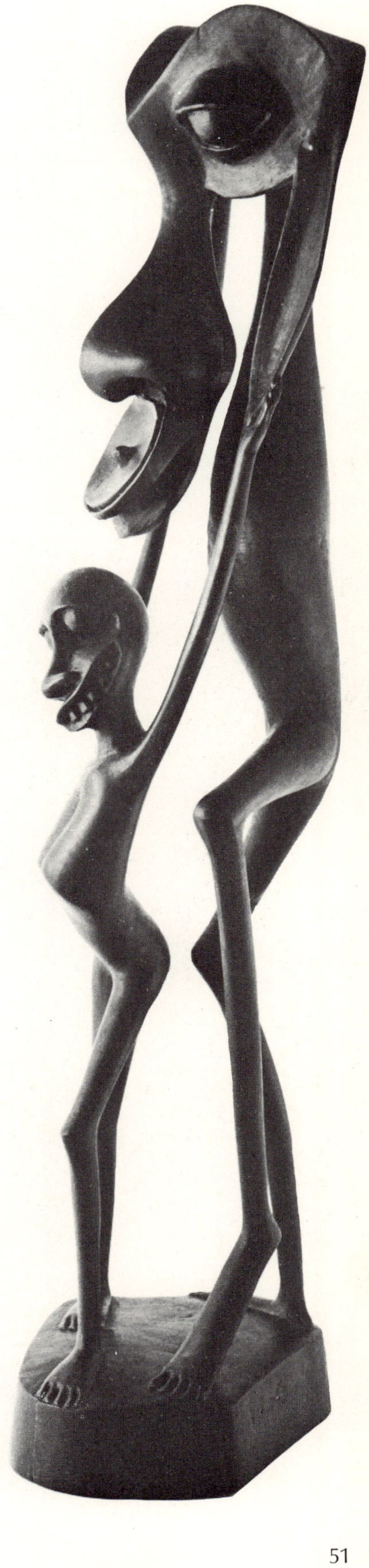

Mask. Portrait of a girl (with characteristic scarifications). Kashimiri Matayo, 1969. 28 cm

Mask. Shetani. Yoseph Francis, 1969. 55 cm

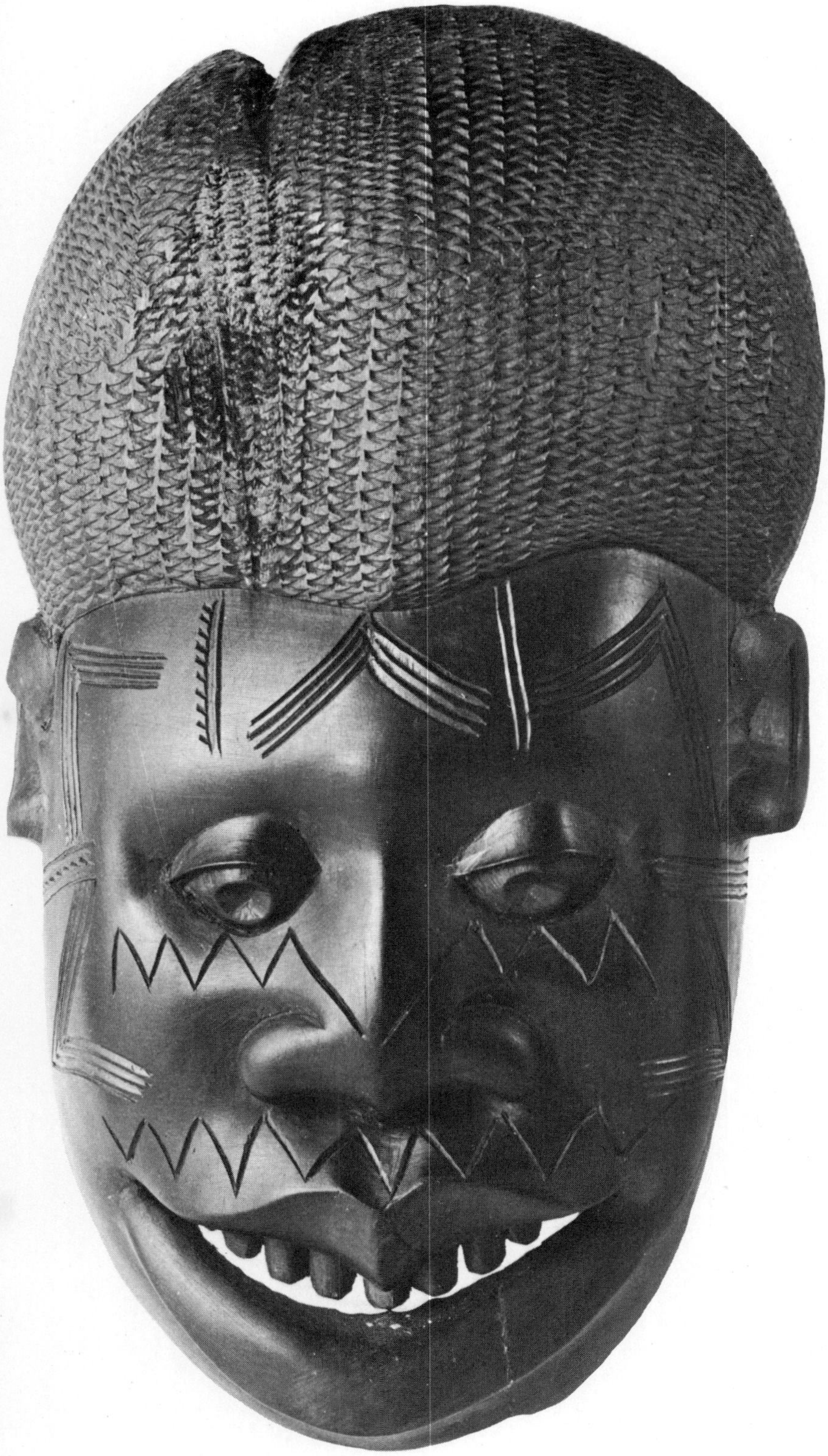

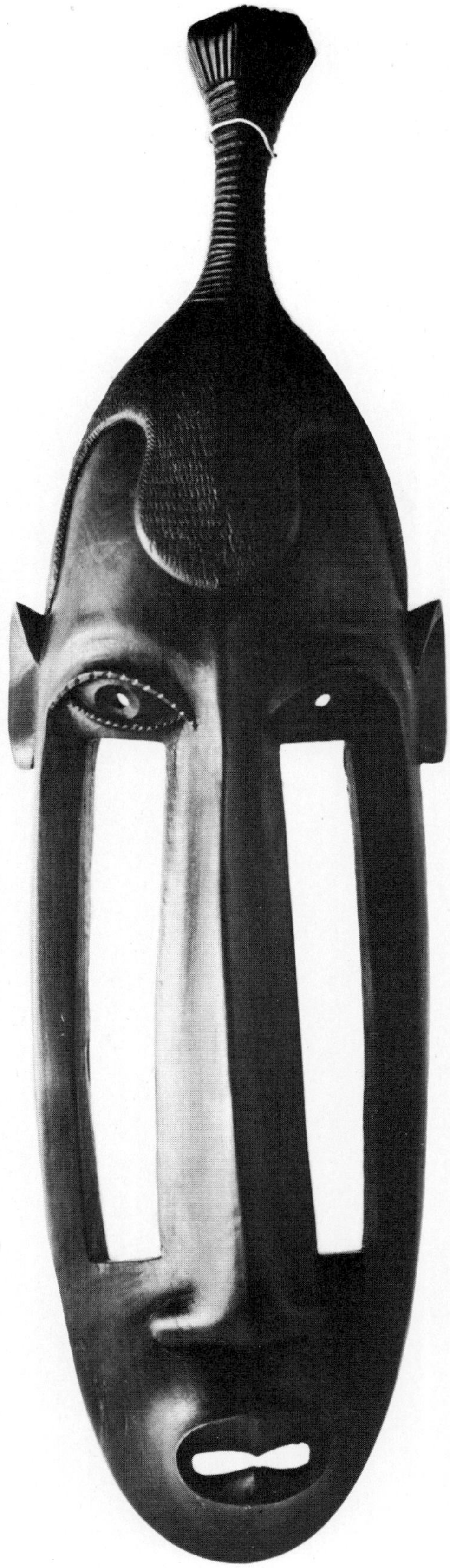

Mask. Male shetani. Kashimiri Matayo, 1969. 46 cm

Mask. Portrait of man. Yoseph Francis, 1969. 47 cm

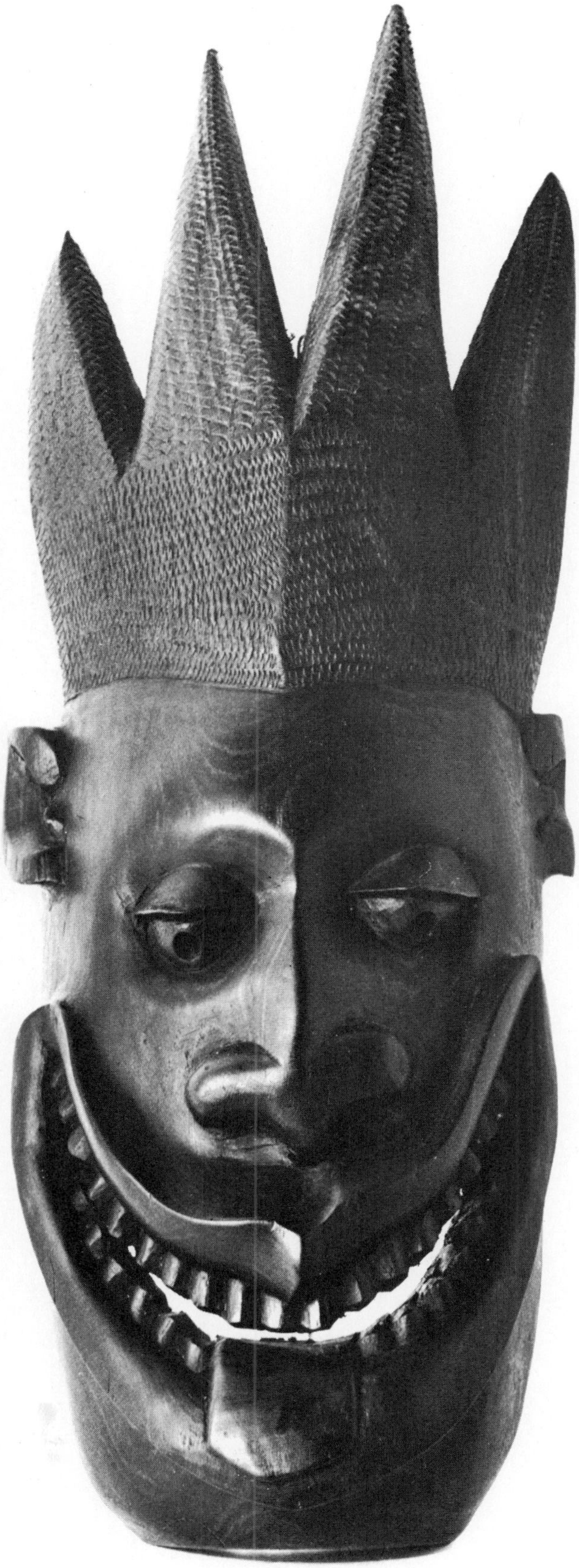

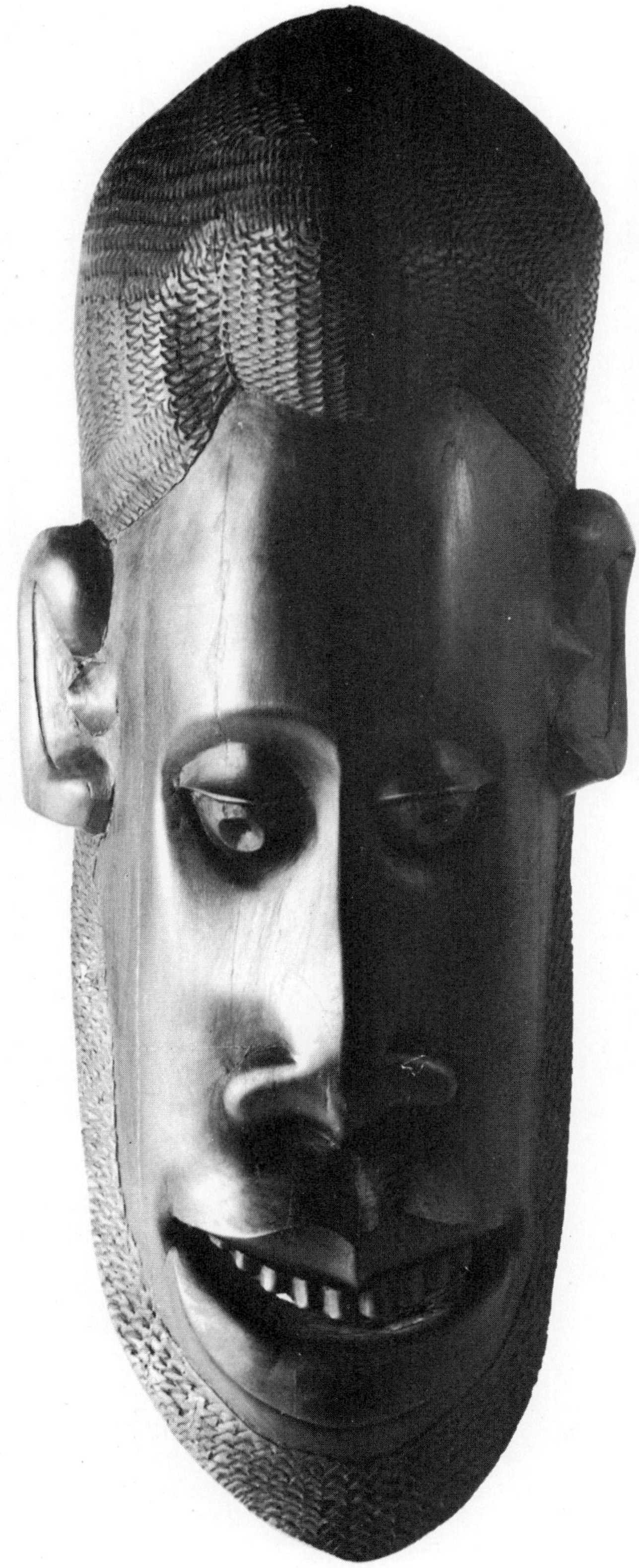

Nafesi Mpagua

Nafasi Mpagua was born in 1933 into a family of traditional wood-carvers in a village on the outskirts of Mueda, Mozambique. Three older brothers are also carvers. As a young boy, Nafasi lived in Mtwara in south-eastern Tanzania. In 1958, he and an elder brother, Gabriel, decided to become sisal cutters on a plantation at Kikonge, 45 miles west of Dar es Salaam. However, the sisal industry was declining at the time and the brothers could not find jobs. At this juncture, Gabriel returned to wood-carving and at the same time taught Nafasi. Since then, Nafasi has worked entirely at his craft. The brothers first set up a workshop near Kibaha, but now live in the nearby village of Pangani.

Nafasi Mpagua

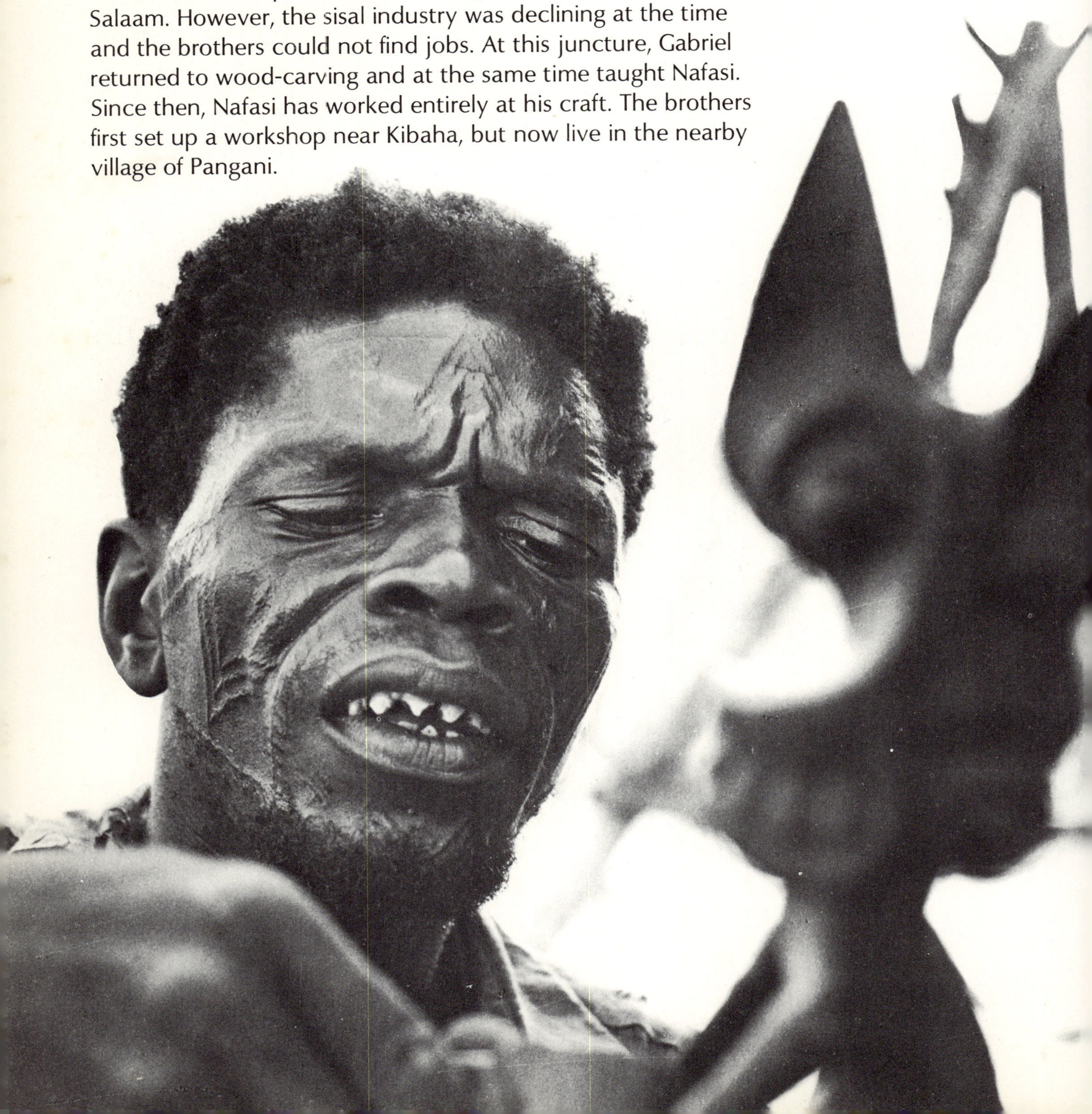

At first they sold their work to a famous curio shop in Dar es Salaam. Later they added expatriates from Kibaha to their list of patrons. Gabriel unfortunately became a drunkard and his skills deteriorated. Nafasi, in contrast, persevered and developed into a hard-working artist. He works alone through all the steps of his craft–from the selection and felling of the tree to taking the finished sculpture to patrons to be sold. He starts to work under his grass roof at about 7 a.m. and does not rest until 6 p.m. An ordinary small sculpture may take him seven days of intense activity to complete. Nafasi abstains from alcohol and drugs during working hours in order to ensure that his brain is alert and his hand steady.

Nafasi's grandfather started the carving tradition in the family. He died when Nafasi was young and is barely remembered by his grandson. Nafasi cannot recall whether his grandfather made sculptures which were said to possess supernatural powers. Nafasi's father never produced such sculpture, nor does Nafasi himself. In his childhood village, wooden figurines were not worshipped. Unlike many of the other Makonde carvers Nafasi never saw such figurines because his clan was continually at war with surrounding people, and he never had the opportunity to venture beyond his village.

Shetani are now the main subject of Nafasi's art and they were very real to him in his childhood. Although he has never seen one in Mozambique or in Tanzania, he feels sure that plenty of them abound in his village near Dar es Salaam. He believes that many species are dangerous, yet passive, and each species has a particular habitat. They are never hurt by an animal that can kill human beings, such as lions and leopards. Due to their short gestation period of, say, only four months, Nafasi believes that the number of shetani in the world is increasing. However, their presence does influence the amount of evil and wickedness in the world, he believes.

As an artist, Nafasi is content to carve shetani from the descriptions given by others. The myths about shetani are his inspiration and he feels free to use them according to his artistic wishes. He explains that his best sculptures start with a dream in which he sees the picture in every detail. He does not see the spirits themselves.

Nafasi does not think that he earns an easy living, although he does make a good income due to his hard work and the aesthetic appeal of his works. His technical skill is well developed and he has an extraordinary ability to copy one of his own successful works. In 1968 he entered about a dozen pieces for a Makonde general exhibition. One was sold before

Small Lidingi shetani–returning home with his prey after a day of hunting in the desert. Nafasi Mpagua, 1968. 45 cm

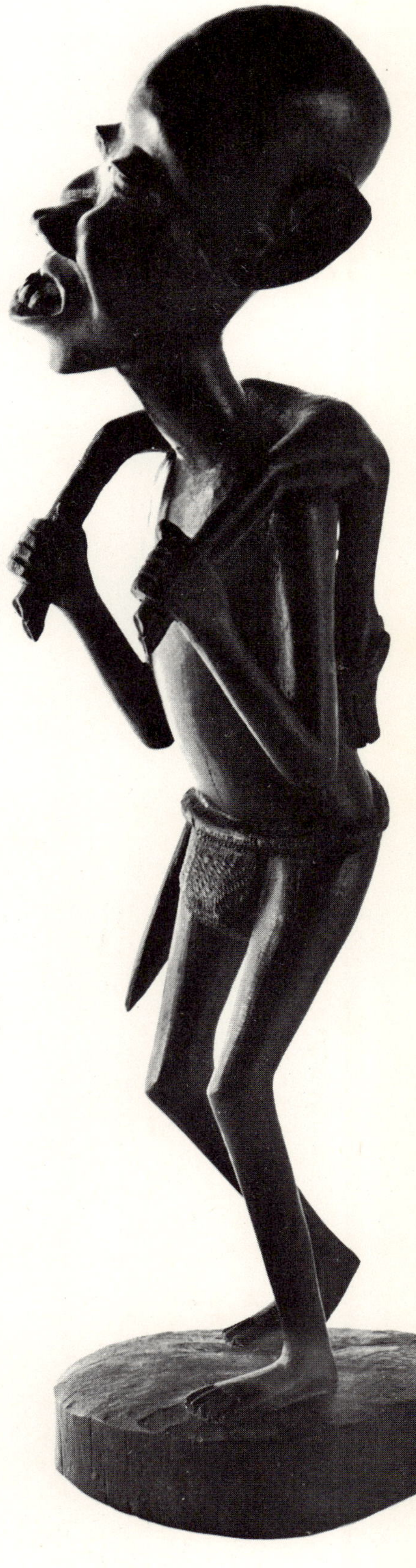

the exhibition opened, and he quickly returned home to produce an exact replica for the show. The peak of his satisfaction occurs when he sees genuine admiration for a new sculpture by a patron. 'I work because I like it and because I know you will like the things I create,' he declares.

Despite his success, Nafasi is worried about his future. He is uncertain what will happen to him and other Makonde carvers when expatriate patrons leave his area. Consequently he has established a small farm of about four acres, and he employs workers to tend his pineapples, cashew nuts and cowpeas. He is the only one in his group of Makonde carvers to have expanded into farming. He says that when his patrons have left Tanzania and when Mozambique is liberated from the Portuguese, he will return to the fertile land of his childhood, where agriculture is profitable.

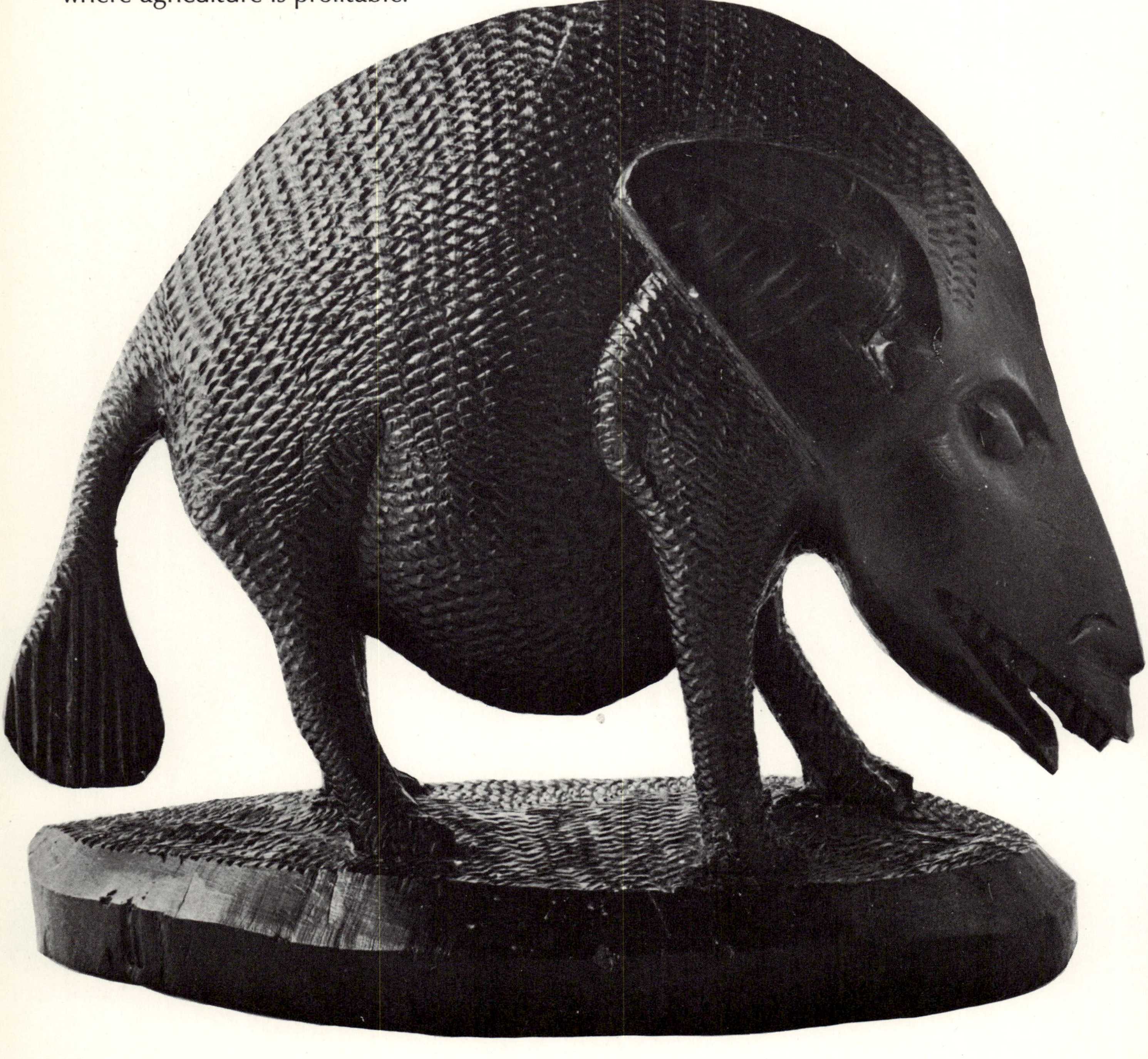

Mbegua shetani. The Mbegua looks somewhat like a common bush-pig. It is a most remarkable creature. To have a glance of a Mbegua means the greatest of luck. Nafasi's father, who was a witch-doctor besides being a wood-carver, was once fortunate enough to see one. Nafasi Mpagua, 1969. 17 cm

Ngenge shetani with a Mbalaza on his head. The Ngenge has just killed a young boy and is now returning to his home to devour him. The Ngenges are huge, horrifying shetani from the bush. The Mbalaza is always seen on the head of the Ngenge, whom it serves as a watch-dog. Nafasi Mpagua, 1967. 70 cm

Small Naliu, a tree-dwelling species of shetani which live from insects. The smell of a carcass will attract the Naliu from far, and it will come to eat maggots. In movements the Naliu resembles a bush-baby more than a chameleon. Nafasi Mpagua, 1967. 23 cm

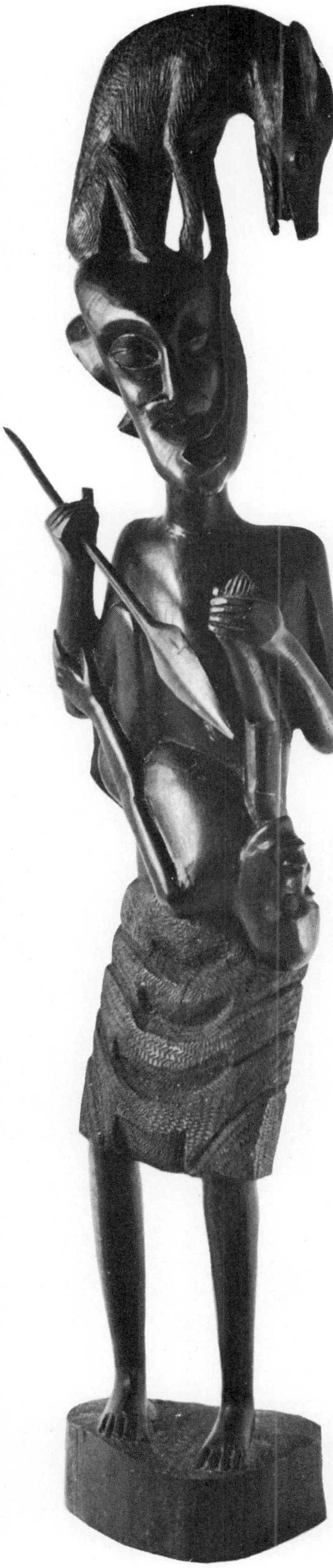

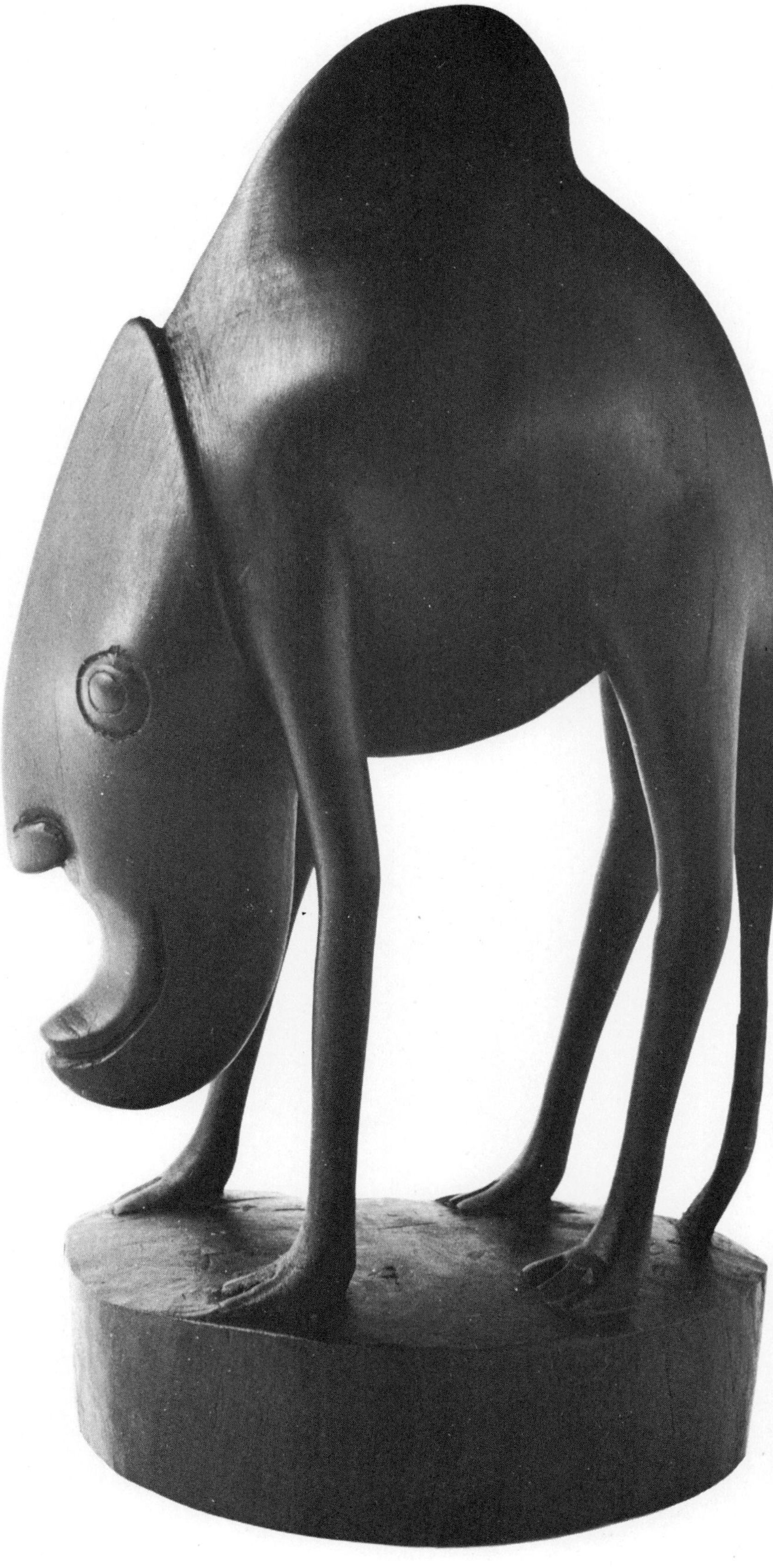

Mmala, a snake-hunting bush-shetani. The depicted snake is a shetani, too. Nafasi Mpagua, 1967. 47 cm

Sitogua shetani. A fish-eating ocean shetani the size of an eight-year-old child. Sitoguas are quite common in the Bay of Mocimboa da Praia, Mozambique. Their meat is tasteless and not good. Here the Sitogua is depicted with a good prey. Nafasi Mpagua, 1968. 40 cm

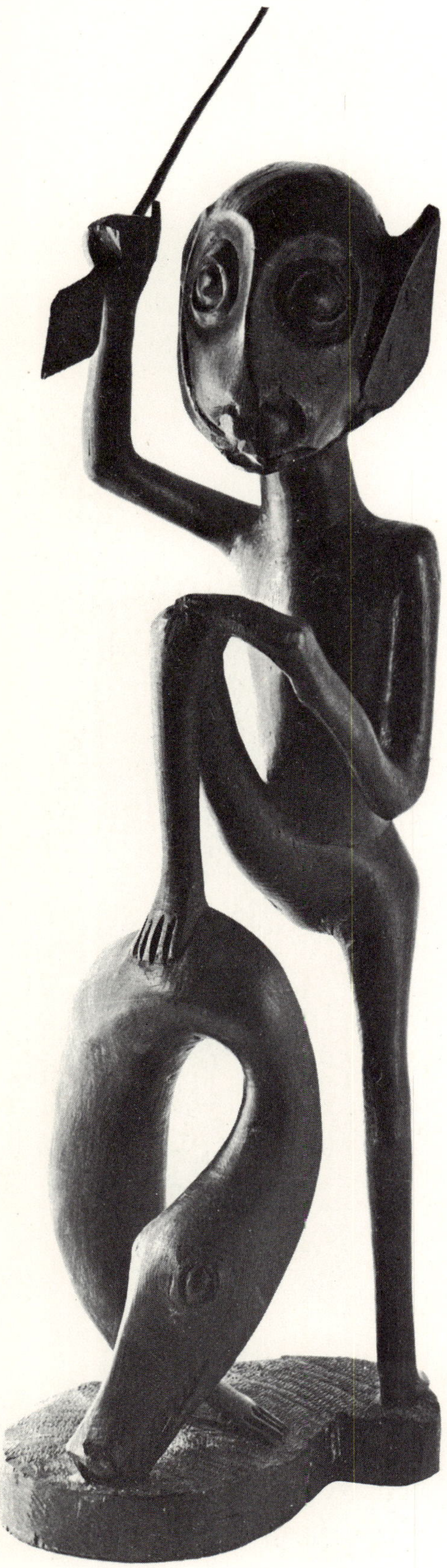

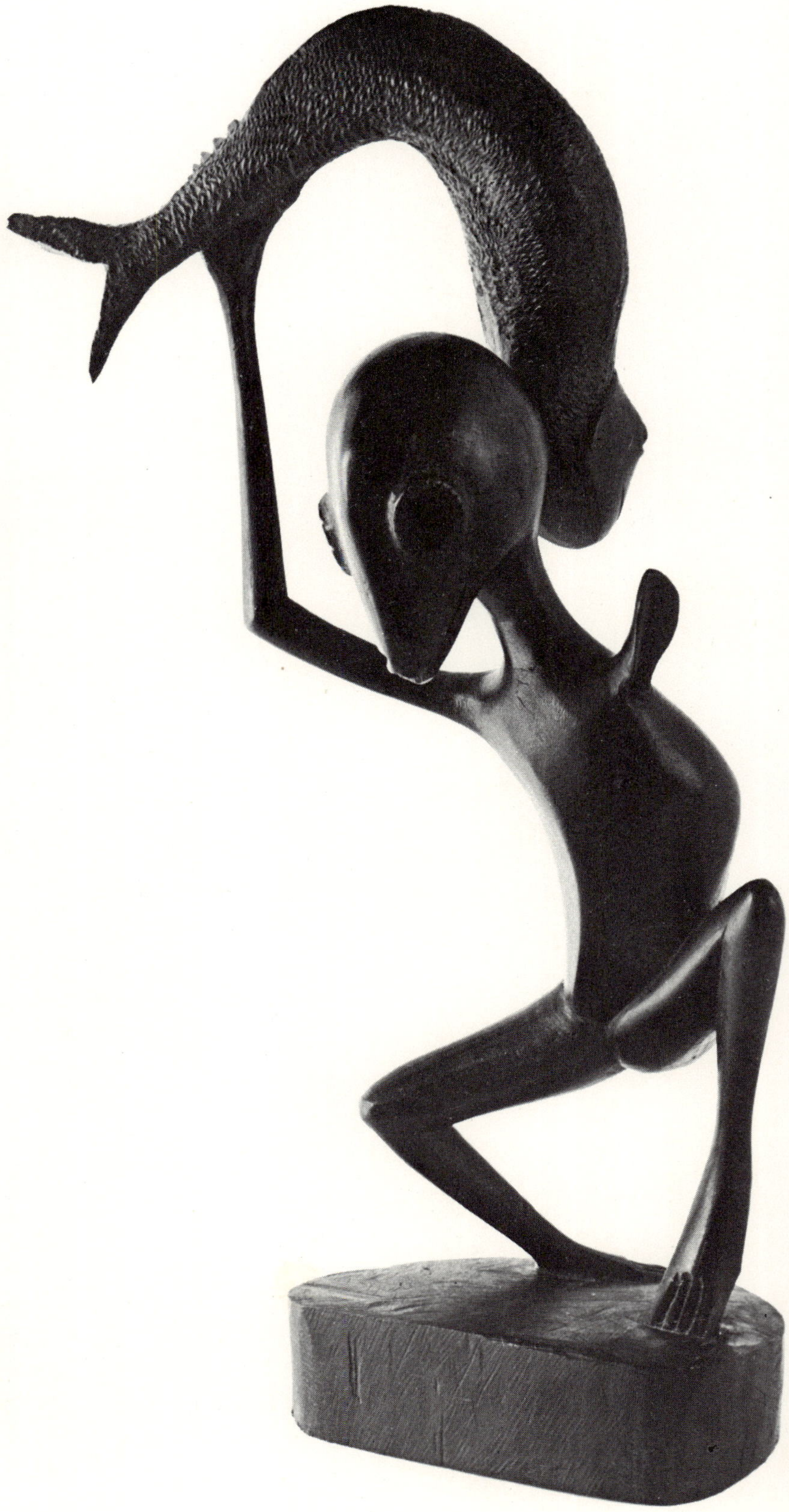

Kamvula shetani unit with double pregnancy. The antelope-like inferior part of the unit feeds on grass and transports the unit. The man-like upper extension of the unit is keeping watch and will feed on fruits. Nafasi Mpagua, 1967. 73 cm

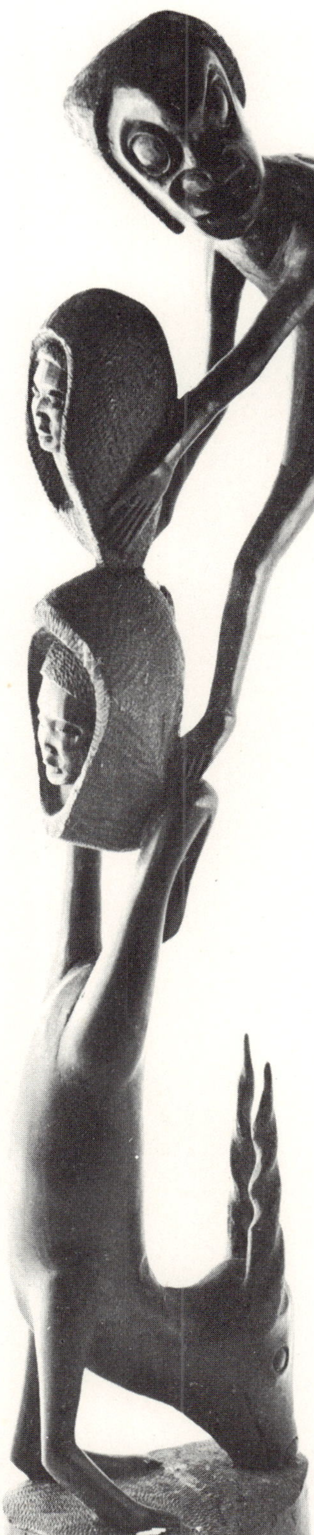

Libwela or Nanu shetani with a Mbalaza-like watch-dog shetani named Nguinnetu. They live symbiotically in wart-hog holes in the savannahs. Nafasi Mpagua, 1968. 50 cm

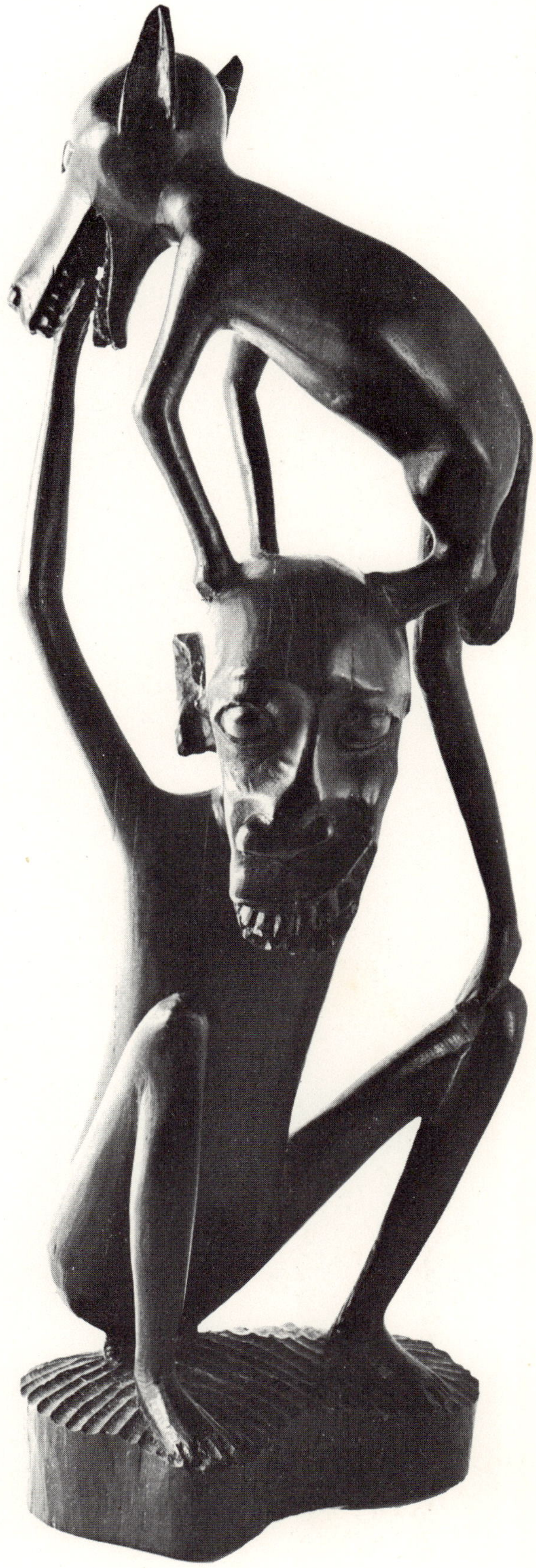

Mwaana shetani in pregnancy. Like so many other species, the shetani of the Mwaana type deliver their babies through bursting open. They stay in deserts. Here, the Mwaana has just filled a calabash with water to take home. Nafasi Mpagua, 1968. 59 cm

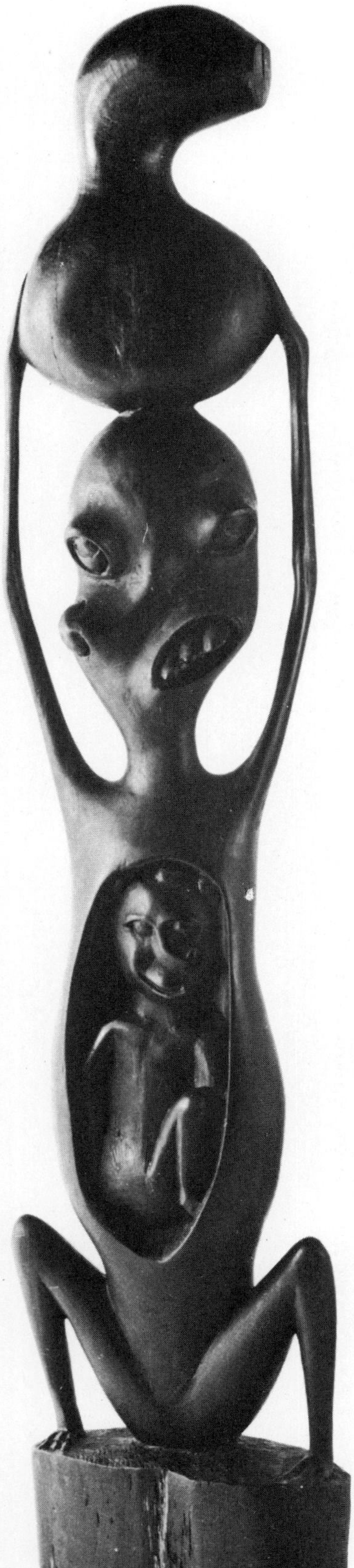

Mtawala shetani. Mtwalas are common in deserts. They are vegetarians who always look happy. Nafasi Mpagua, 1969. 44 cm

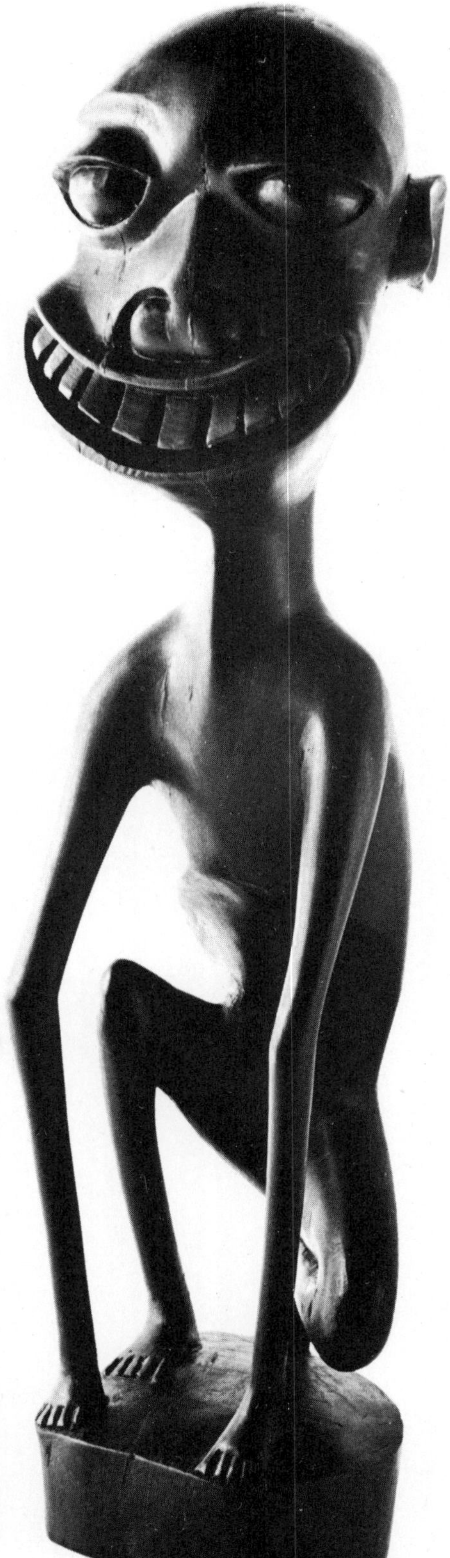

A Ngange shetani unit with a Mbalaza, which serves the unit as a watch-dog. Ngenges are herbivores, harmless to man. Nafasi Mpagua, 1968. 56 cm

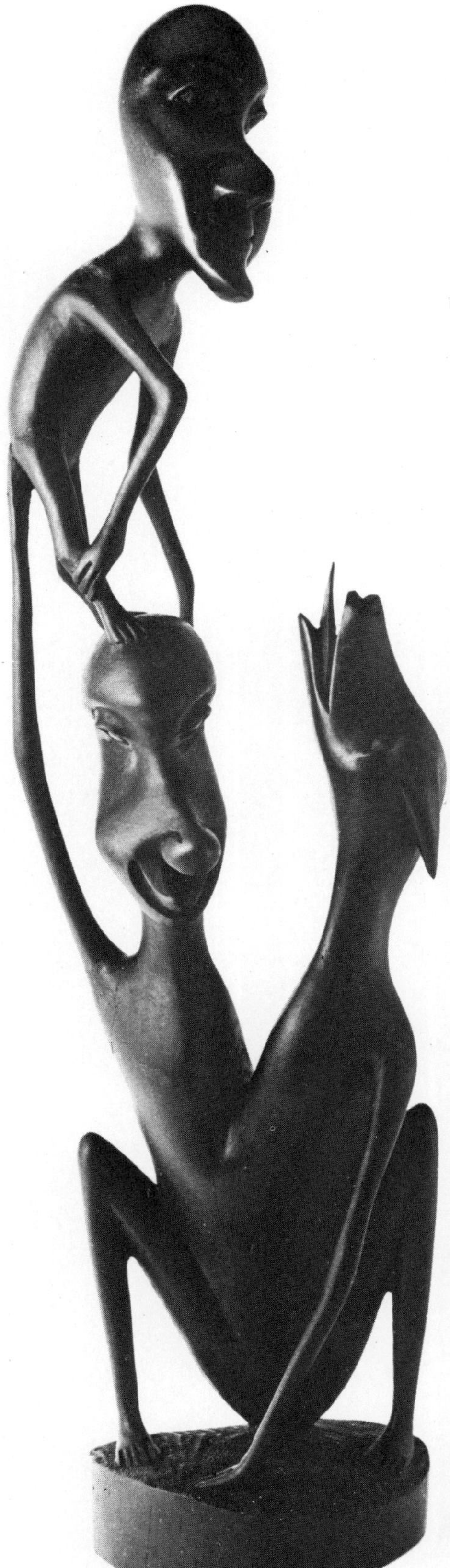

Nansheto shetani. The Nansheto couple—of which the male is the larger one—quarreled so bitterly that they eventually threw spears after one another. Both weapons missed, but the Nanshetos caught them in the air. The sculpture shows the Nanshetos the moment they are turning around to hit one another again after their first unsuccessful attempt. Whenever a shetani is hurt, friends will apply magic herbs and the victim will invariably recover. Nafasi Mpagua, 1968. 42 cm

An enormous Mmaka shetani with his victim, an old man. The picture shows the true relative size of this cruel shetani species which is a cave-dweller. Nafasi Mpagua, 1967. 57 cm

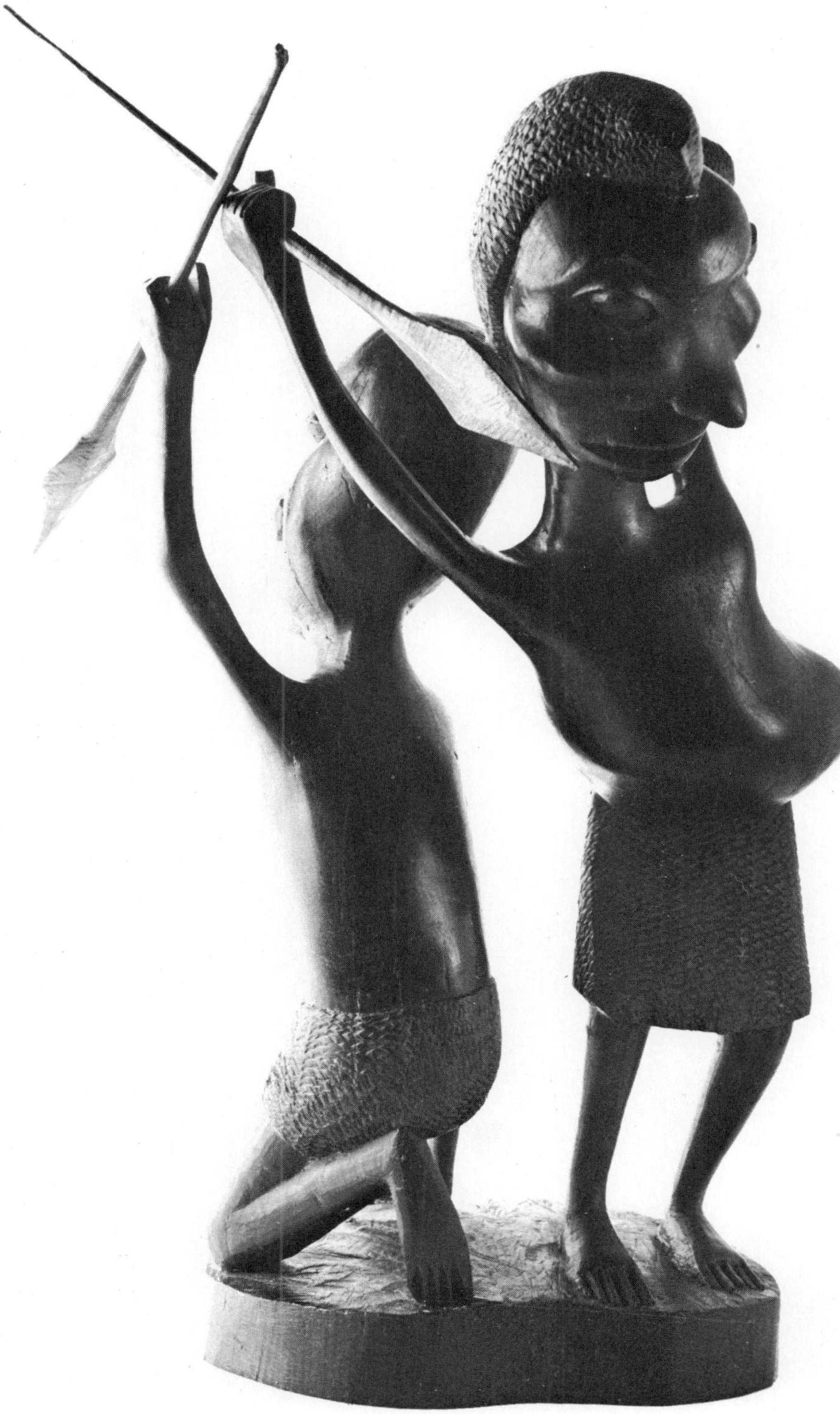

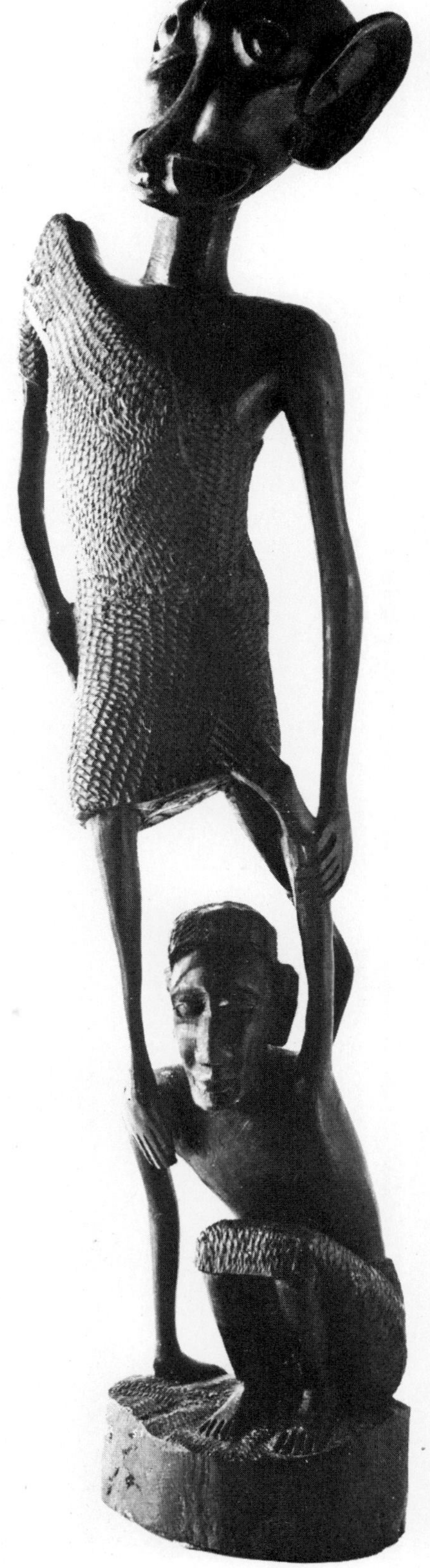

Nantipi and Nantundila (right). These two forest-shetani are always together. Like puppies, the merry small shetani will dance and jump and play as they travel along. Nafasi Mpagua, 1969. 42 cm

A Mmaka shetani—cruel cave-dweller from the forest. Nafasi Mpagua, 1967. 42 cm

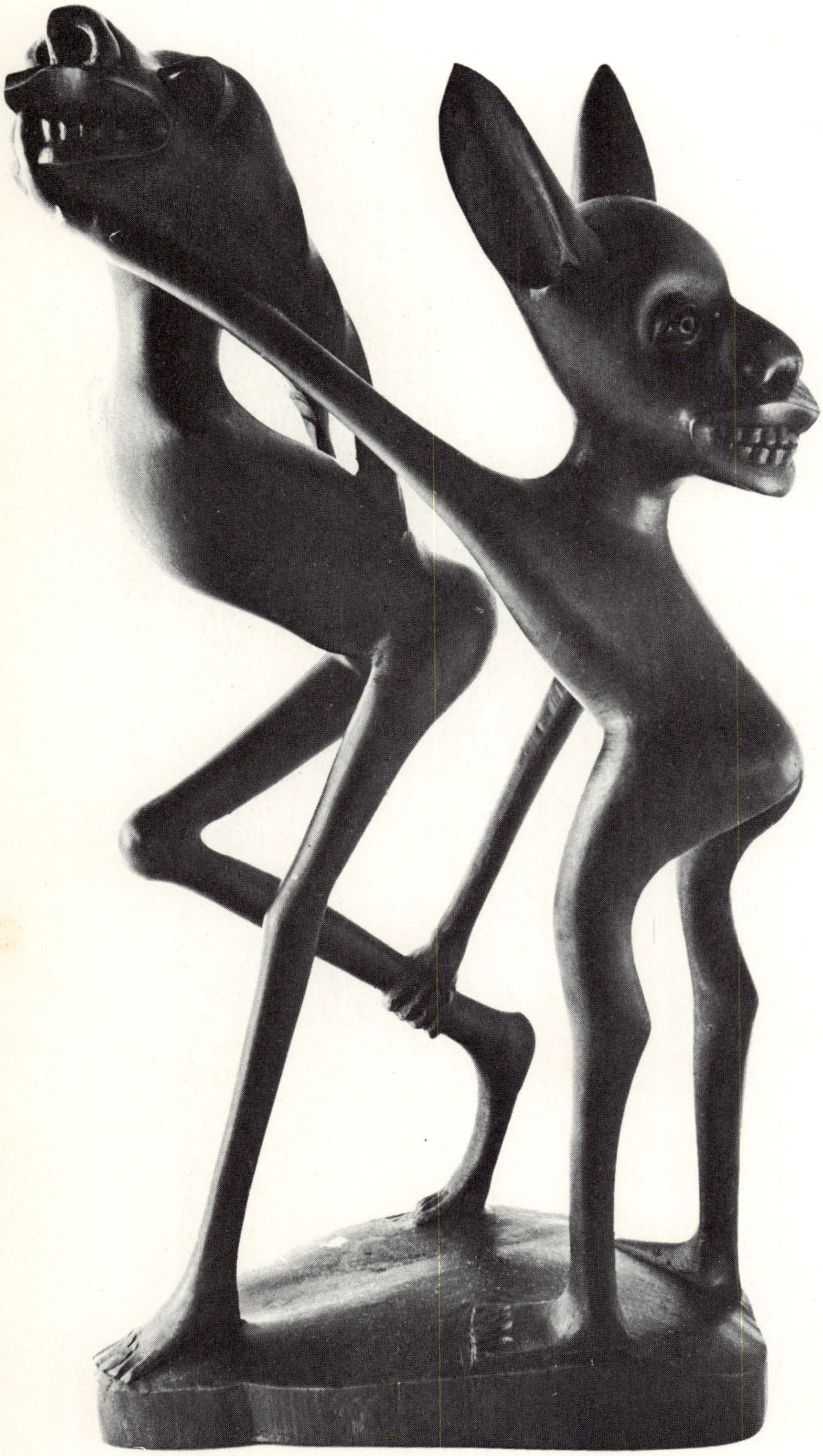

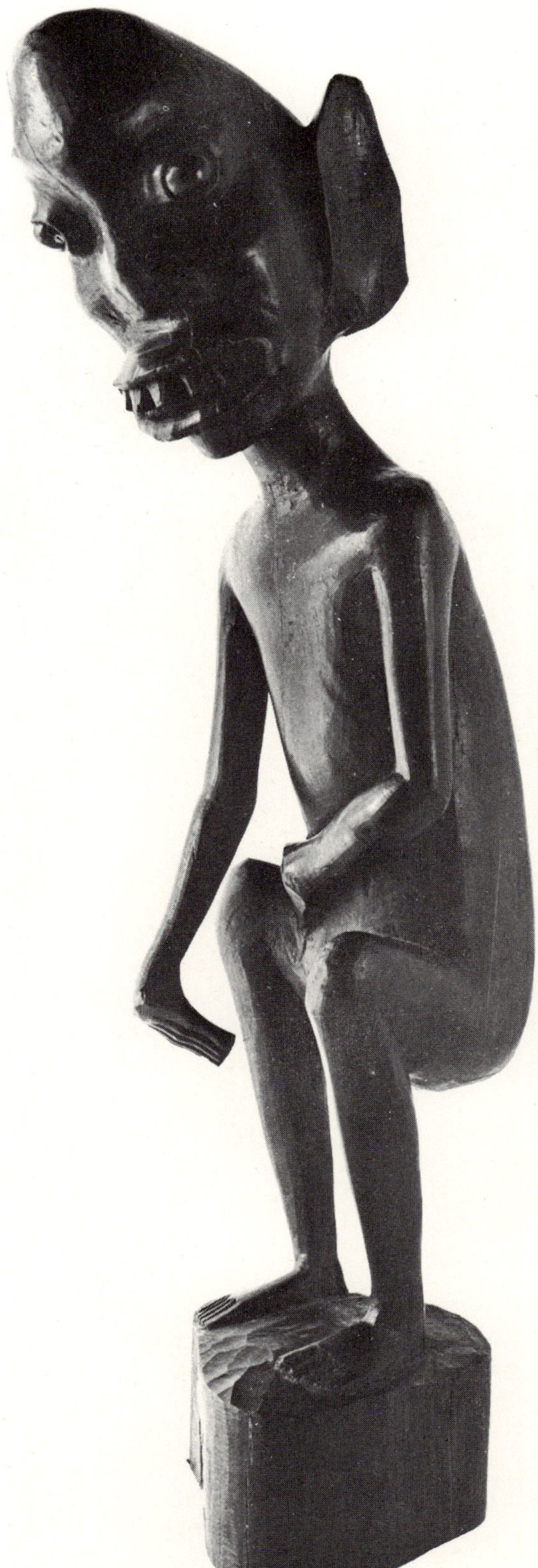

Two Nabwamwa shetani and a (man-like) Ngwile. The Nabwamwas are of two sub-species—goat-sized, peaceful shetani who prefer maize as their main food and consequently cause some havoc in the gardens. The Ngwiles prey on small animals which they hunt with spears. Here the three shetani are depicted in a situation surrounded by enemies. Nafasi Mpagua, 1969. 52 cm

Yomba and Ndikitii. The Yomba carries the calabash for water. Yombas are herbivore swamp-shetani. Ndikitii is a coprophage species, and the sculpture shows Yomba about to defecate straight into his mouth. Nafasi Mpagua, 1969. 49 cm

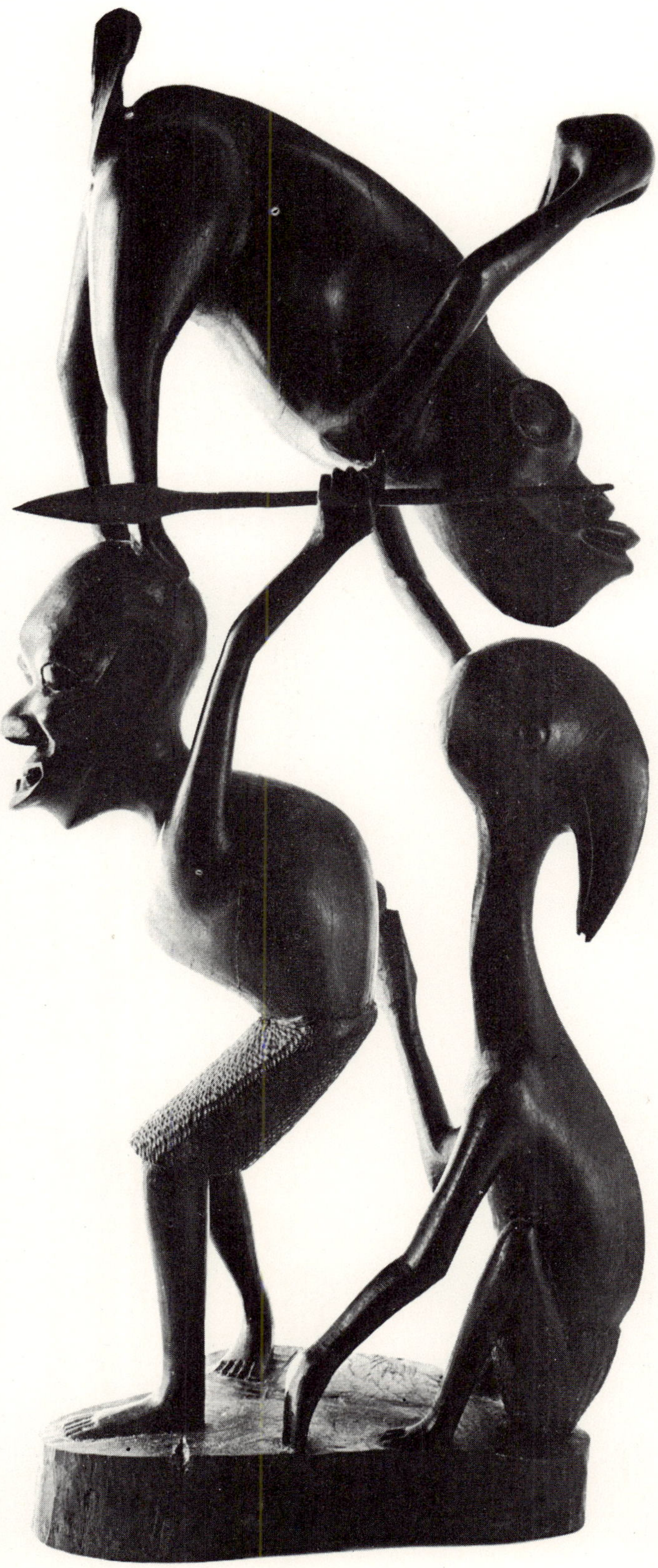

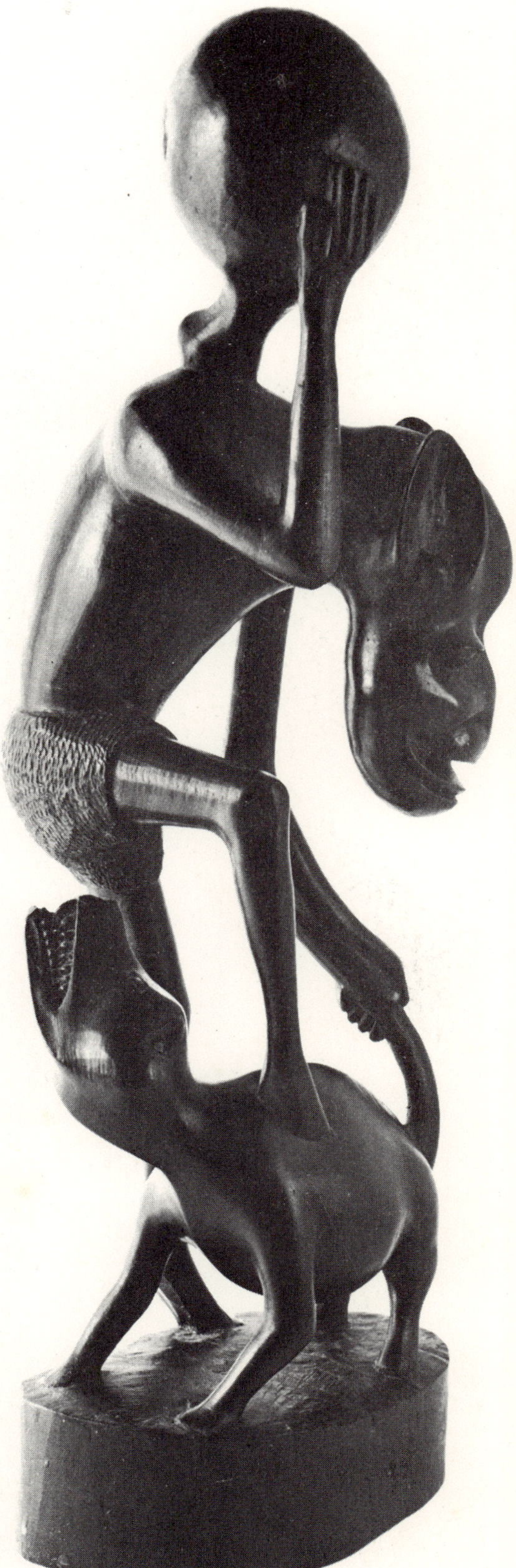

Hossein Anangangola

Hossein Anangangola was born in the village of Ulerezeboa, Mozambique about 35 years ago. In his early years, he moved with his family to the homestead of his grandfather in Diaka near Moçimboa Praia on the northern coast. Both his father and grandfather were wood-carvers, and Hossein began learning from them as a young boy. The men sold their sculpture to Portuguese living in the area or to villagers who used their wooden figurines in ceremonies.

Hossein Anangangola

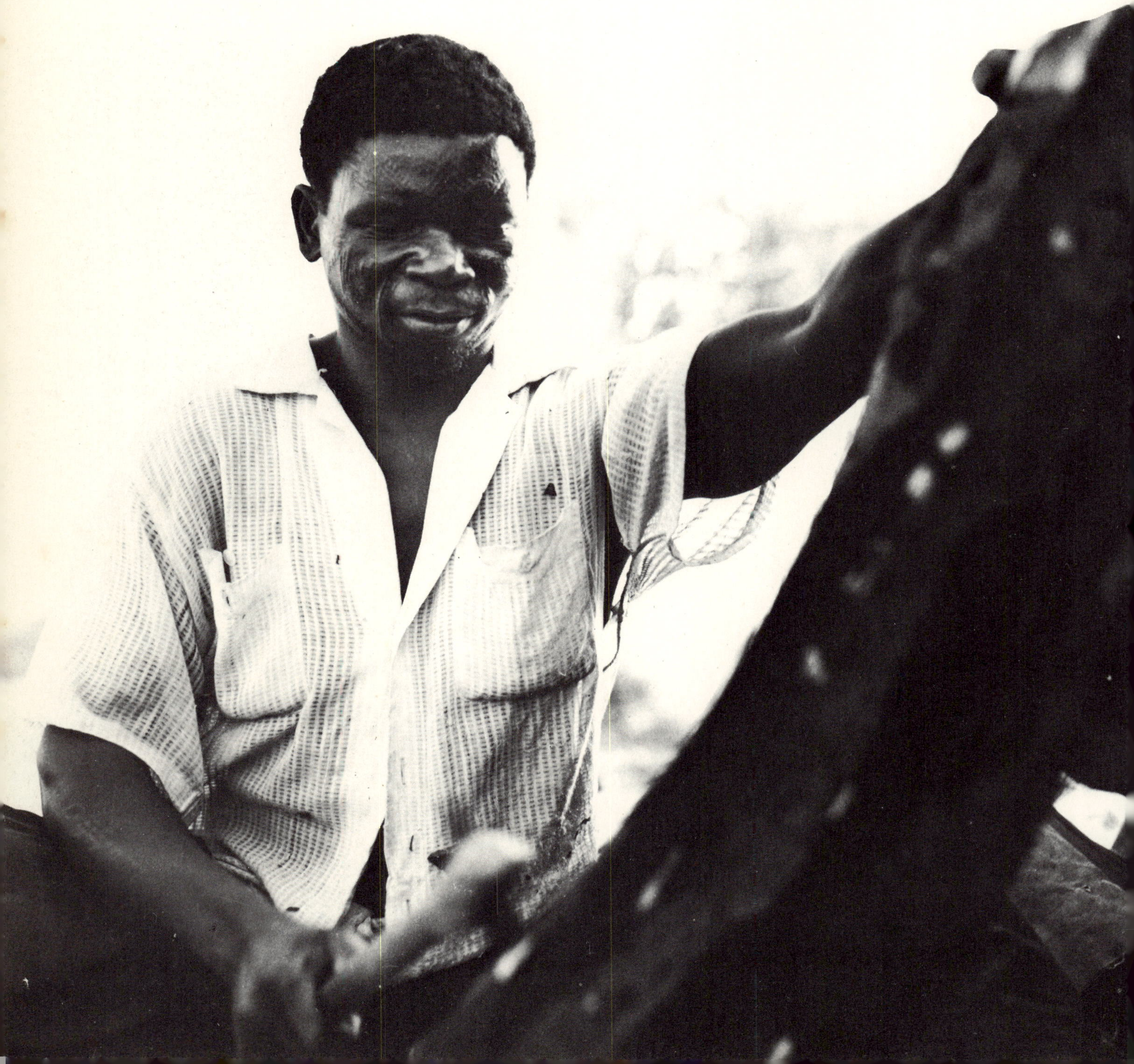

In the 1960s Hossein joined the enlargening stream of political refugees from Mozambique and migrated to Dar es Salaam. He says that he left Mozambique of his own free will in search of a better market for his carvings. Soon after his arrival in Dar es Salaam, Hossein sold five sculptures to one of the best known curio dealers. With the money earned, he moved out of Dar es Salaam and joined his sister in Lulanzi near Kibaha. He has a family in Lulanzi and one in Mozambique.

Hossein's name is common to Islam, but he is not a follower of the faith. In 1968, he undertook religious instruction from Roman Catholic priests and was baptized that year. He confides that he would change the subject of his carvings if told to do so by the priests. Although illiterate, he signs his sculptures OΣN which he intends to stand for his name–quite an achievement, he feels.

As one of a third generation of sculptors, Hossein is the perfect craftsman. He is meticulous about anatomical detail, and is probably the only Makonde carver who can carve the hardwood into sheets the mere thickness of paper. His sculpture displays great virtuosity and some pieces are extremely complicated and refined.

Hossein works alone on his sculpture from the selection of the log to the incredibly sleek finish of his sculpture. He is the only carver in the Lulanzi area who can carve a perfectly straight line, a skill of which he is proud. The largest sculpture he ever carved showed a classroom in a village school with a teacher, some naughty-looking boys, the blackboard and other details–all inside the school building of which every single line looked as if it had been measured by a ruler.

Hossein believes that carving to the satisfaction of his patrons will bring in the largest income, so that is his objective.
He makes no pretensions about his artistic ambitions. His inspiration comes from the world of spirits and myths that were related by members of his grandfather's large family. When he feels that a subject is appreciated, he tends to elaborate on the theme until it is exhausted in his mind. Apart from his depictions of chameleons, none of his works possesses magical or supernatural powers. He carves shetani, and although he has never seen one, he is certain that they exist.

To him, most shetani are dangerous. If someone is unlucky enough to meet one, he would probably die on the spot, his blood coagulating in his veins. The shetani he carves are derived from his grandfather's descriptions, according to which most shetani were the size of a mango tree and had eyes that glowed like torches.

Hossein often carves shetani defecating–or delivering–a

Mask. Portrait of a young man.
Hossein Anangangola, 1969. 28 cm

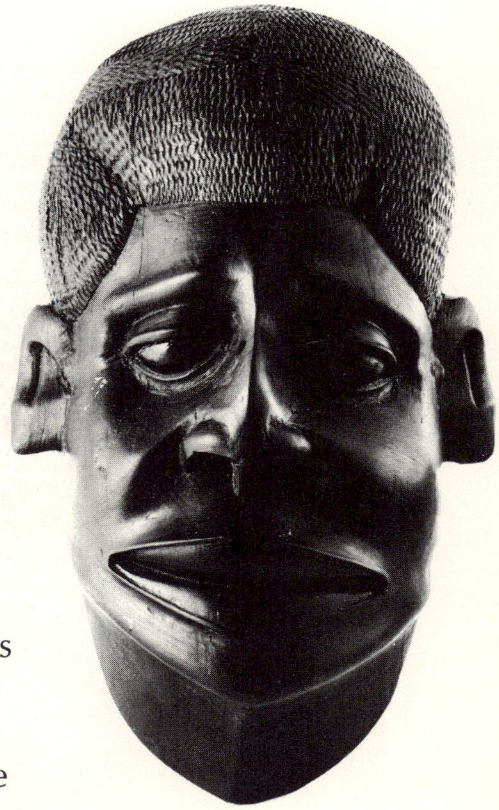

Chameleon fighting small snake-shetani. Hossein Anangangola, 1969. 11 cm

Anonymous shetani delivering a baby which is immediately devoured by a large fish. Hossein Anangangola, 1969. 40 cm

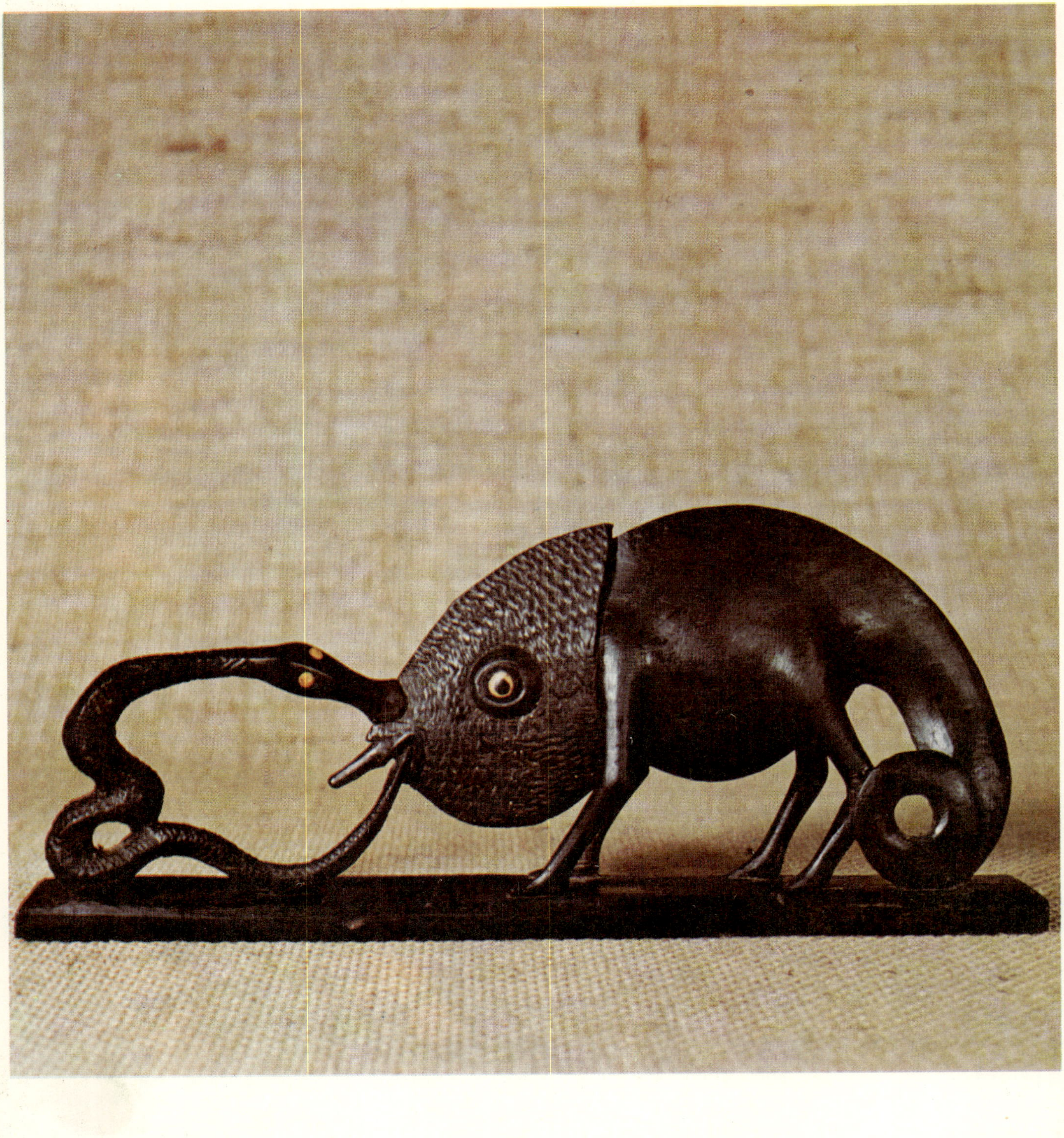

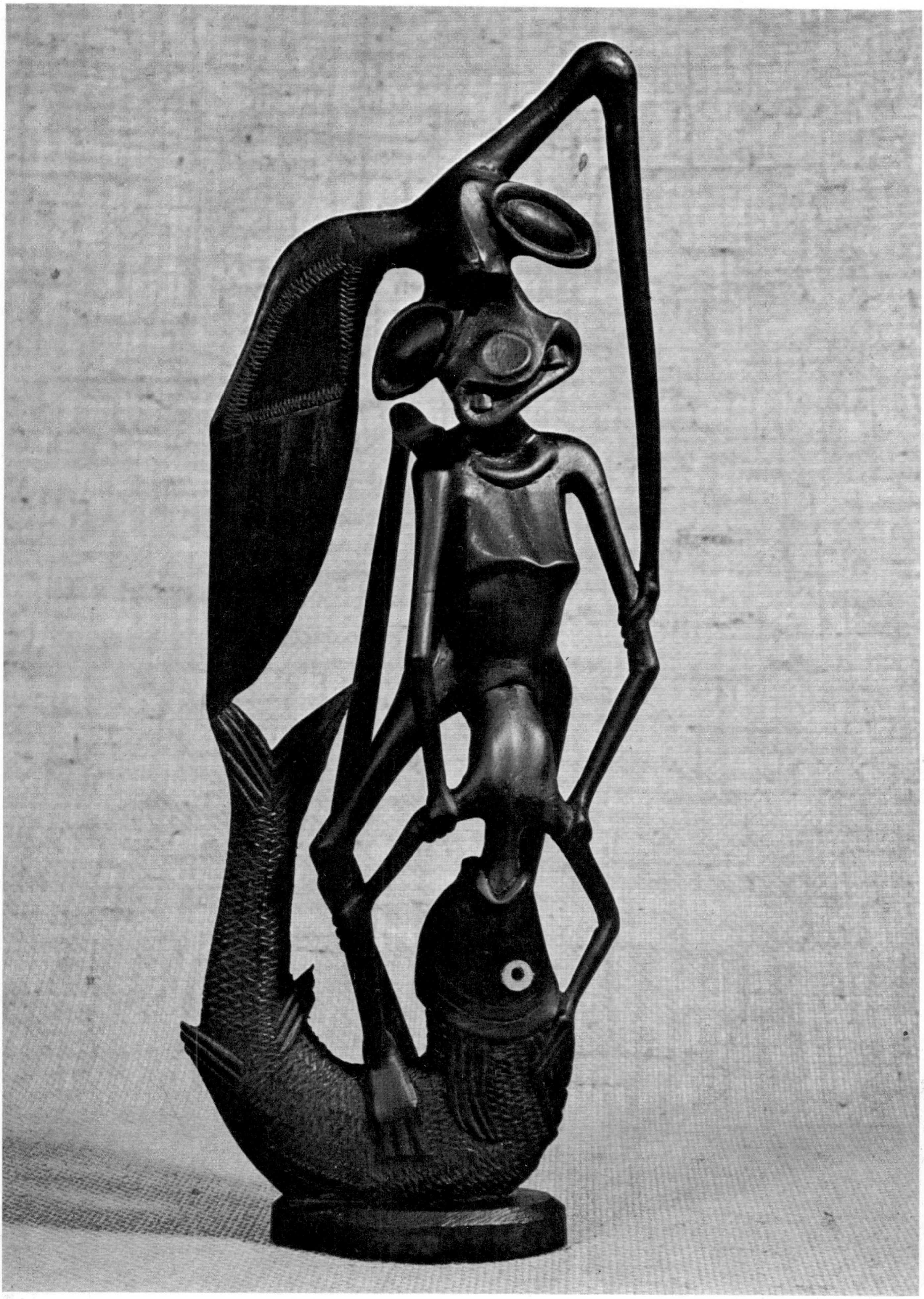

child in the shape of a snake that curves upwards and sucks at the shetani's breast. Occasionally he sculpts shetani with no anterior abdominal wall and with all the viscera exposed. An enlarged spleen, the cardinal sign of malaria, is usually accurately depicted. Other Makonde carvers were vague about the meaning of these shetani with open abdomens, but Hossein explains that they are less vicious than most shetani.

Due to the spread of Islam and Christianity in Africa, Hossein believes that the shetani fauna will eventually disappear. They have such a long gestation period, he says, that they cannot procreate quickly enough to counter the forces of eradication.

A father protecting the child from seeing a shetani. (An example of Hossein Anangangola's naturalistic art.) Hossein Anangangola, 1969.

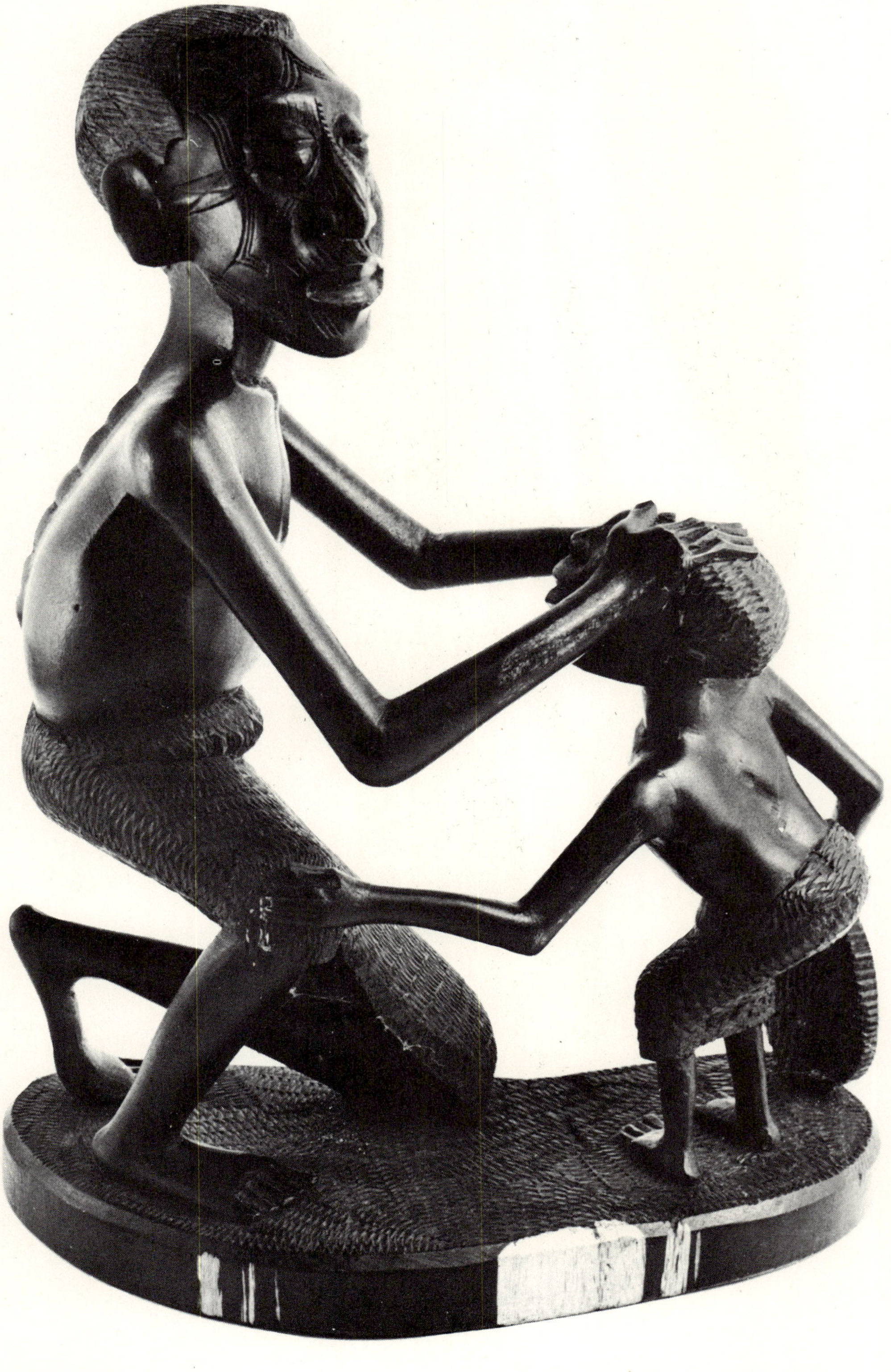

Wimbo shetani, with new-born snake-shetani baby sucking. Hossein Anangangola, 1969. 39 cm

Nancheto shetani with her baby. Nanchetos are harmless and prefer to live close to villages. Hossein Anangangola, 1968. 28 cm

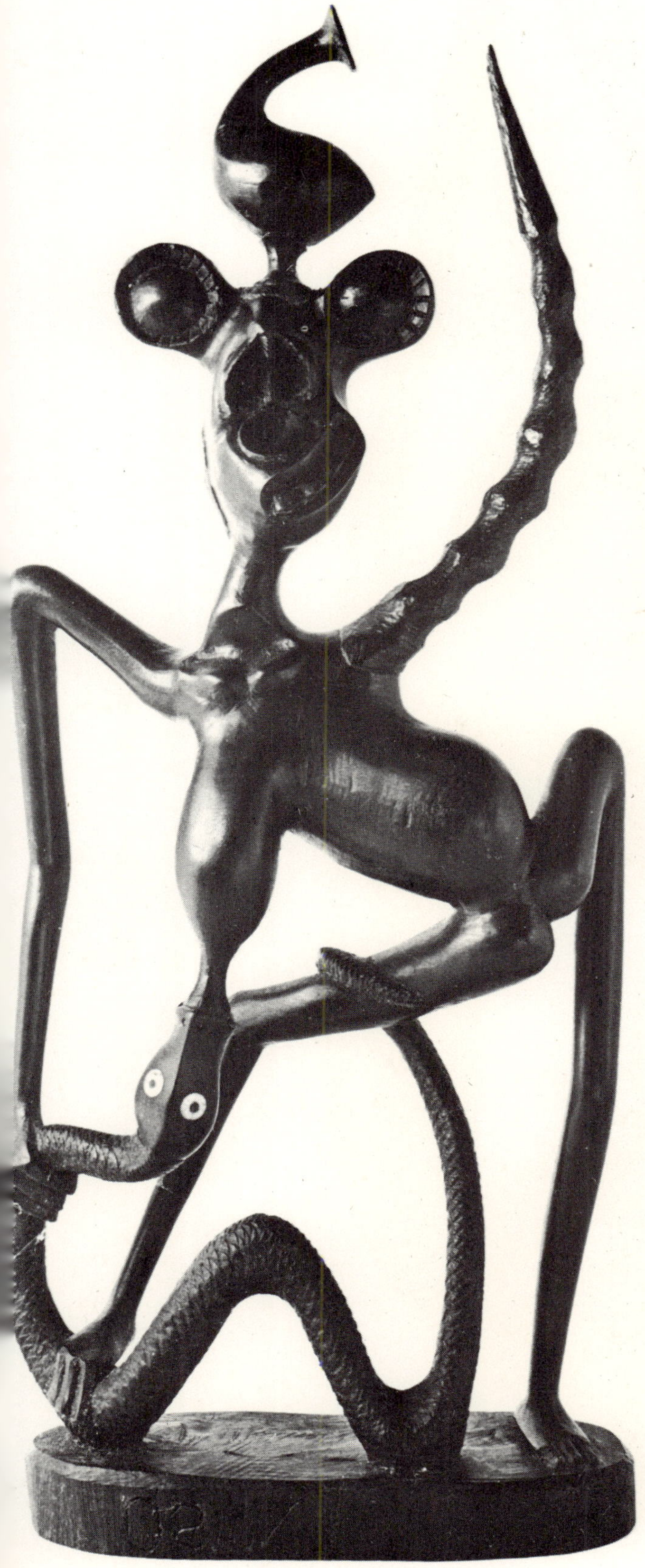

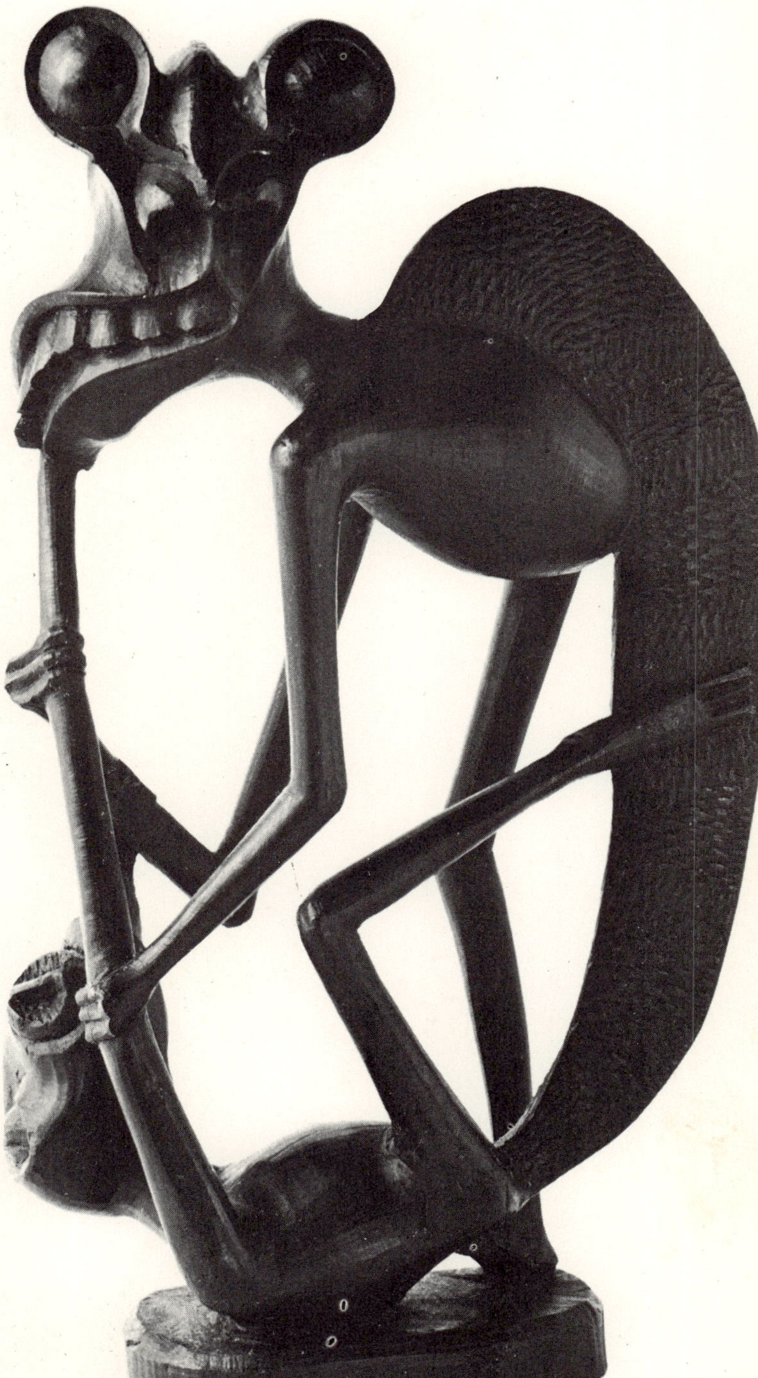

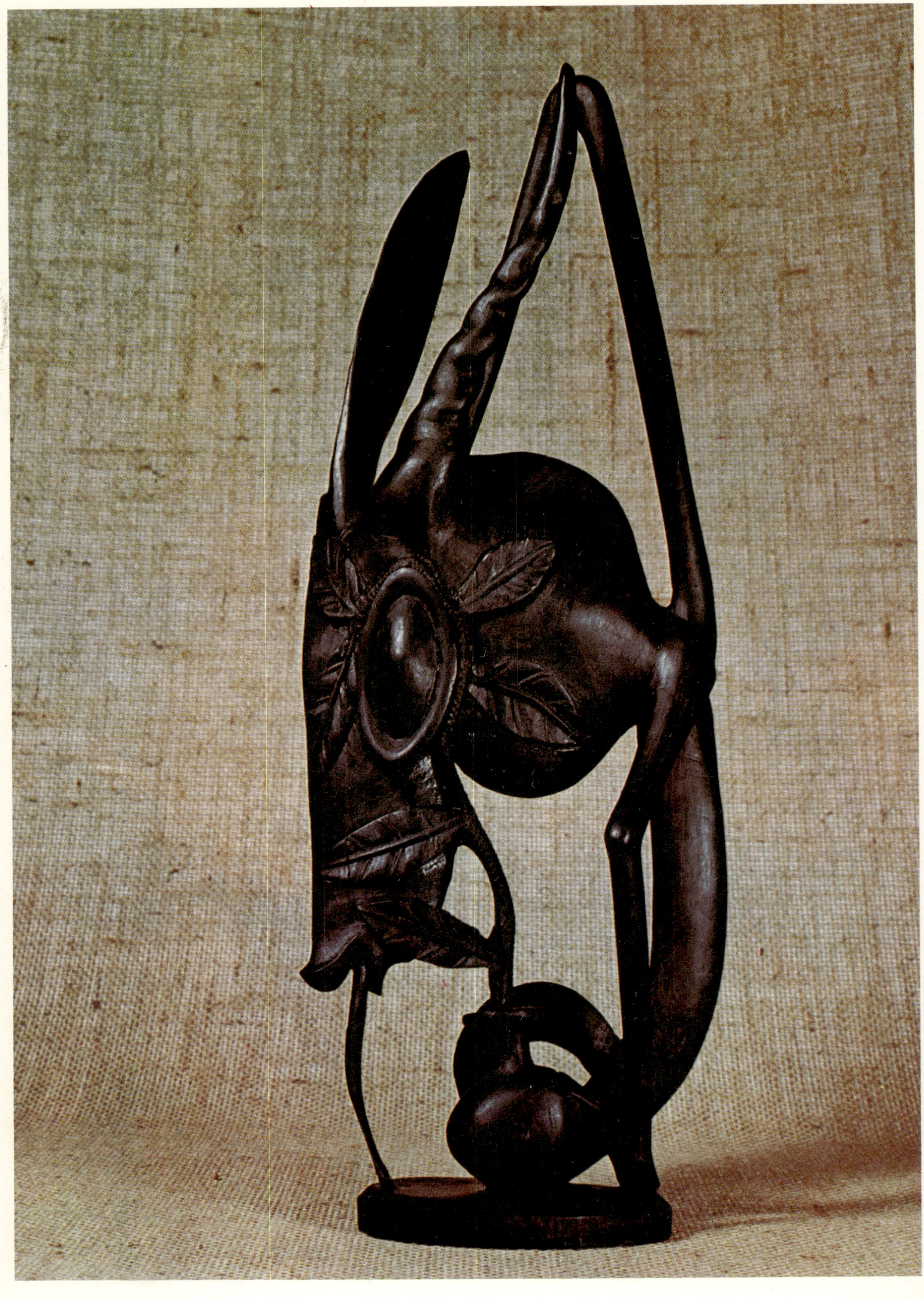

Anonymous shetani of a species which collects medicine-herbs. Hossein Anangangola, 1969. 43 cm

Kamanya shetani unit with a chameleon shetani. There exists a symbiosis between the two species. Kamanyas live in the Mozambique bush-land and are shetani of prey. Hossein Anangangola, 1969. 44 cm

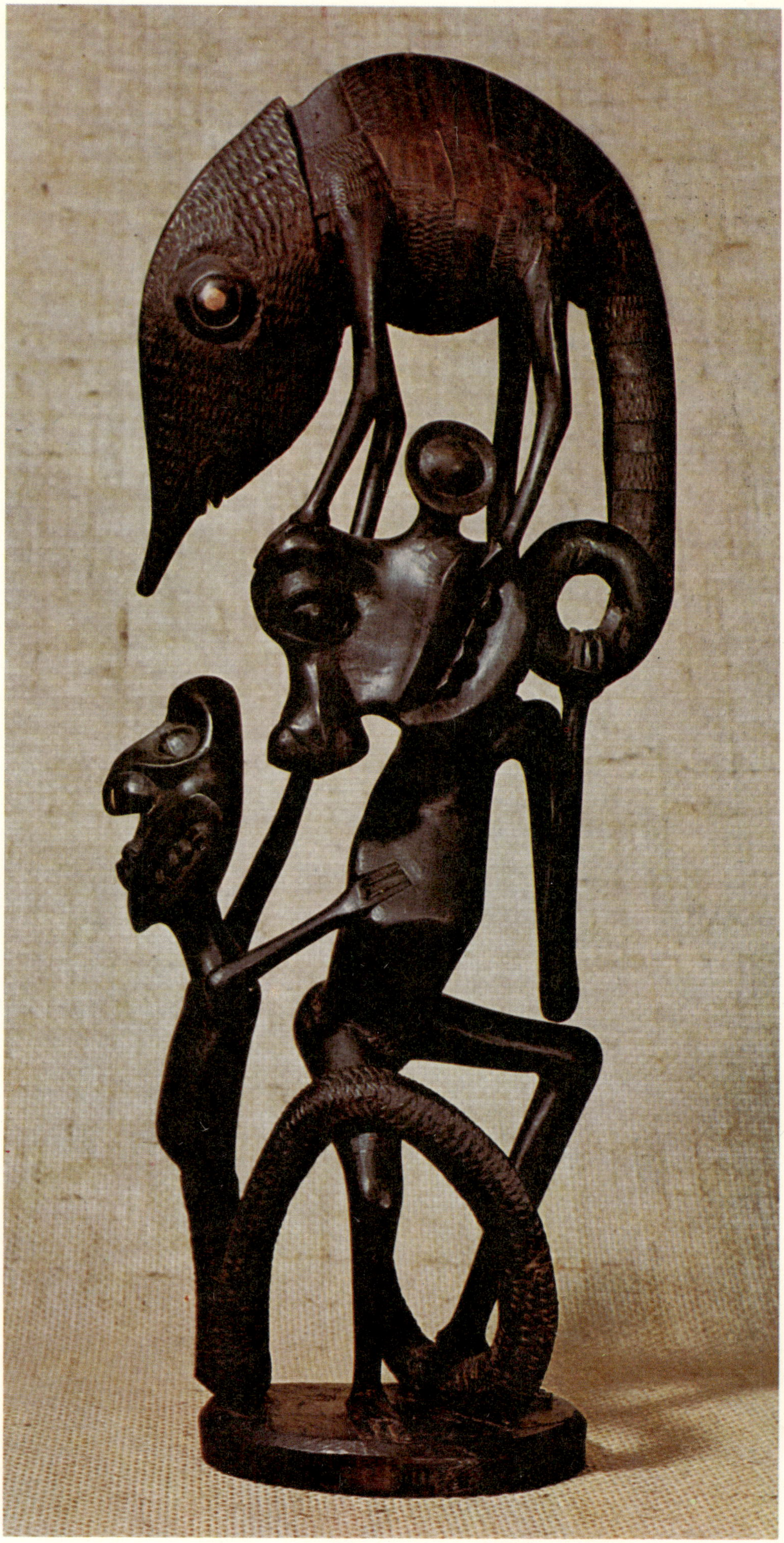

Wimbo shetani, suckling her new-born snake-baby. Wimbos are carnivores. Hossein Anangangola, 1967. 22 cm

Chingwele shetani and her child. The Chingweles are mountain-dwellers which subsist mainly on snakes. The knife-like extension of the right upper extremity is used when hunting. Hossein Anangangola, 1969. 33 cm

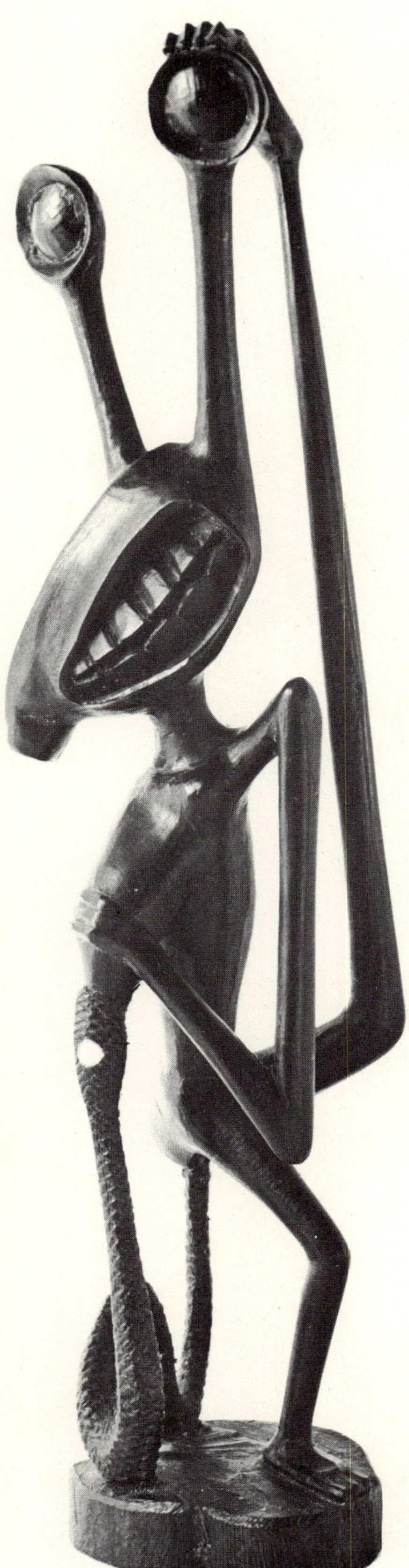

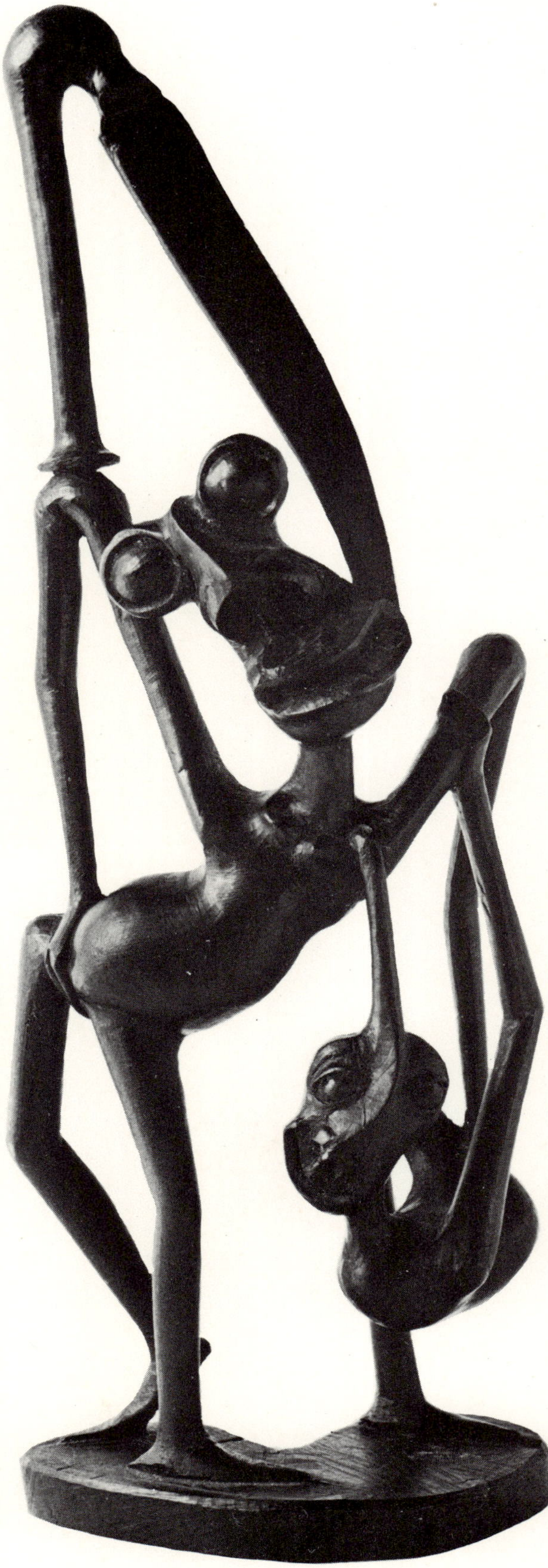

Chameleon shetani, eating a screaming frog. Hossein Anangangola, 1969. 18 cm

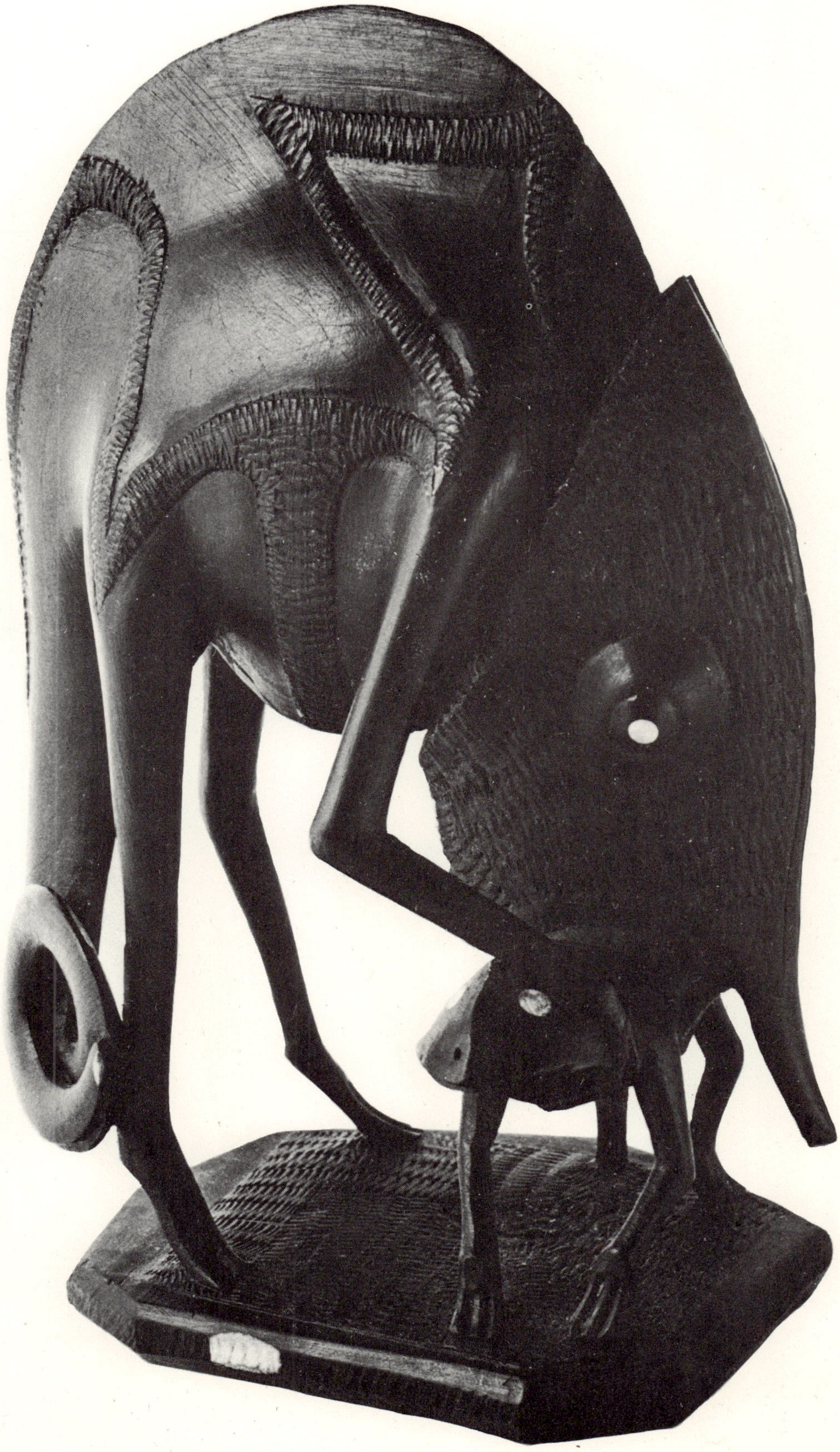

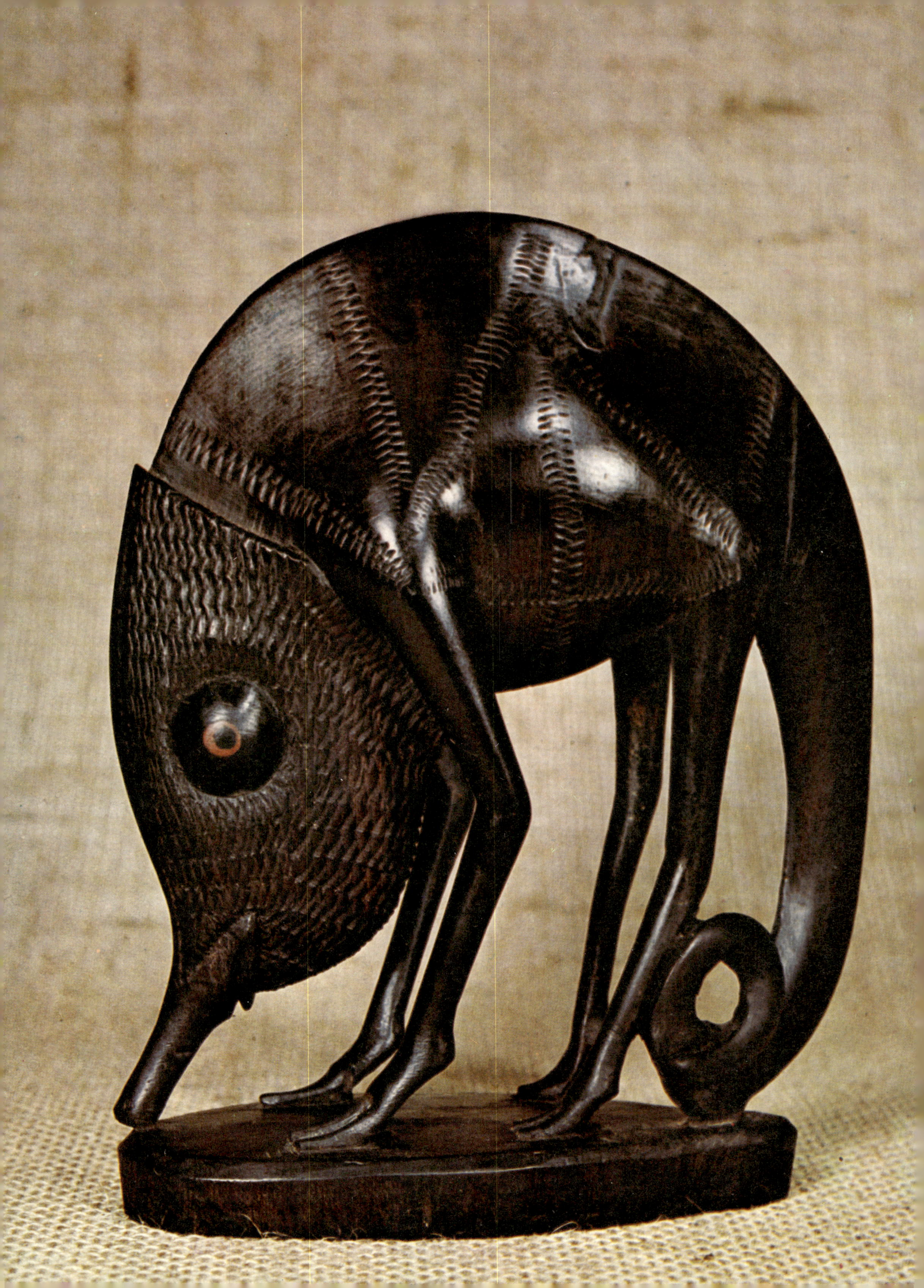

Chameleon shetani. Hossein Anangangola, 1969. 18 cm

Kundola shetani (with lip-plug), nursing her child. Kundolas are a harmless and ubiquitous species of sweet-water shetani. Fish is their main food. By night the Kundolas will come out of the water and walk around on dry land, their large eyes glowing like torches. Hossein Anangangola, 1967. 55 cm

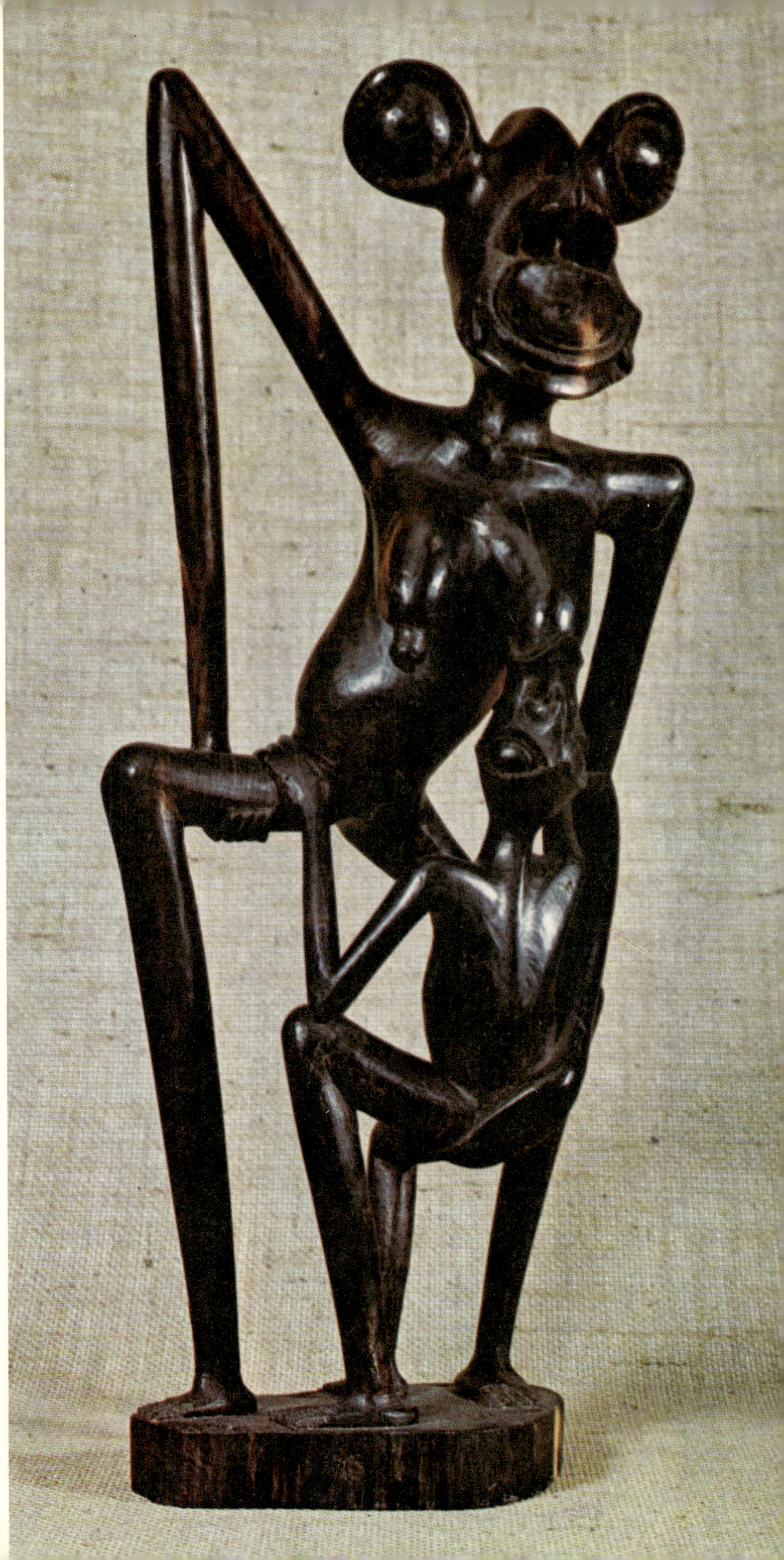

Kundola shetani, nursing her child. Hossein Anangangola, 1968. 44 cm

A shetani fighting a chameleon shetani. Hossein Anangangola had forgotten the name of this shetani, about which his father told him many stories. Whenever the two species meet, a bitter fight ensues. This time, they bounced into one another near a water-hole. Hossein Anangangola, 1969. 38 cm

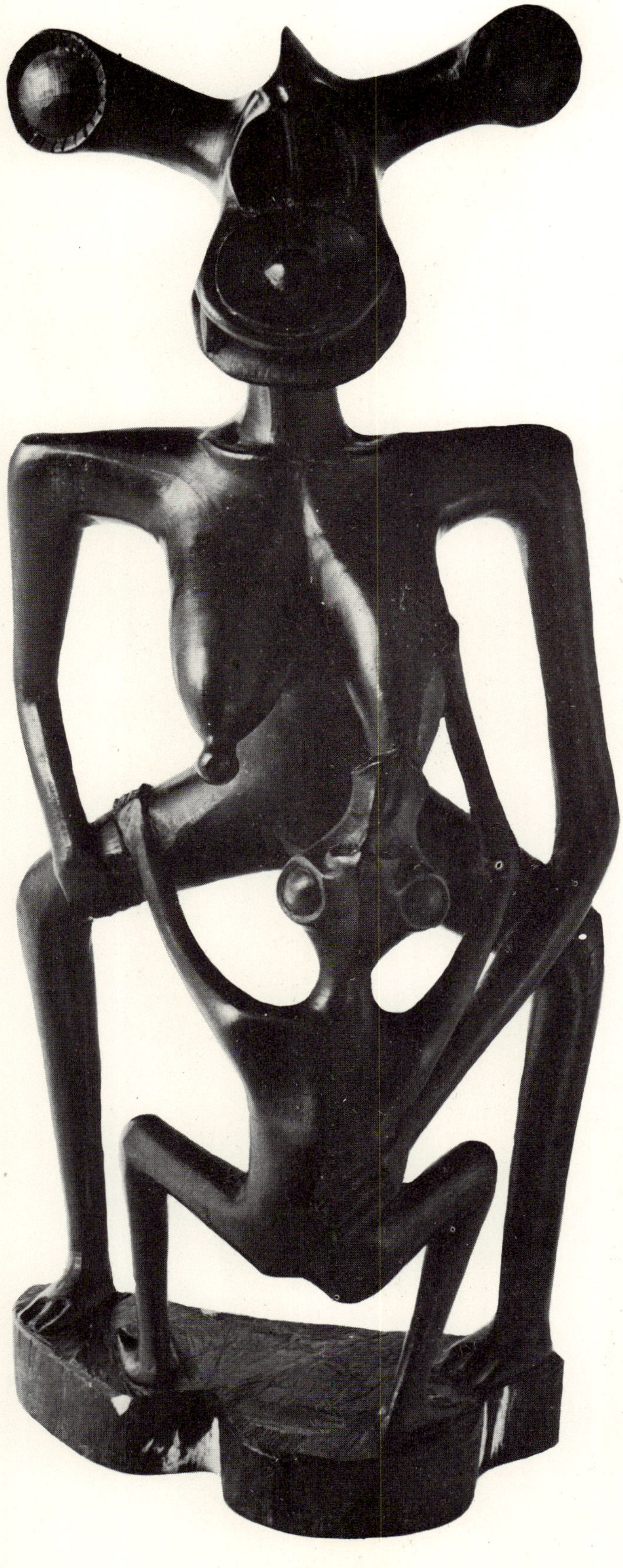

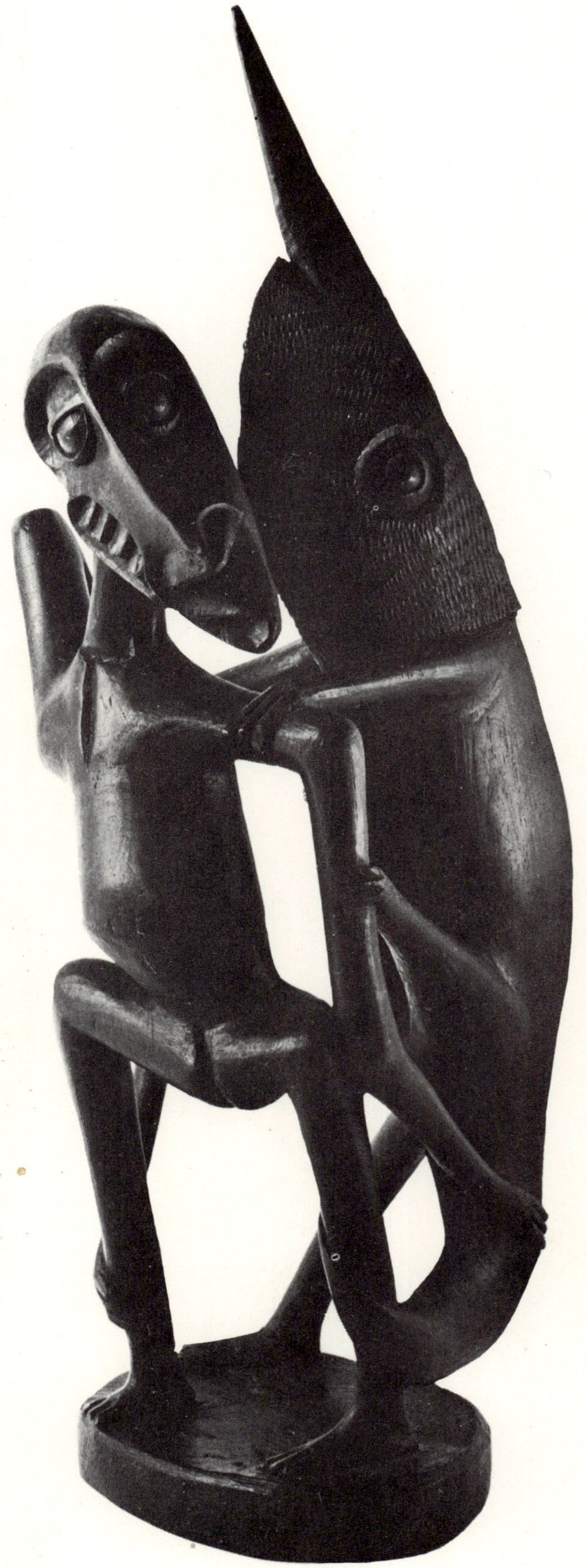

below left Changu shetani, playing a brass flourish for other shetani, 'As in the olden days in Mozambique'. Hossein Anangangola, 1969. 48 cm

below right Kutumbo shetani (tumbo means abdomen in Swahili), with young one. The Kutumbos always lack their interior abdominal wall. They look horrifying, but are harmless. Here depicted as they walk about in search of food. Hossein Anangangola, 1967. 37 cm

bottom A decorative relief with flower- and beer-shetani. Hossein Anangangola, 1968. 18 × 53 cm

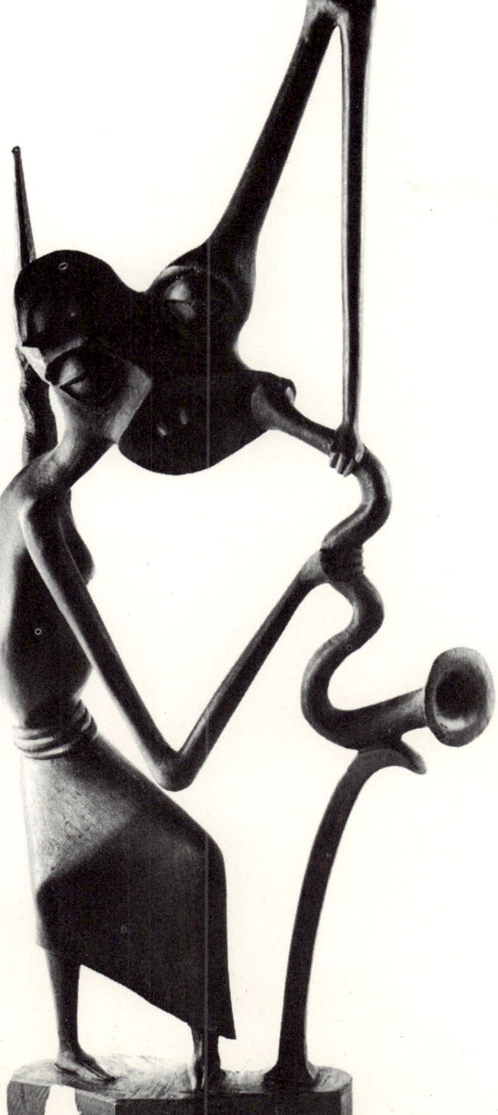

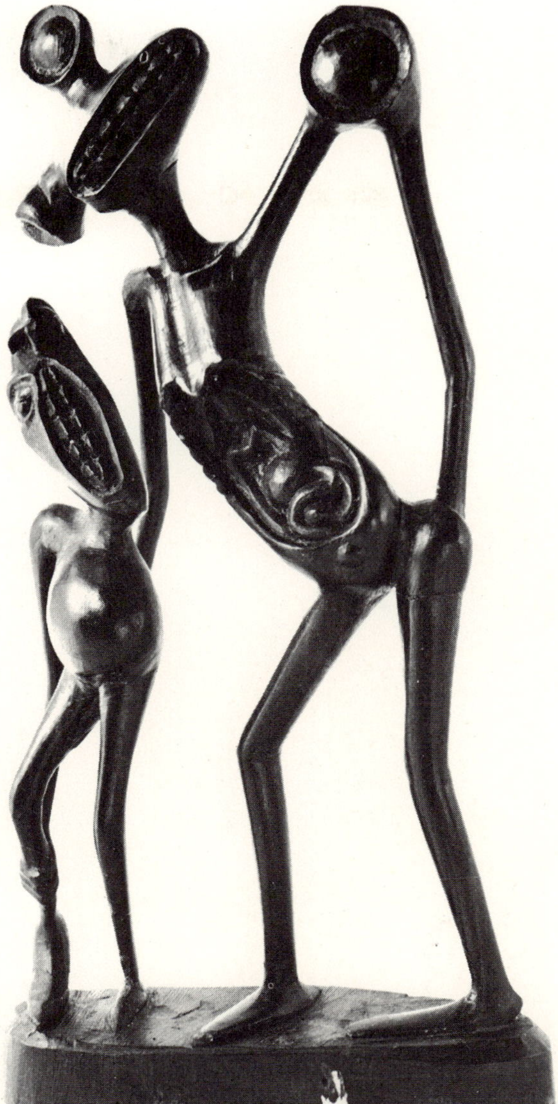

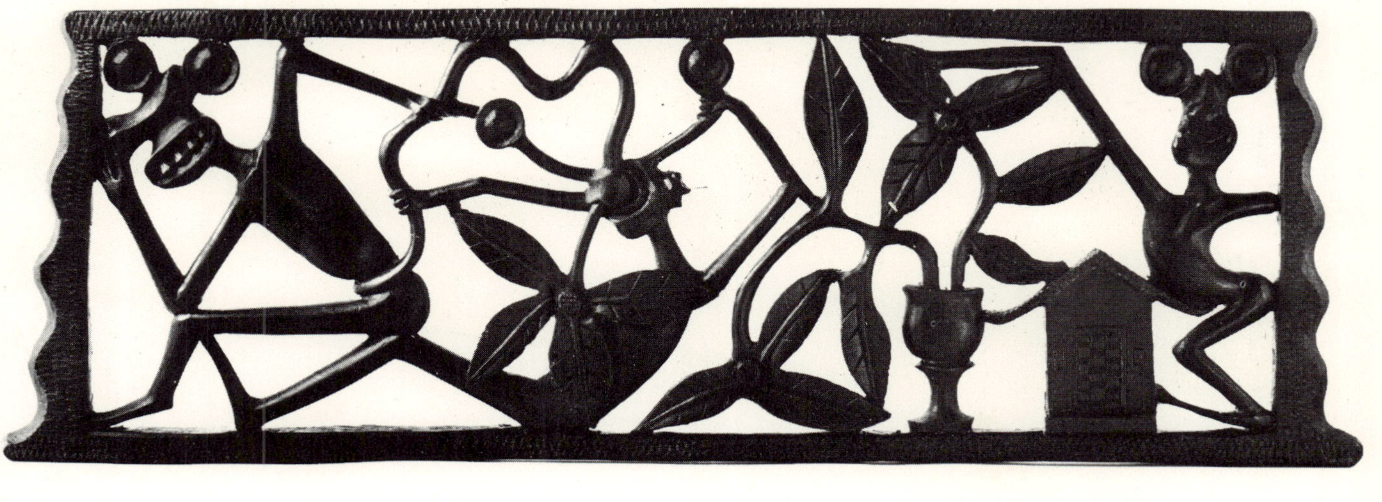

below Mating couple of anonymous shetani suffering the interruption by a third shetani. Hossein Anangangola, 1969. 7 × 42 cm

right Erotically excited female shetani. Anonymous. Hossein Anangangola, 1969. 9 cm

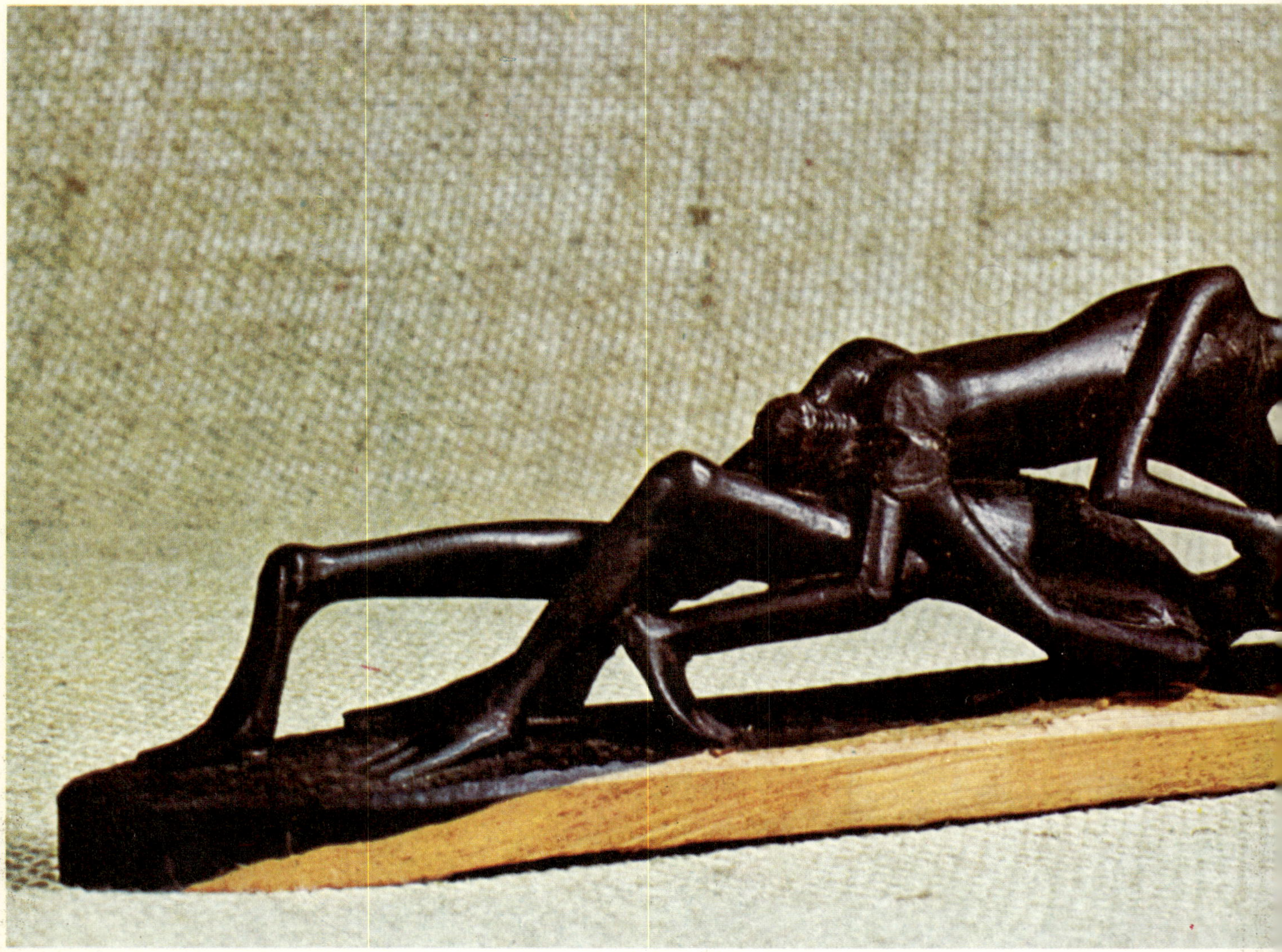

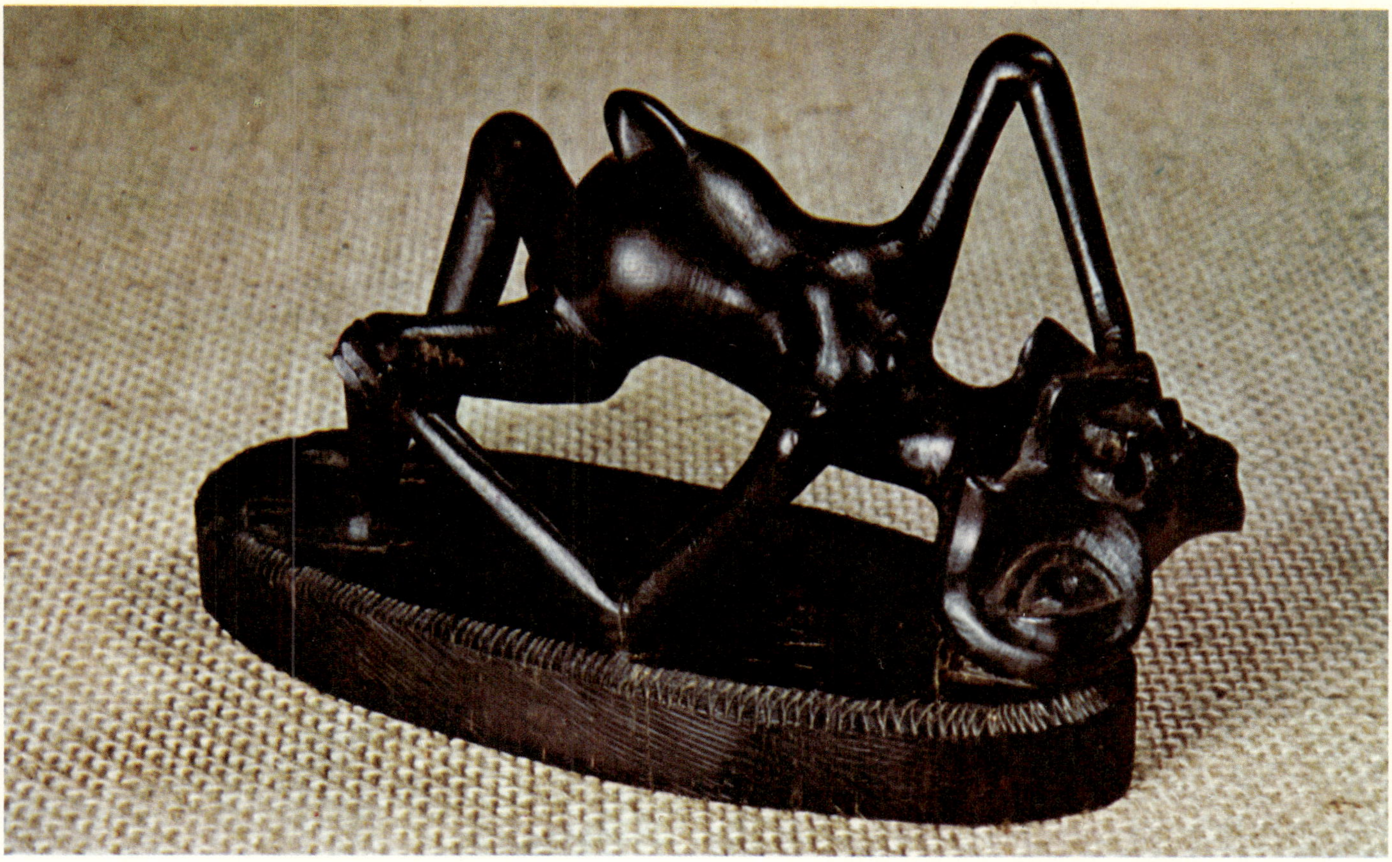

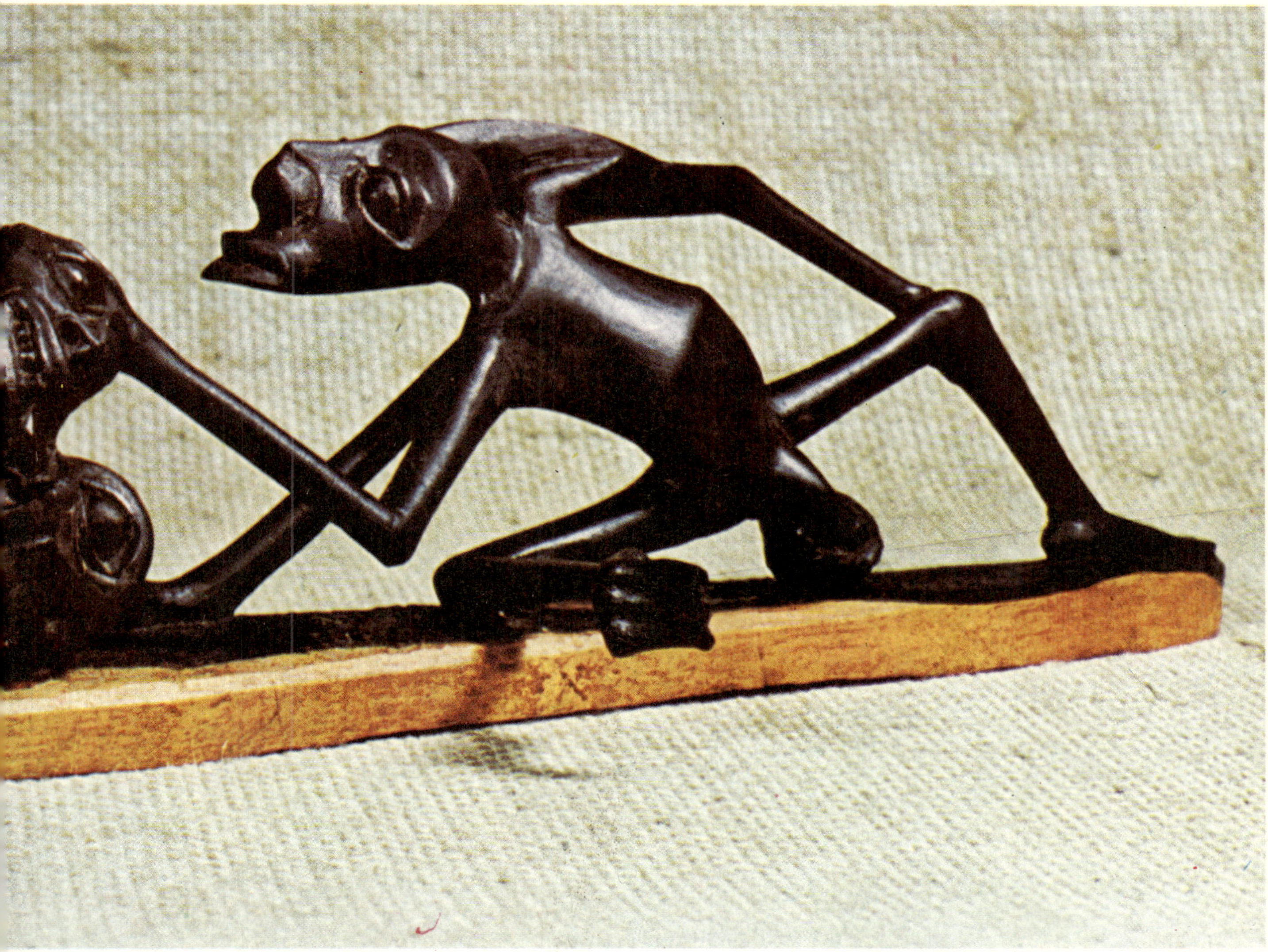

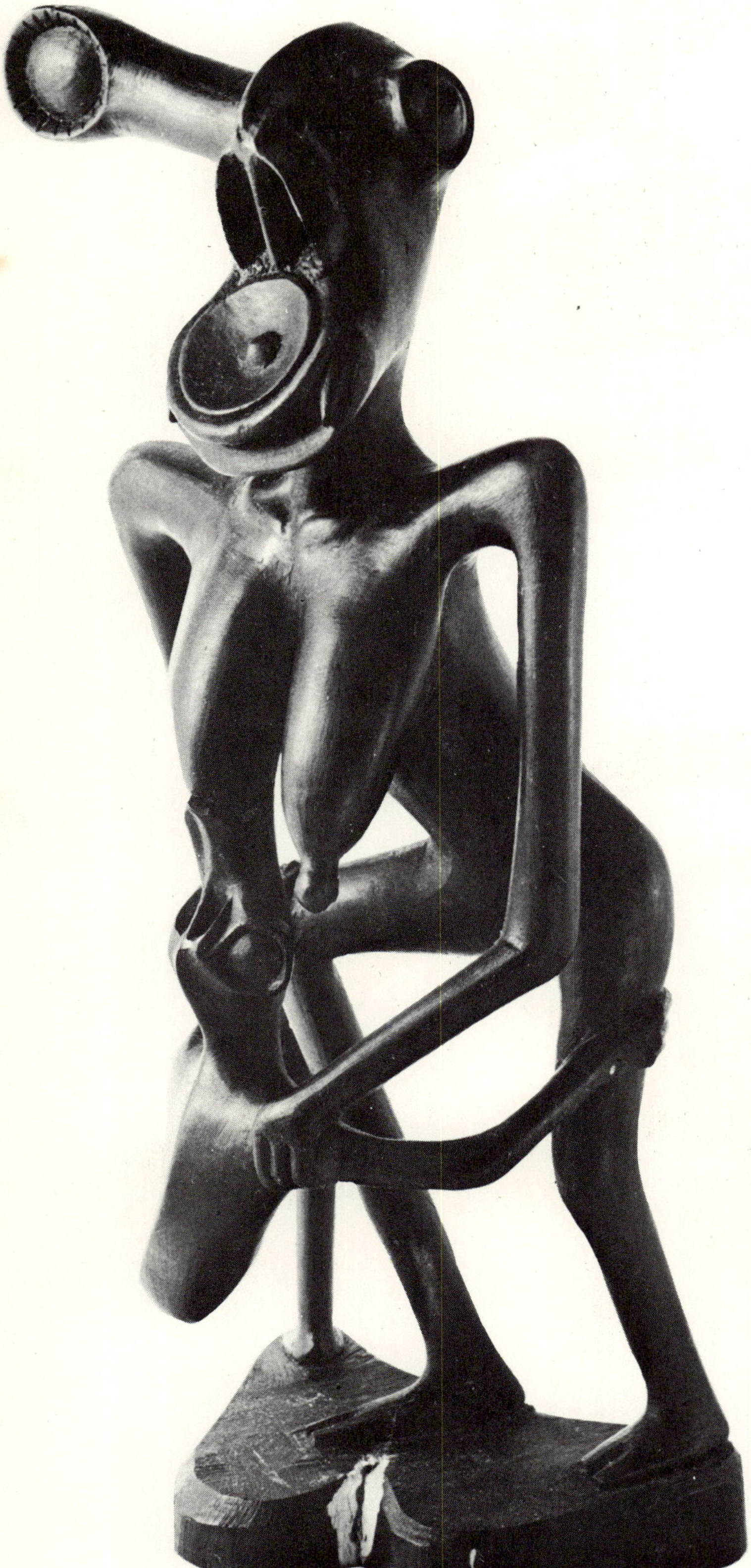

Kundola shetani nursing her baby. Hossein Anangangola, 1968. 55 cm

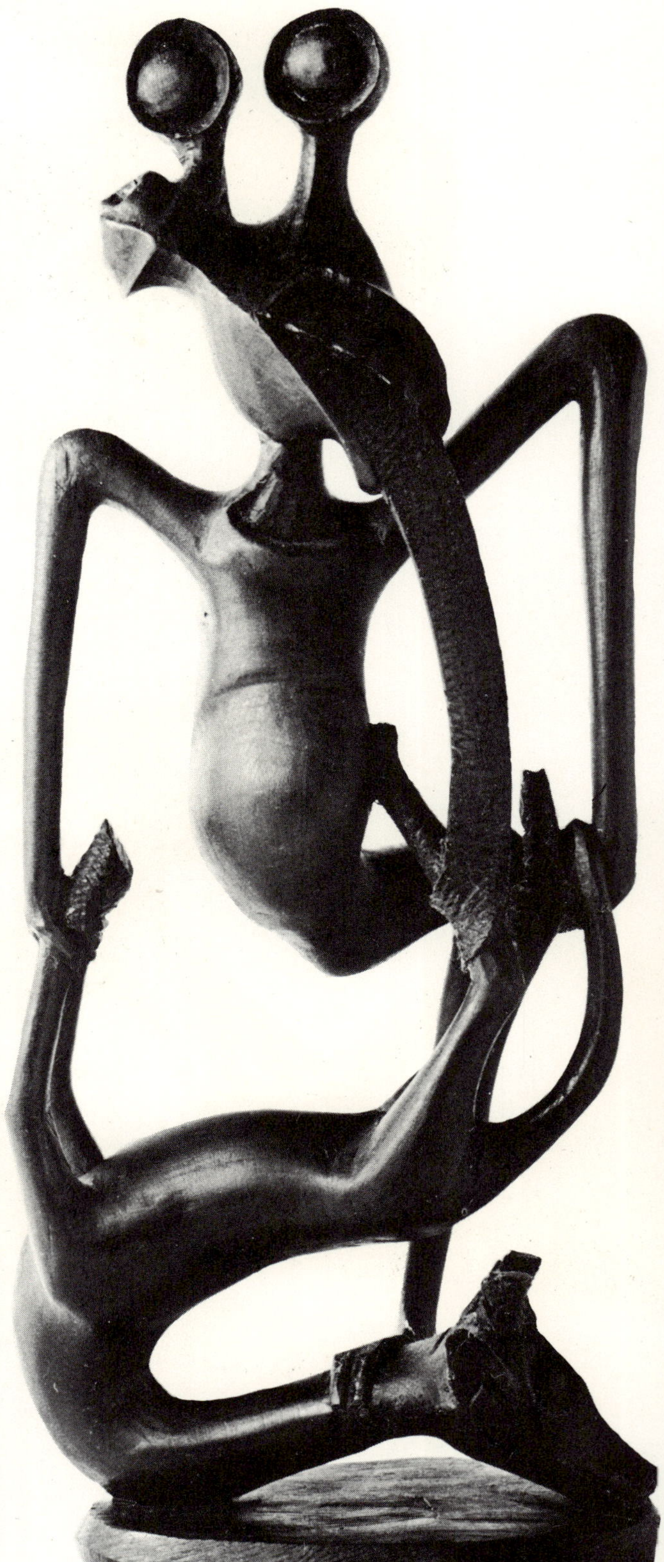

Likambale, a huge, fierce forest shetani. Here the Likambale has killed a giraffe which he is going to eat. To man, the Likambales are generally not harmful. Hossein Anangangola, 1968. 32 cm

Kamanya female with a chameleon. Hossein Anangangola, 1969. 35 cm

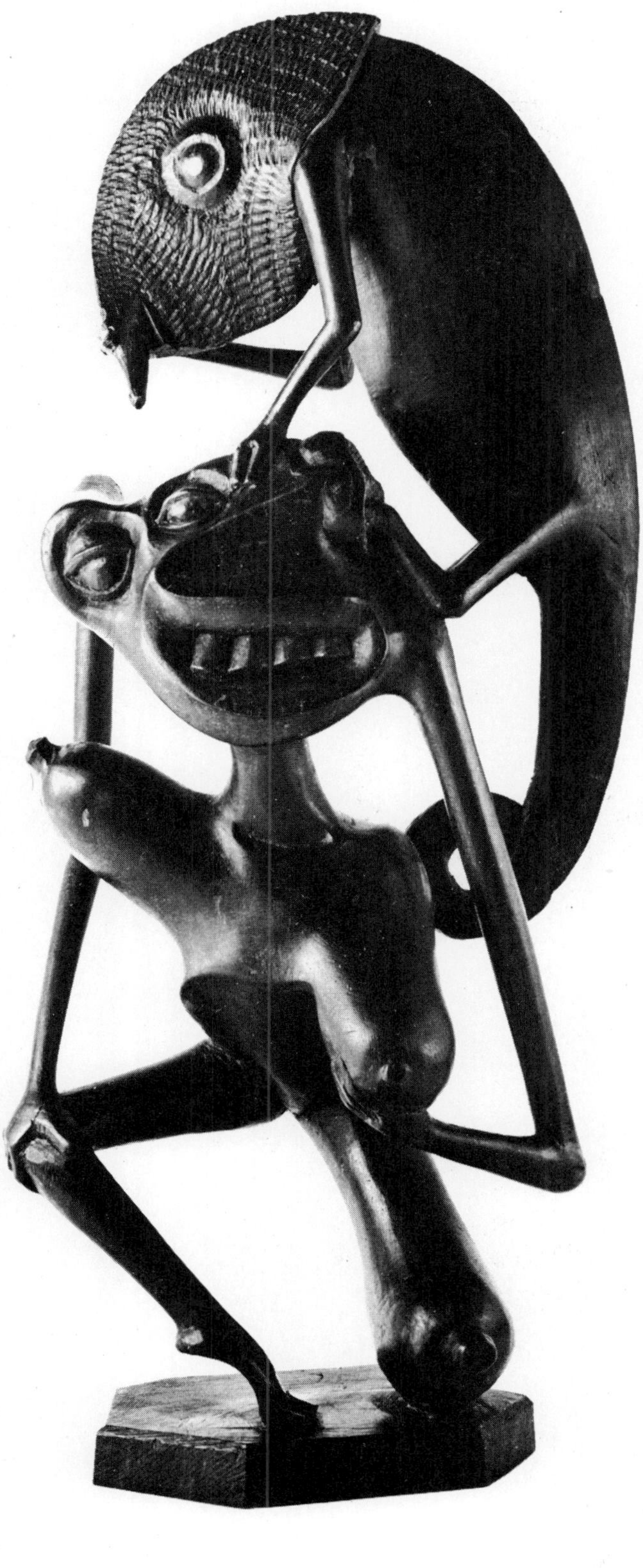

Kanyole shetani unit. A snake-eating species from high altitudes in Mozambique. Hossein Anangangola, 1969. 52 cm

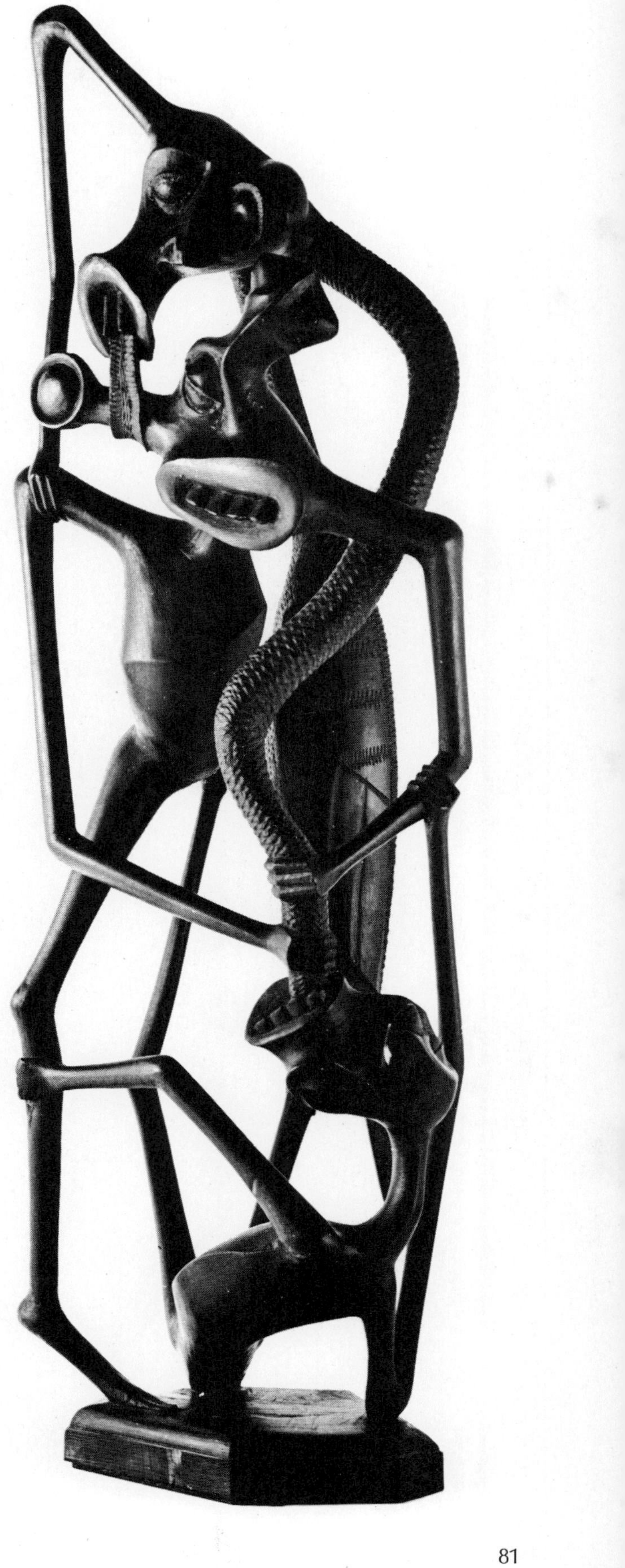

A shetani couple. One shetani is sick. Since medicine herbs did not cure the disease, the other shetani is now performing an uvulectomy on his friend, licking her face for comfort. The species is Tulambane, a bush-shetani. Hossein Anangangola, 1968. 43 cm

Chuni shetani. A flying species from the forest but generally found close to villages. The Chunis catch their prey with their hands while flying. They can even in their flight catch small mammals like mice with their lower, head-like extension which will sweep over the ground as the Chuni flutters along in the darkness. Hossein Anangangola, 1969. 35 cm

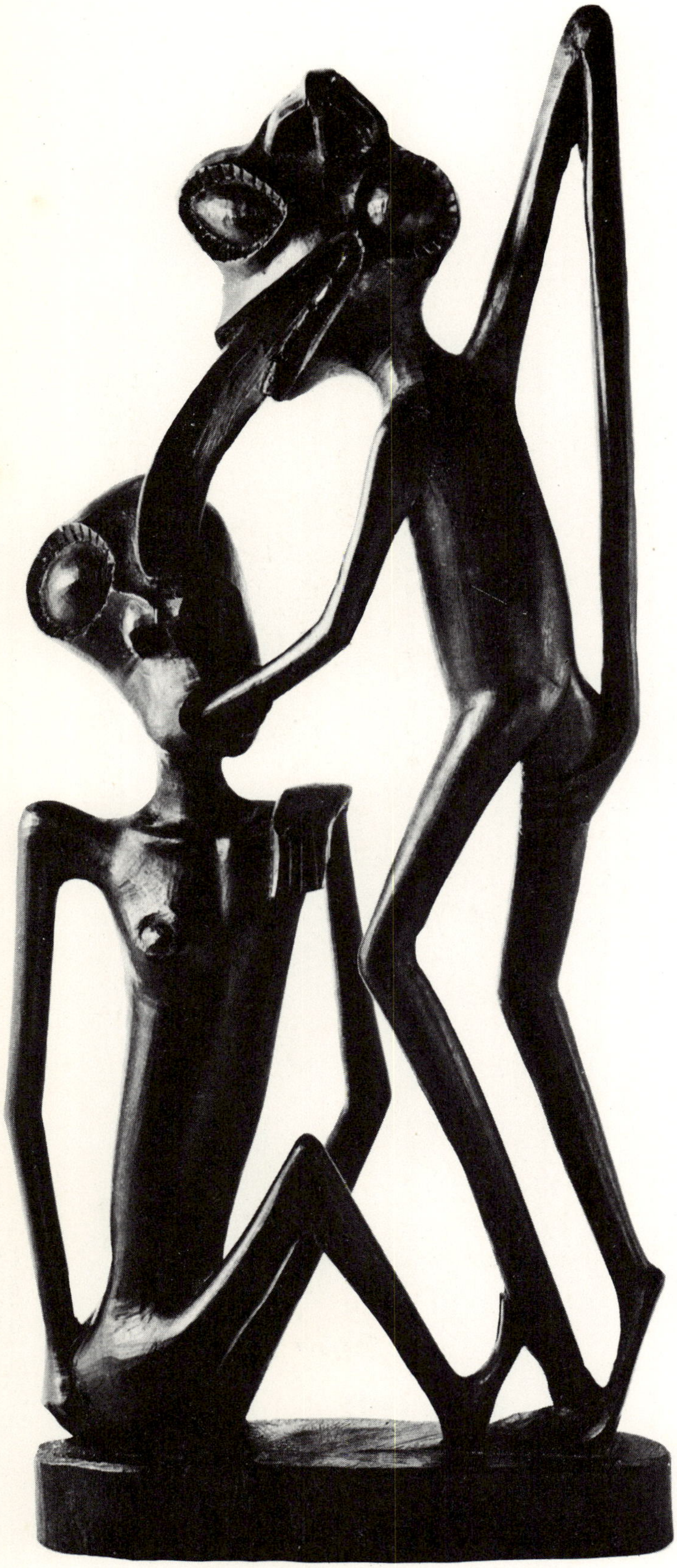

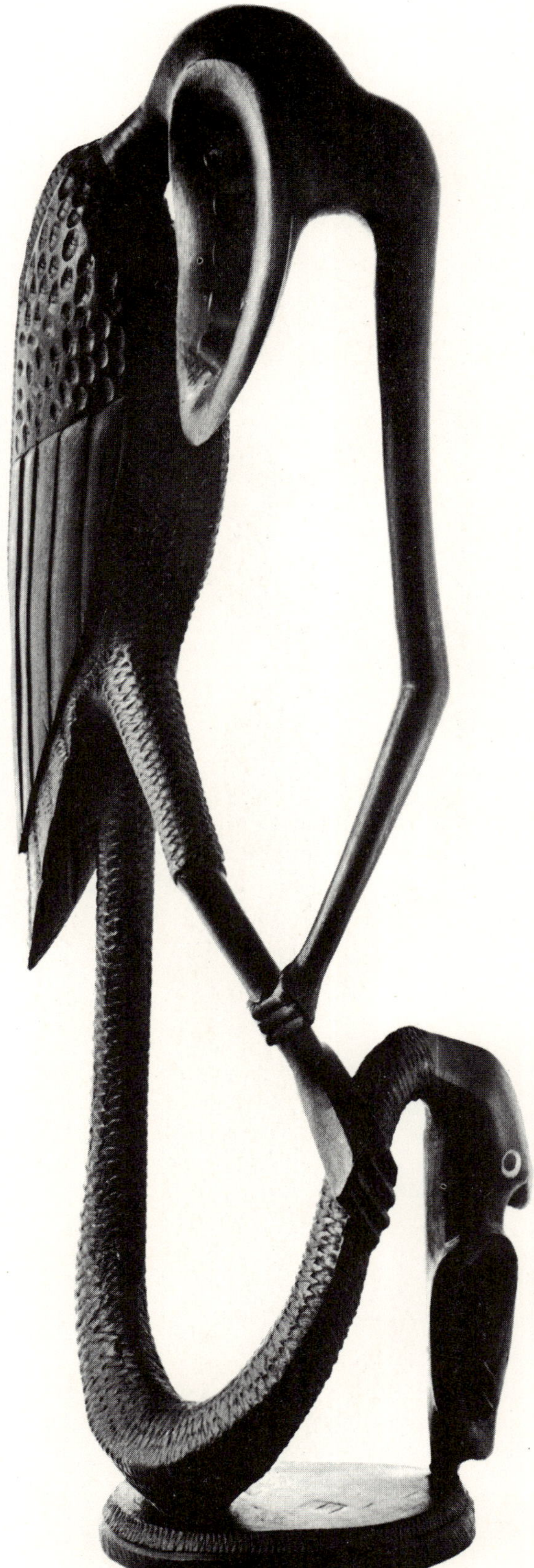

Anonymous shetani unit. Hossein Anangangola, 1969. 54 cm

Likutu shetani, mother with two babies. The Lijutus are tall like giraffes. The adults are easily recognized by their single large ear. Hossein Anangangola, 1968. 38 cm

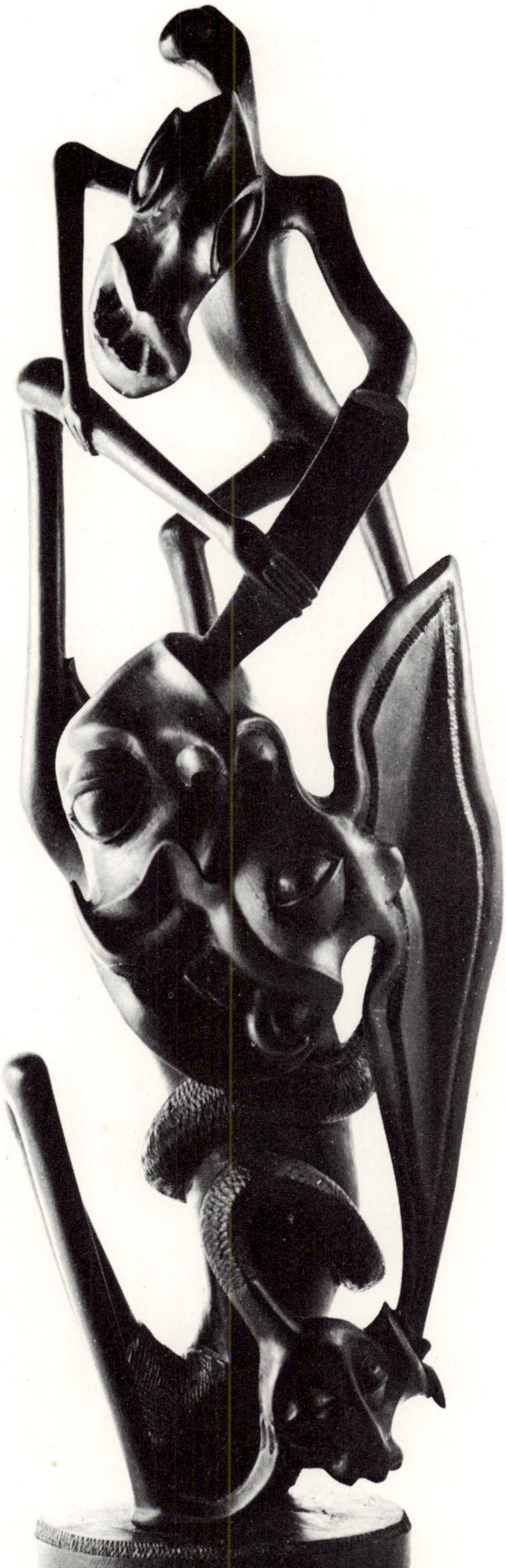

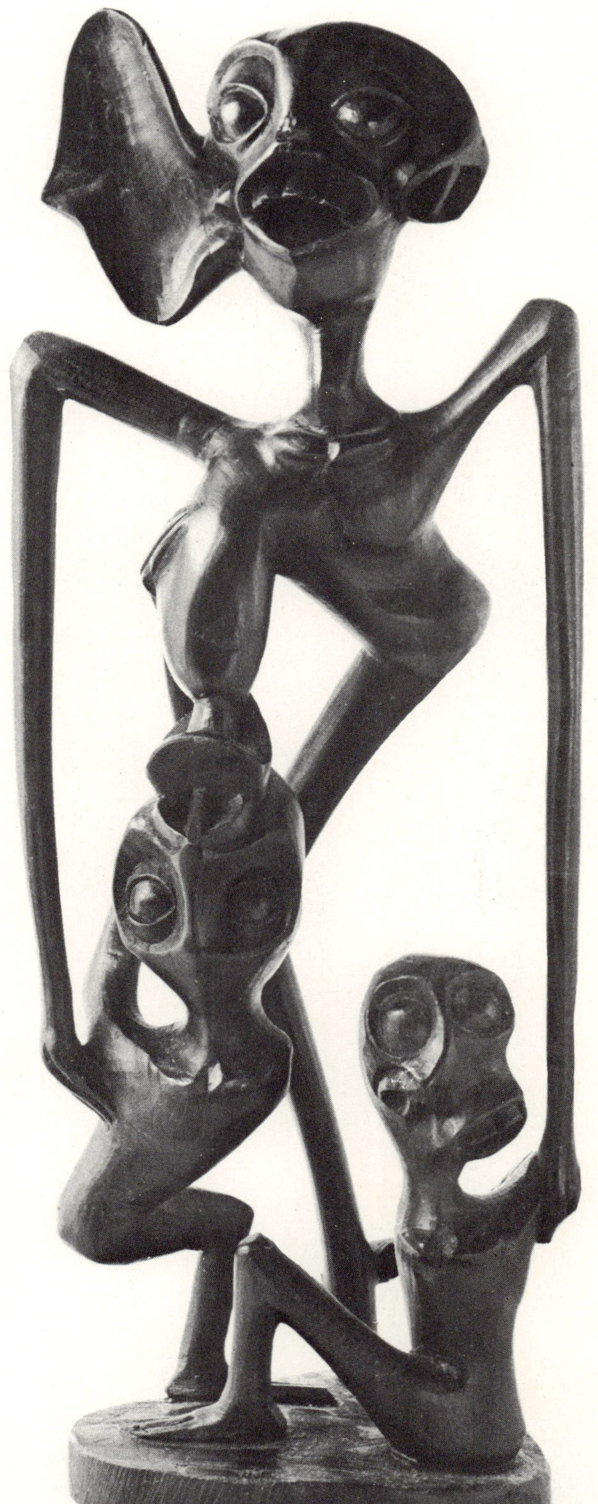

Kwinama, a common sweet-water shetani. The Kwinamas feed on dry land like the hippopotami. When a human being happens to pass them, they will bend their head down and stand quietly. They do not harm men. Hossein Anangangola has seen few shetani with his own eyes. Kwinama is one of them. Hossein Anangangola, 1968. 41 cm

Shautumbo, a small, harmless forest shetani. Hossein Anangangola, 1968. 32 cm

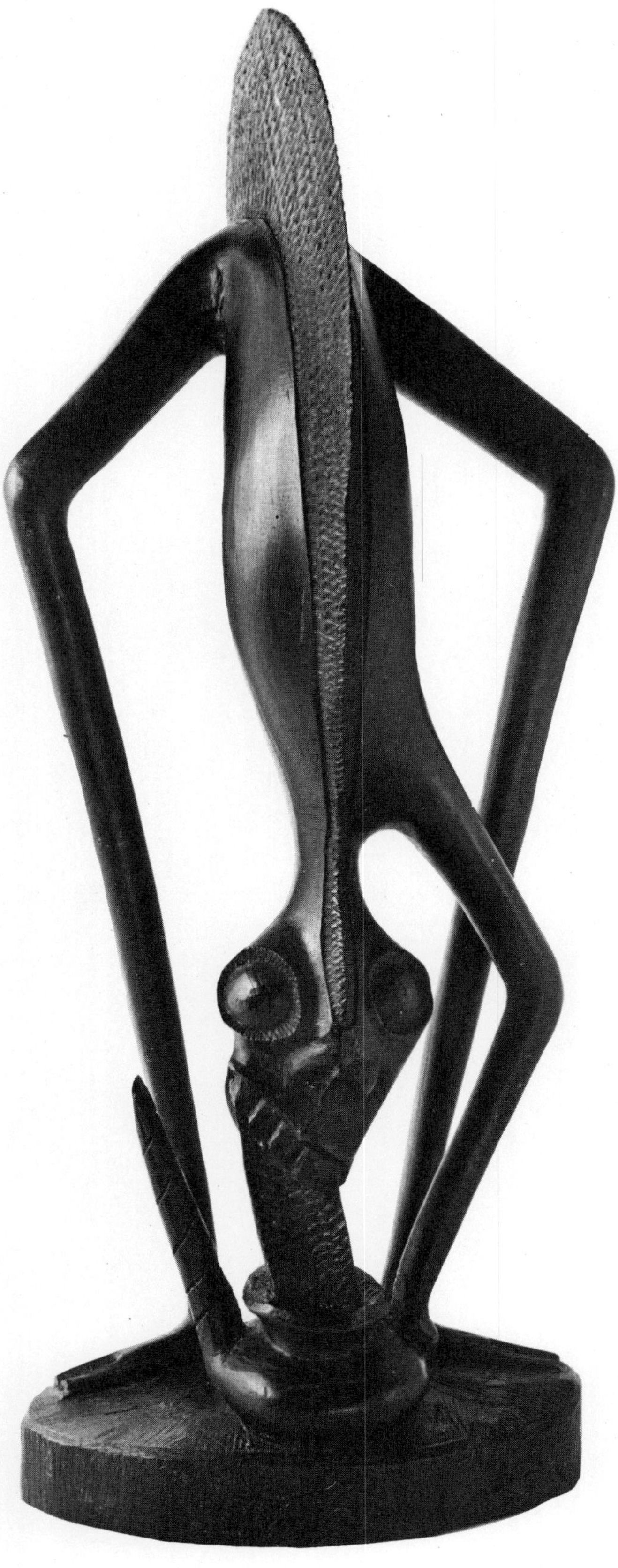

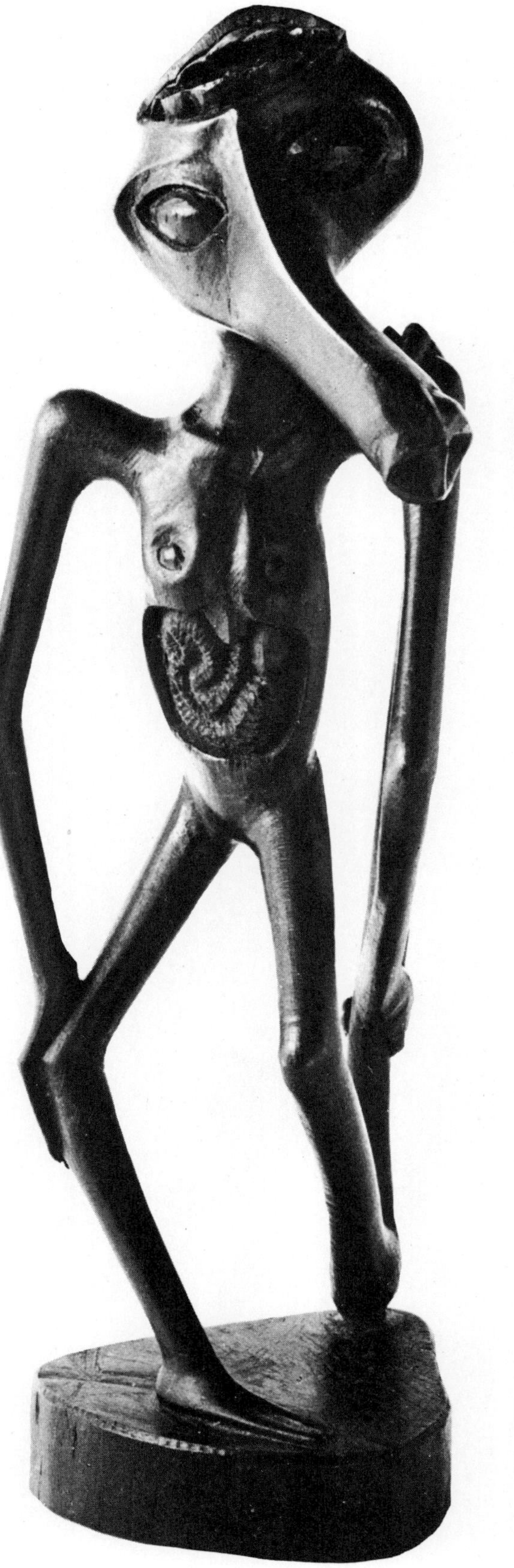

Kibwenge shetani unit. Mother and two children. Shetani of prey which live in the bush and dwell in holes in the ground. Hossein Anangangola, 1968. 43 cm

Nkalikole shetani unit. Mother and two adolescent children which are being nursed before the unit sets out for hunting. Nkalikoles are similar to Kibwenges, but smaller, only the size of a goat, and less dangerous to human beings. Hossein Anangangola, 1968. 46 cm

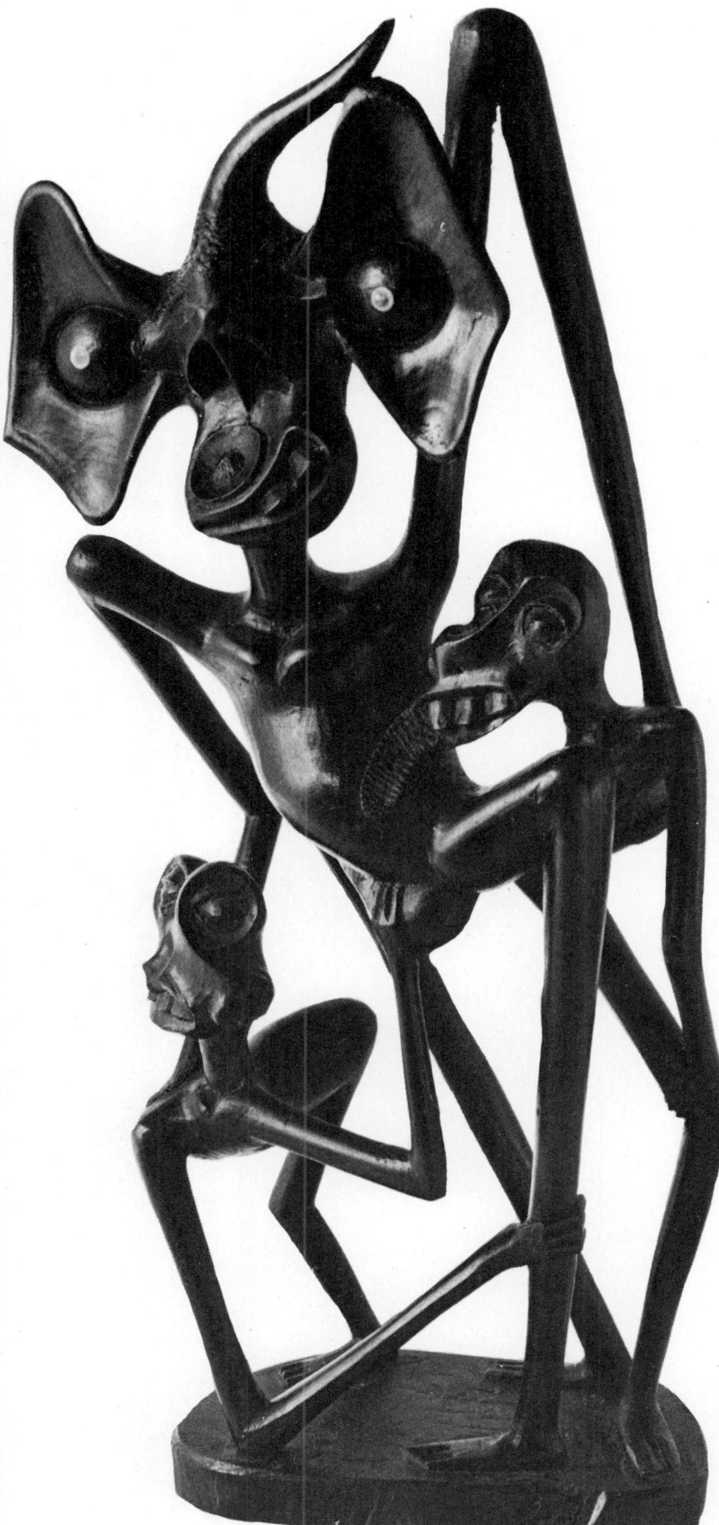

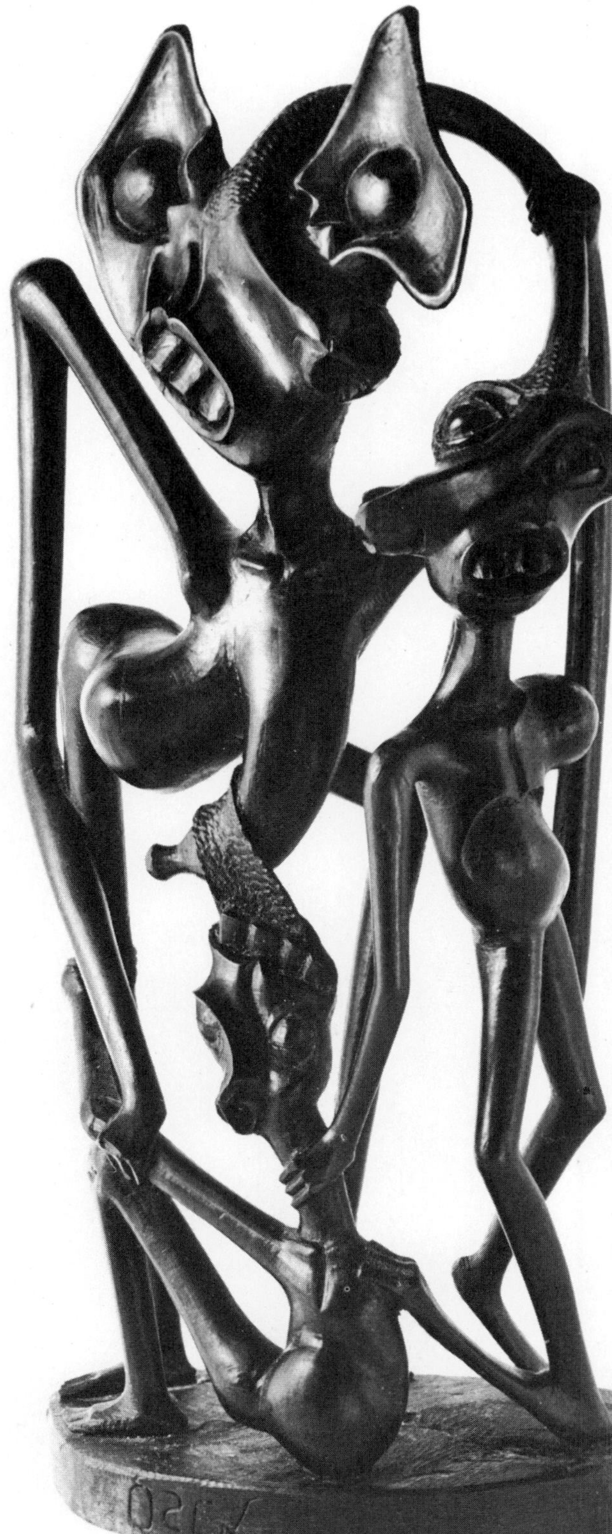

Kibwenge shetani unit, mother with two children. The adult Kibwenge unit is taller than a man. The Kibwenge is a nocturnal species, and extremely quarrelsome. Dangerous to man. Hossein Anangangola, 1968. 58 cm

A couple of anonymous mountain shetani, resting and making love in their strange way. Hossein Anangangola, 1967. 42 × 13 cm

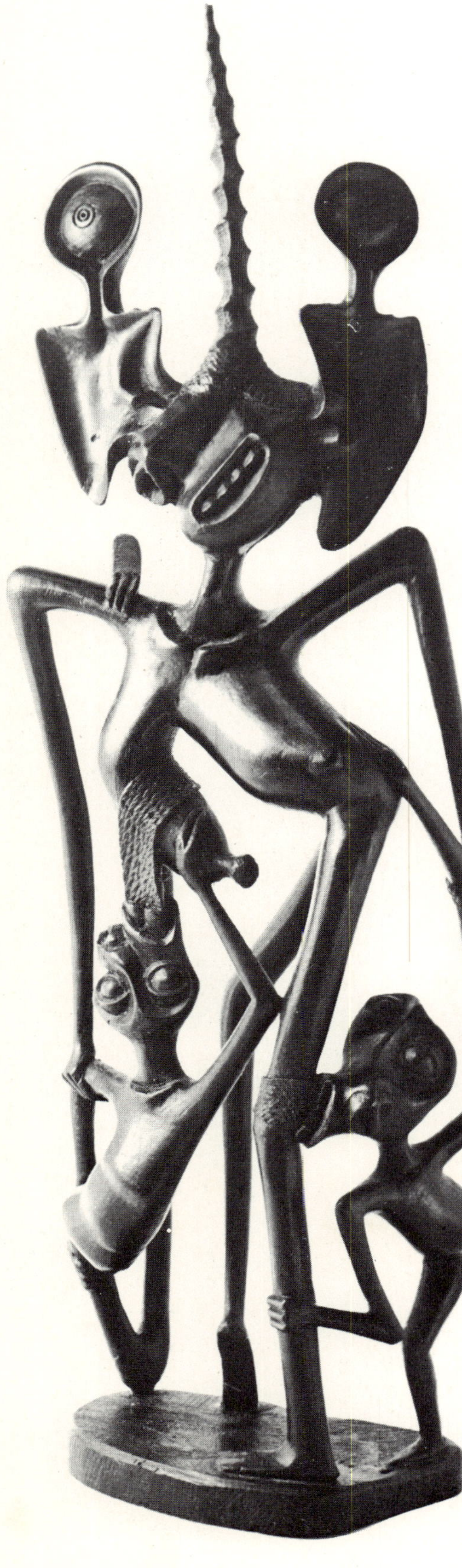

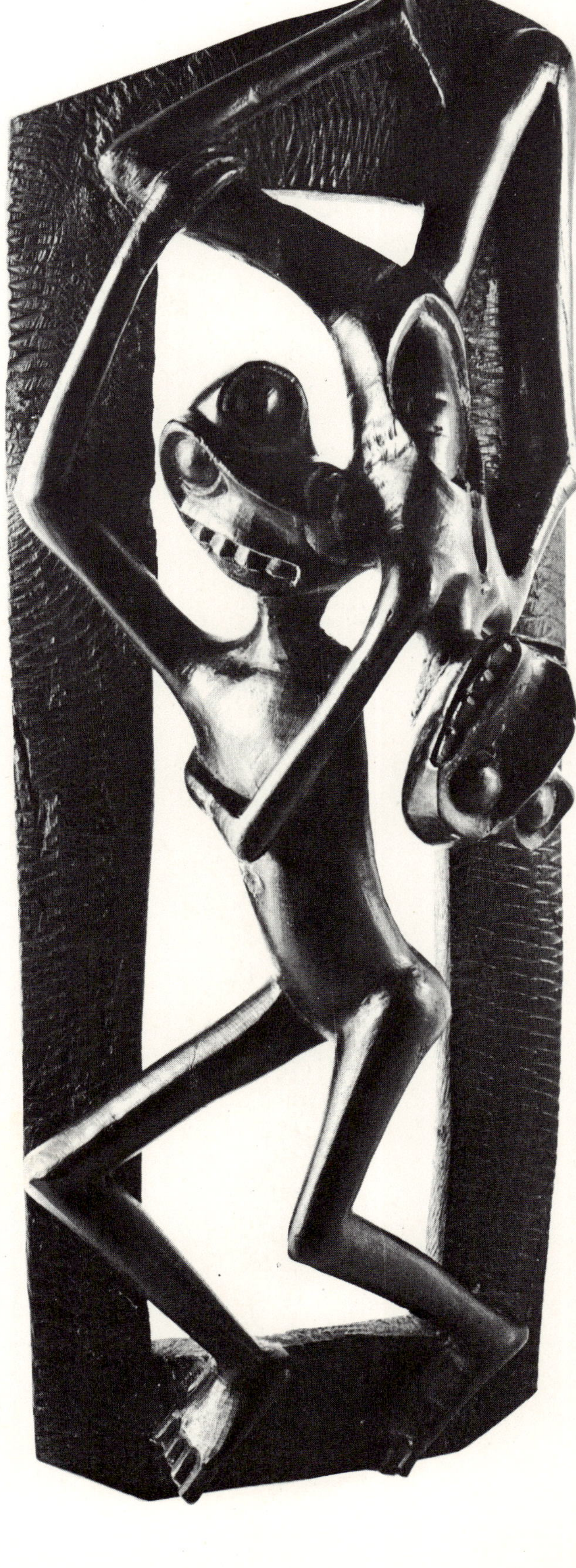

Nchila shetani mother with child. Nchilas are snake-hunters. Like the Chingweles, the Nchilas have one knife-like upper extremity. They live in the mountains. Hossein Anangangola, 1969. 37 cm

Anonymous shetani unit. Hossein Anangangola, 1969. 52 cm

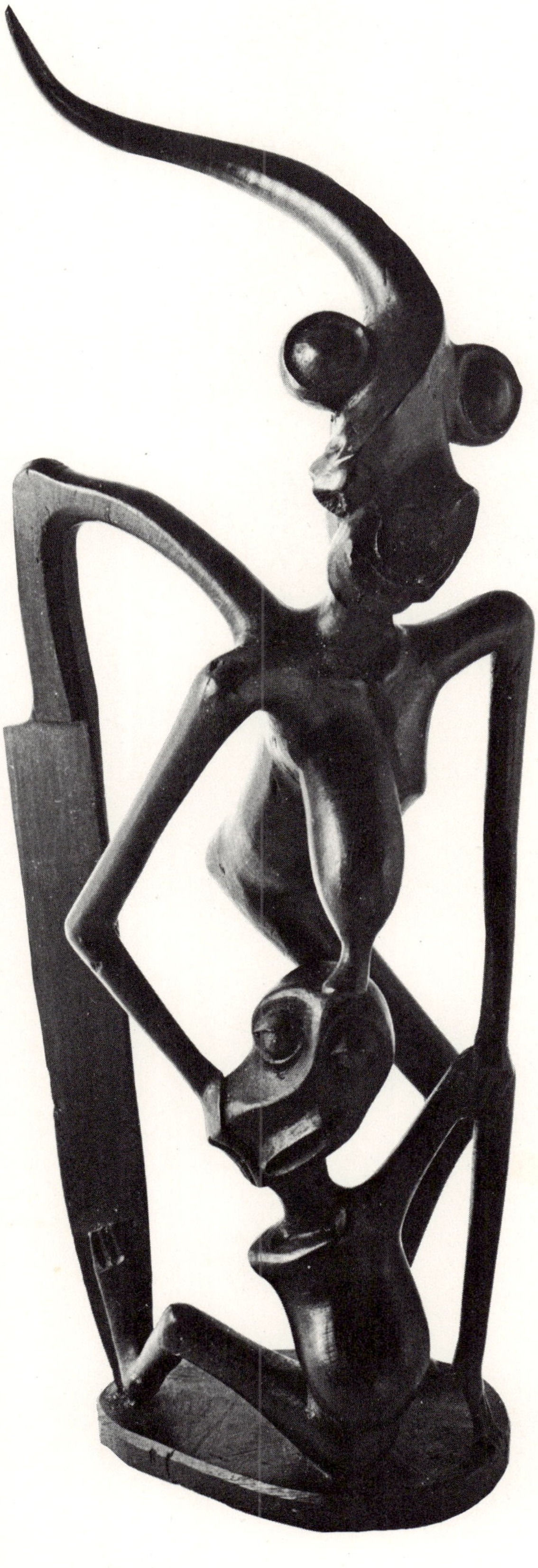

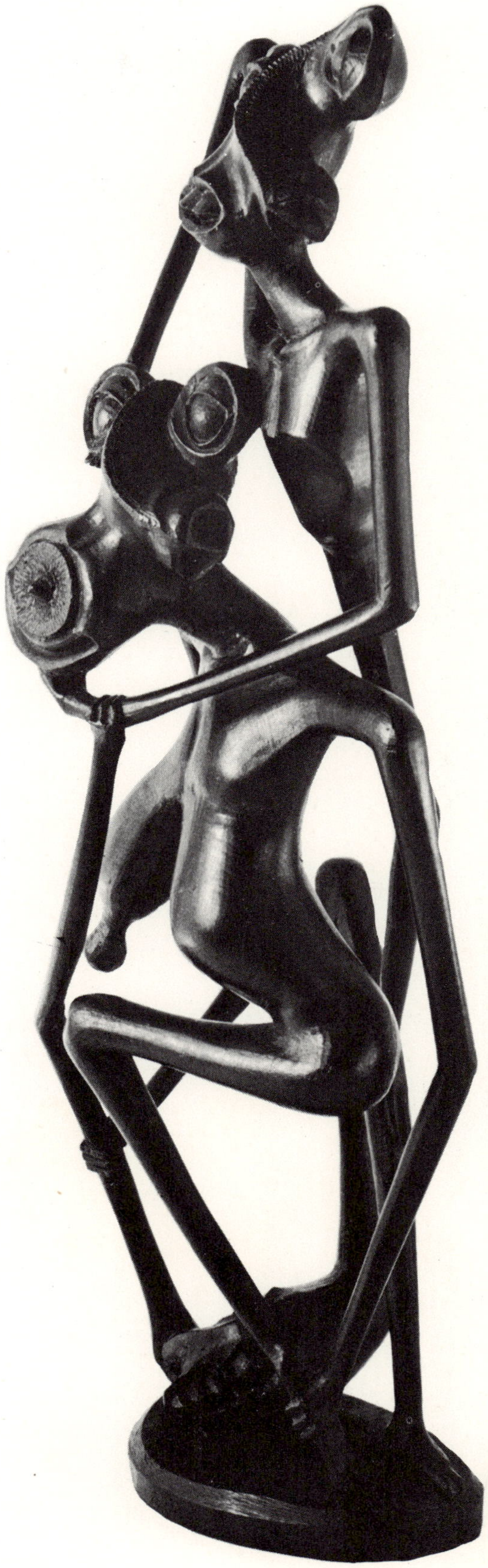

The wood of Makonde sculpture

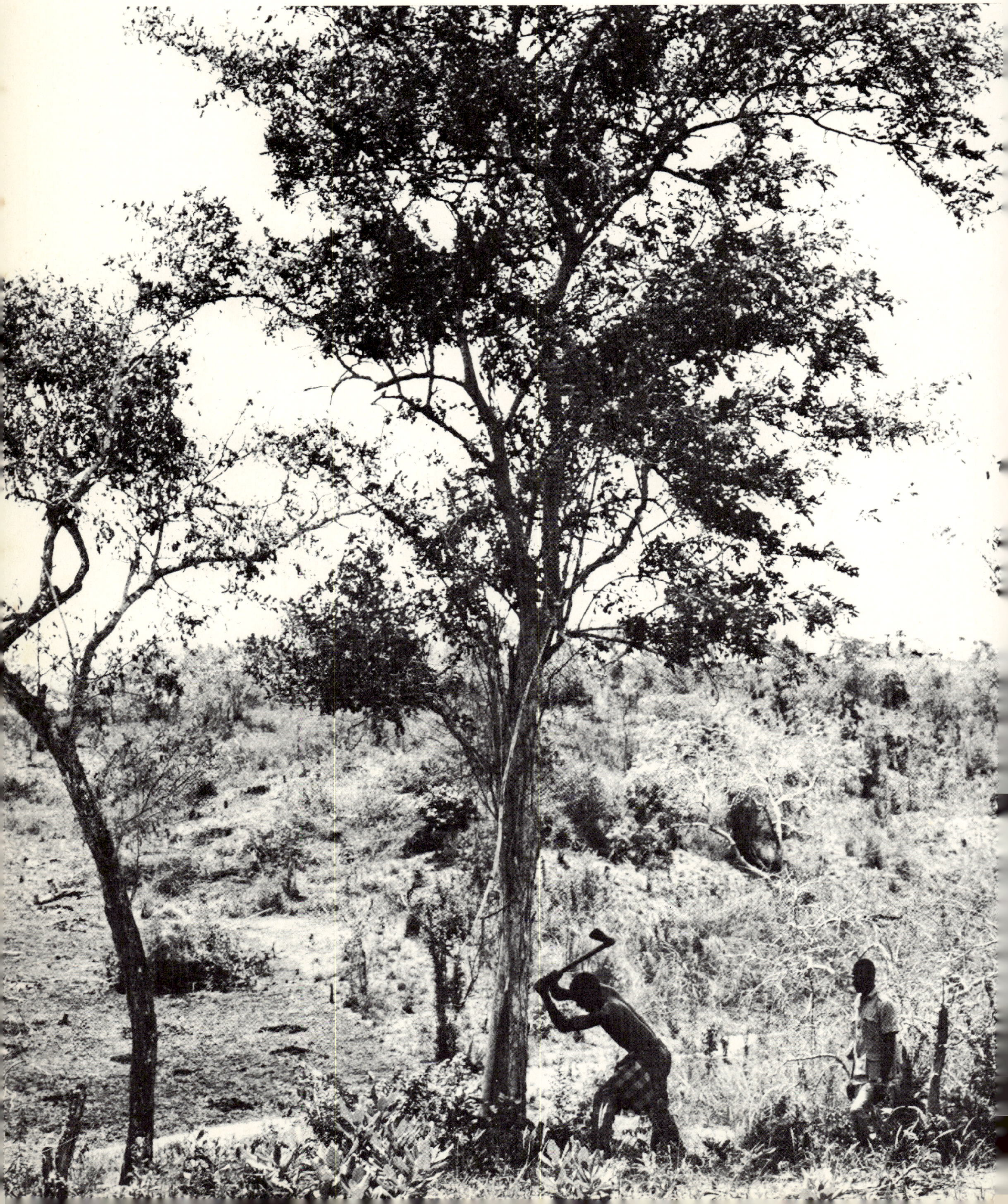

A mpingo tree

The Makonde craftsmen find their wood in the local shrub forest. People called it ebony for centuries although it is not from the true ebony tree which also grows in the area. The ebony tree does not usually develop much of a black core in these regions, so the Makonde carvers use wood from the African blackwood tree. It is called mpingo around Dar es Salaam, and in Mozambique grenadilla. The tree is common all over Africa south of the Sahara, and is found particularly on old ant-hills in the coastal savannah. The trees are small, untidy and spiny with leathery leaves somewhat similar to those of the ash. Their trunks are short, deeply ridged and irregular, with greyish, flaking bark. The logs often have a rotten heart or contain pockets of stone and sand or inclusions of bark. These irregularities are often used to effect by the craftsmen in their completed sculpture. So also is the layer of yellowish sapwood, a half to an inch deep, which surrounds the hard brownish-black core. Occasionally the sapwood just shows up in peripheral parts of a sculpture obviously intended to be all black.

African blackwood is a heavy wood of dense texture. It is much appreciated all over the world by the makers of musical instruments. When seasoned there is little tendency for the wood to crack or warp, and no distinct grain will disturb the chisel, although tools will soon blunt on it.

An object from African blackwood is practically imperishable for it is not attacked by insects or fungi. However, a certain menace to Makonde sculpture is to be found in the fact that the carvers will choose their wood straight from the forest and set to work long before it is seasoned. In the damp coastal climate where the majority of the Makonde carvings are made, the wood dries out slowly, and consequently it is less likely to split or warp. But when the sculpture is abruptly transferred from an atmosphere of more than 90 degrees of relative humidity to the dry air of European houses there is a risk that spontaneous cracking of a new work will occur. This can be prevented by sealing the pores of the wood-surfaces with an application of oil, wax or plastic emulsion. The effect is to make the wood much darker and there may be an unavoidable loss of texture. Nevertheless, the sculpture may gain in clarity because the reflected light accentuates details with small highlights. Black shoe-polish is applied by some of the Makonde carvers to their products to give a highly polished finish that repels most art lovers. (The surfaces of the sculptures photographed for this book were all lightly impregnated with a solution of bees' wax in turpentine oil.)

Where to find Makonde art

Workshop sign boards

As implied in the introduction, the homelands of the Makonde people in Mozambique or their villages north of the Ruvuma river are not the places to find modern Makonde art of the type presently favoured. The craftsmen have migrated to their markets, and the artists are amongst them.

The centre of Makonde sculpture is Dar es Salaam. Thousands of carvings can be seen in that city, and the bulk of the export goes from there. On a trip of some 30 miles along the northern roads from Dar es Salaam you will find several Makonde workshops, the craftsmen working in small groups under a palm-leaf roof. The village of Boko, on the Bagamoyo road, is famous for sculptures in the Jamaa style. Also, up-country in Tanzania, Makonde sculpture is offered along the tourist routes. Naturally it is possible to find interesting objects in that multitude of carvings, and if you wanted to contact the artist personally he could surely be found.

Since 1970 Tanzania has tried to nationalize the business of Makonde sculpture. With the aid of Mr Peera, who was mentioned above, The National Arts of Tanzania was created, with an art gallery in Dar es Salaam and an exhibition of Makonde sculpture by Dar es Salaam artists in which the works are for sale. But in recent years Nairobi, the capital of Kenya, has attracted several Makonde artists amongst whom are Rashidi bin Mohamed and Hossein Anangangola.

The rapidly growing awareness of values in modern Makonde sculpture has offered opportunities for some of the artists to pursue their individual intentions free from commercial pressures. A snag, however, is still to be found in the absence of any permanent contact between the artists and their audience abroad. Without that contact they are at risk, in spite of all, and are tempted to yield to the whims and value judgements of dealers, officials, and temporary patrons. In the mind of the public, Makonde sculpture is identified with a multitude of anonymous craftsmen from the Dark Continent. Yet one cannot do a greater service to the Makonde sculptors than acknowledge their artistic integrity, a problem as long as so few of them have adopted the idea of a signature, and as long as scholars of Africana maintain the attitude that Makonde art is an ethnographic phenomenon rather than one aspect of contemporary art.

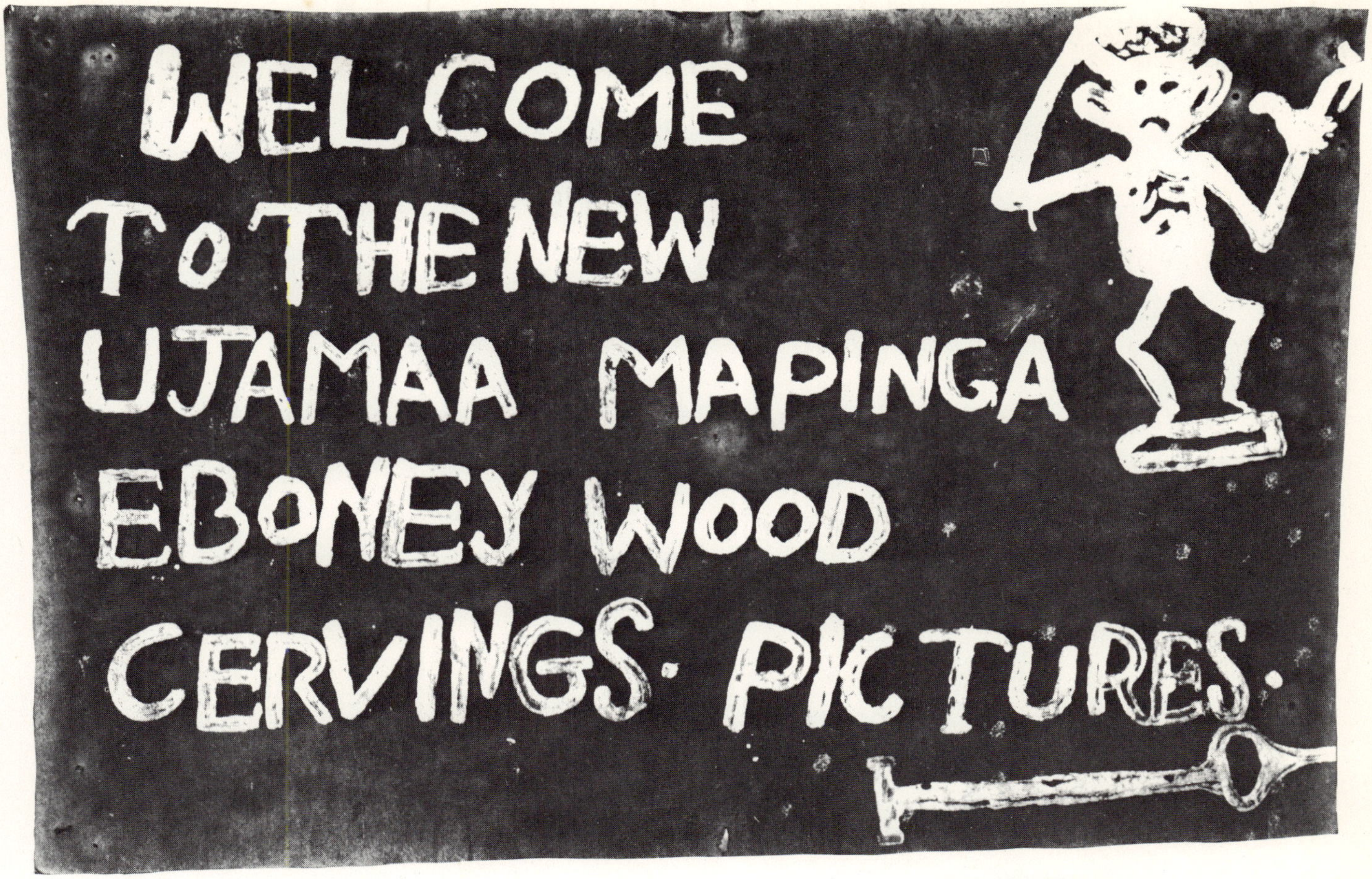
WELCOME
TO THE NEW
UJAMAA MAPINGA
EBONEY WOOD
CERVINGS. PICTURES.

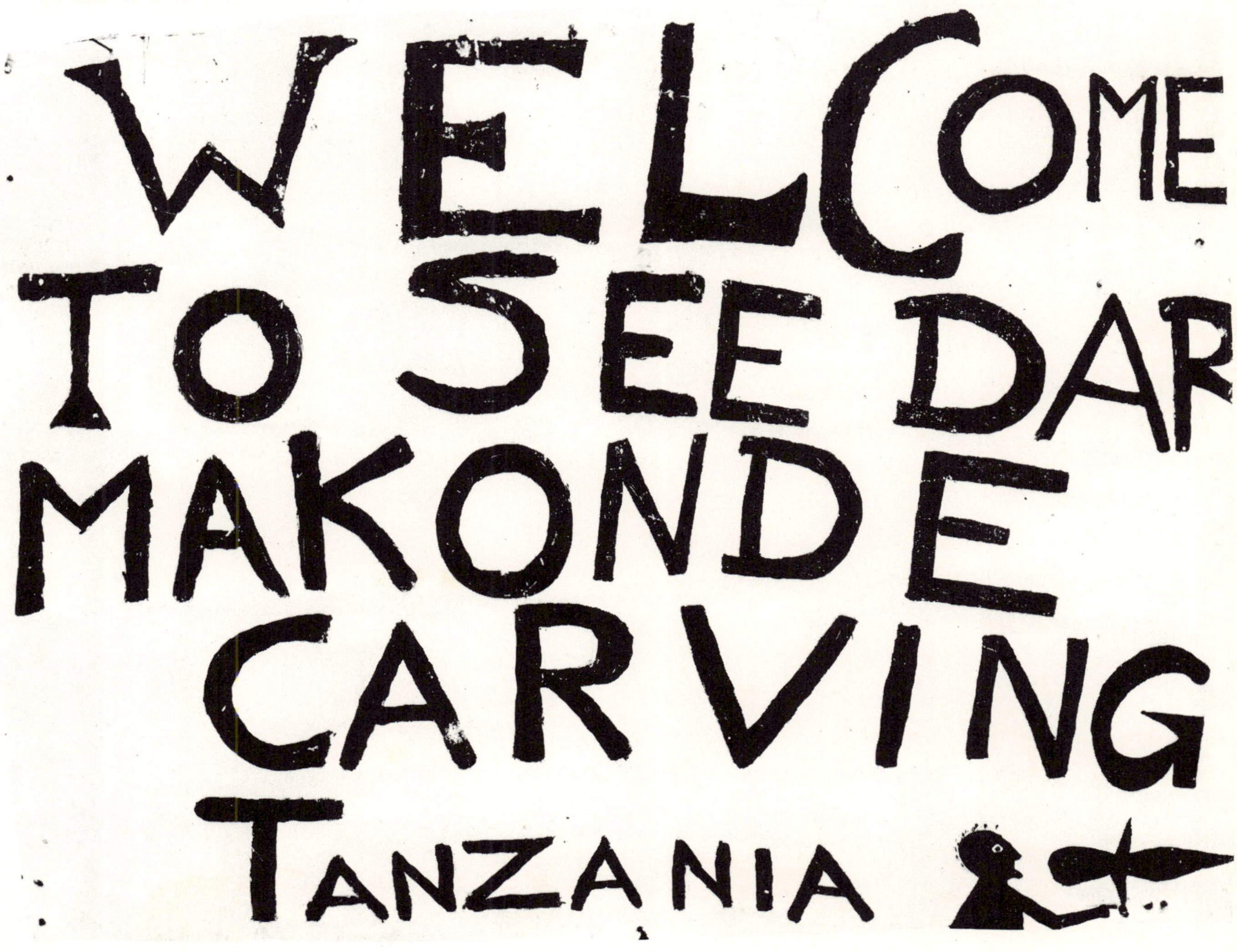
WELCOME
TO SEE DAR
MAKONDE
CARVING
TANZANIA

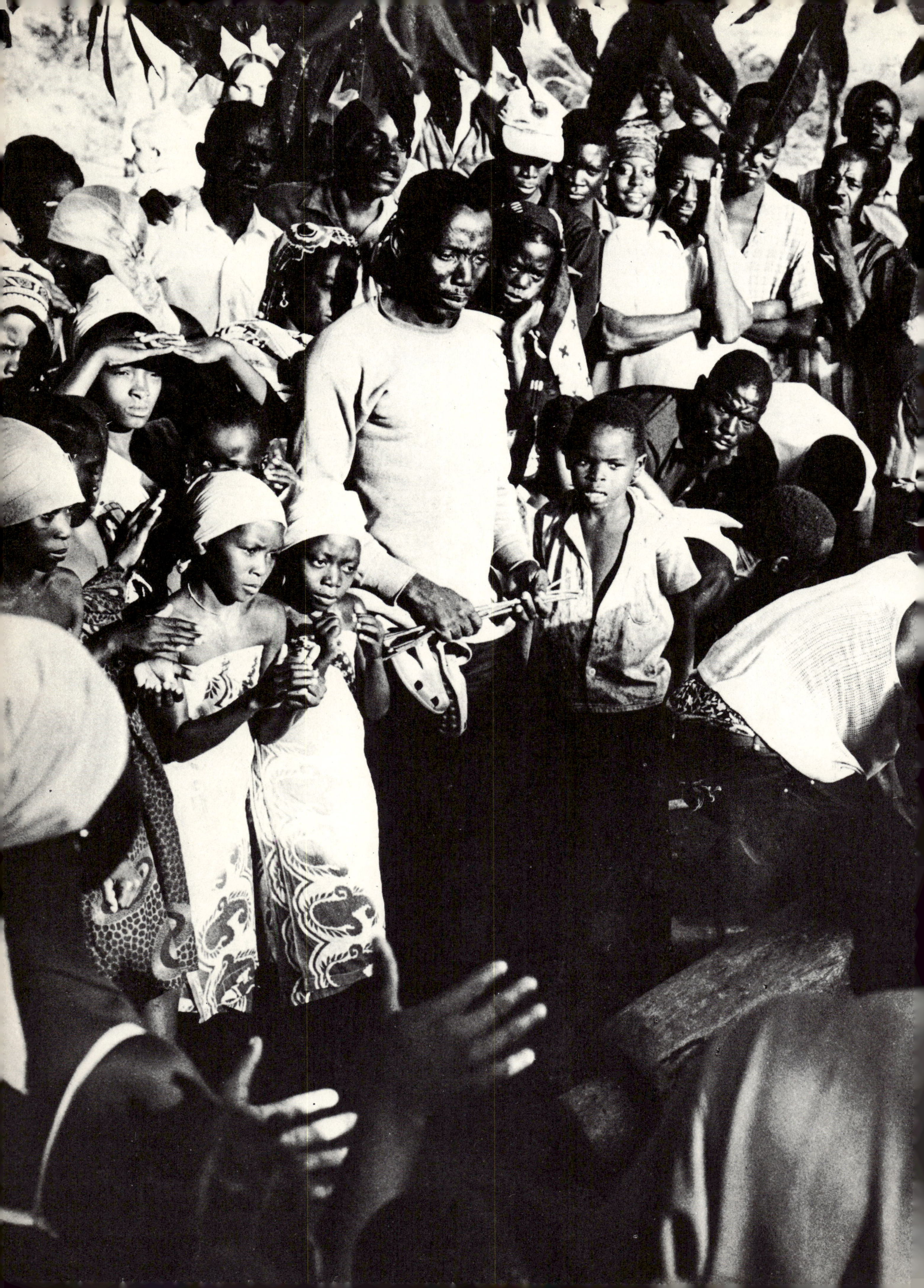

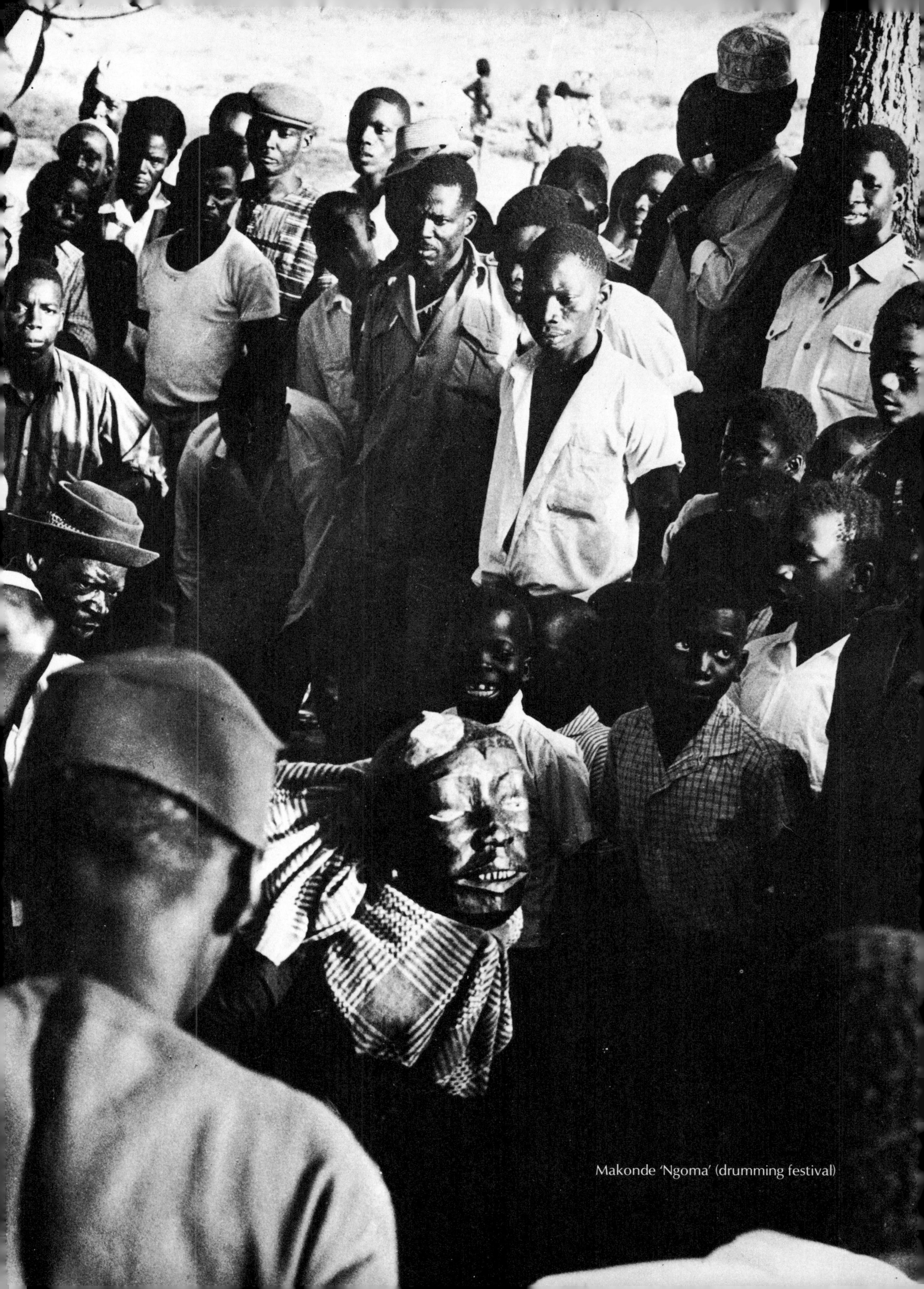

Makonde 'Ngoma' (drumming festival)

Bibliography

Literature exclusively on modern Makonde art is scarce but rapidly increasing in quantity and quality, a fact of which the artists themselves are largely unaware.

To date, the most important book is a revised catalogue of an exhibition held by Mr J. Anthony Stout, who collected Makonde art while stationed in Nairobi. The book was published there in 1966 under the title of *Modern Makonde Sculpture*. Kibo Art Gallery Publications, Nairobi/R. P. Dutton, 125 Lowell Ave, Newtonville, Mass. 02160, USA.

In 1971, Roger Fouquet published in Paris a document which gives much attention to the background of the art: *La Sculpture des Makondés,* Nouvelles Editions Latines, Paris, and in 1972 the book appeared in an English translation through the efforts of The National Arts of Tanzania, Dar es Salaam.

In Baessler Archiv, Neue Folge, Band XIX, Mrs Elisabeth Grohs, of Berlin, presented a thorough survey of modern Makonde art, unfortunately with few illustrations: *Moderne Makonde Plastik*. Verlag Dietrich Reimer, Berlin.

In newspapers and periodicals the world over, the topic of Makonde sculpture appears. Let the following magazine quotation stand for an assumption probably contradicted above: 'Like children, these artists seem unable to do any wrong' (*Newsweek*, April 22nd, 1968).

Here a comprehensive list of references is not included. Such documentation is available from the Institut für Auslandsbeziehungen (Forum für Kulturaustausch), Stuttgart, Mai 1971: *Makonde, Eine ostafrikanische Dokumentation,* ed. Hermann Pollig, with more than 300 titles of which one third touch upon art.

In University libraries of East Africa are several theses on the subject of Makonde art and culture.

Acknowledgments

All sculptures illustrated in this book are from The Jörn Korn collection with the exception of that on pp. 46–47 which belongs to Jesper Kirknæs.

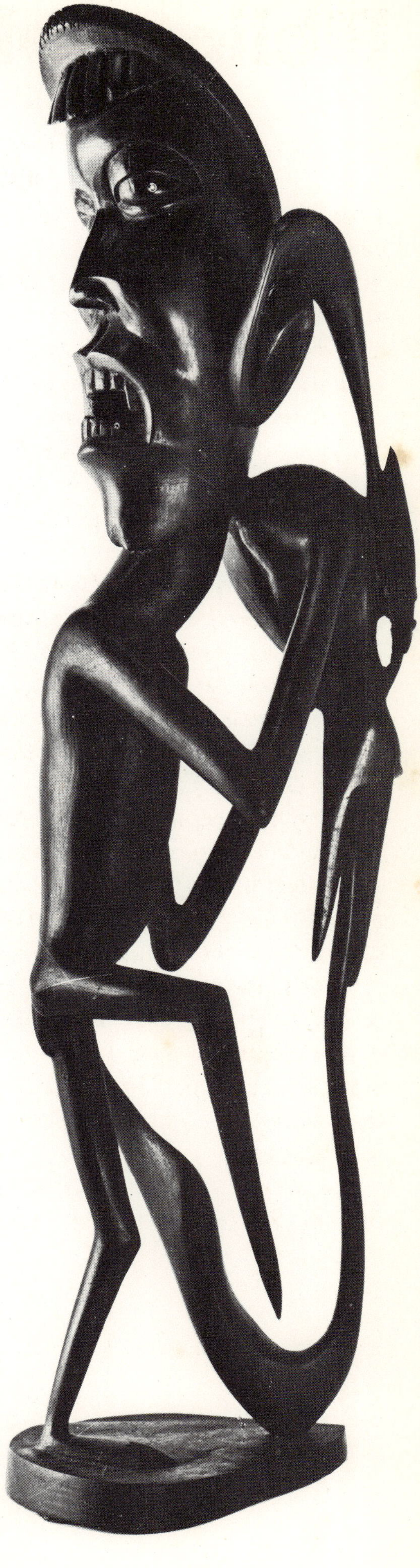

Modern Mozambique shetani. This large shetani will walk around in the streets by night, pretending to be a policeman. He is always accompanied by a snake shetani. And his hand is shaped like the head of a cruel monster. Rashidi bin Mohamed, 1969. 58 cm